The
Almanac
of
Anniversaries

The Almanac of Anniversaries

Kim Long

ABC-CLIO

Santa Barbara, California
Denver, Colorado
Oxford, England

Library of Congress Cataloging-in-Publication Data

Long, Kim.
    The almanac of anniversaries / by Kim Long.
    Includes bibliographical references and index.
    1. Anniversaries—Calendars.   I. Title.
    D11.5.L64   1992   394.2—dc20   92-28945

ISBN 0-87436-675-5

99 98 97 96 95 94 93 92   10 9 8 7 6 5 4 3 2 1

ABC-CLIO, Inc.
130 Cremona Crive, P.O. Box 1911
Santa Barbara, California 93116-1911

This book is printed on acid free paper ∞.
Manufactured in the United States of America

70280052

CONTENTS

CONTENTS

INTRODUCTION

Dis aliter visum —Virgil

With the passage of time, the events and notable people of an era often seem to gain importance and stature. In art and literature, in fact, it is often only the passage of time that separates the really significant from the momentarily interesting. Such notables as Mozart and Jefferson, for instance, were known and appreciated in their time but only acquired the status of legend centuries later.

The retrospective appreciation of people and events makes the celebration of anniversaries an enduring phenomenon. Initially, it is not merely the excuse for a holiday or party that turns ordinary citizens into adulators, but recognition of the contributions of the past. This trait has been noted even in the earliest cultures. In time, however, anniversaries can become so common in their celebration that the excuse for a holiday becomes the major issue, and few who participate actually take time to appreciate what the date means in history.

Several things can interrupt this inevitable consequence. One is the arrival of significant milestones in anniversary celebrations—the marking of periods of time such as 50, 100, or 150 years from an original date. Another is the prospect of celebrating forgotten or little-known anniversaries. Both of these rationales form a primary purpose for *The Almanac of Anniversaries.*

Although the birthdays of important figures and a myriad of other historical events are often noted every year on specific dates, it is the arrival of significant anniversary milestones that makes most historical events especially appreciated. These milestones, at least in western cultures, are characterized by their age in round numbers, with figures such as 50, 100, and multiples of 100 thought of as markers of considerable value.

Why these figures should be significant, rather than numbers such as 27 or 83, is related to a long history of decimal-based arithmetic—a system of counting not inconsistent with the number of fingers on the human body. The additional significance of such "odd" numbers as 25 and 75 in this litany of milestones is most likely related to innate counting methods, where such numbers as these are most easily distinguished as midpoints on the way to larger numbers, 50 and 150 for example. In fact, Latin names for ordinal numbers such as 25th or 50th are translated literally as meaning "quarter" or "half" of 100.

In the history of anniversary celebrations, the rule of thumb is: "the older the anniversary, the bigger the celebration." Exceptions abound, however, with many milestones finding greater appreciation closer to their occurrences. In these cases, time can numb the original impact of such things as the invention of the printing press or the telegraph—technology that is significant in history but supplanted in the popular mind by later discoveries and widespread, unconscious usage. Also, the meandering path of progress can leave behind the accomplishments of some and uncover the heroics of others. Especially in the current cultural climate in the United States, such reevaluation of history is thrusting new figures from the past into the limelight while discarding others previously favored. When the 400th

INTRODUCTION

anniversary of Columbus's discovery of America was marked in 1892, his actions were not in dispute. The 500th anniversary, celebrated in 1992, on the other hand, created as much dissension as accolades.

The contents of this book generally follow the conventions of traditional celebrations, but additional dates are included when available to allow for a wider interpretation of some historical milestones. Also, there is increasing pressure—often from marketing and advertising sources—to "jump the gun" and mark the arrival of milestones in advance. Thus, a building might be recognized as 75 years old from the date of the laying of its cornerstone rather than from the date of the building's completion, often a gap of several years. Driven by the overwhelming size of their population group, baby boomers have also been increasingly responsible for marking milestones with little regard for the appropriate passage of time. For example, some of the original participants of the Woodstock Festival, held in 1969, chose to revive its memory with an anniversary celebration twenty years after that date—in 1989—rather than wait for a more traditional twenty-fifth fete in 1994.

Furthermore, many events and historic figures are increasingly being lauded over prolonged periods of time. In 1992, an entire year was spent marking the arrival of Columbus in the Americas; in 1989, the 50th anniversary of the creation of Bugs Bunny was celebrated throughout the year. Entries in *The Almanac of Anniversaries* are not prejudged for their potential exposure, but they are marked as the calendar dictates.

The criteria used for including information in *The Almanac of Anniversaries* was primarily the accepted importance of anniversary dates as already celebrated in this country. While the United States is the focus, additional entries indicate people and events from elsewhere in the world that literate Americans might acknowledge as having an important influence on subsequent generations.

Anniversaries included are as follows:

- The general history of the United States
- Specific entry dates for states into the United States
- Births and deaths of important people
- Foundings of noted businesses
- Creations and patenting of important inventions
- Publication and creation of important literary and musical works
- A general miscellany of unusual events

The quincentennial—500th anniversary—is the oldest milestone observed in *The Almanac of Anniversaries*. Looking as far back into recorded history as is possible, it should be the case that the most significant of events are the oldest ones that still have contemporary meaning. Using the standards of major milestones, this would include those marking their 1,000th anniversary, an almost mythical point in history. Unfortunately, virtually nothing can be verified about the activities of our ancestors 1,000 years ago, the result of the fog of time and the relative lack of written records. Millenial celebrations that would qualify for inclusion in this book—events occurring from A.D. 993 to 1000—could not go much beyond the arrival of lemons in Spain (carried by Arabian adventurers), the first use of bells in churches in Europe, and the invention of the crossbow.

Among the few more specific events of 1,000 years ago that are recognized by established celebrations are the voyages of Leif Eriksson, a legendary Norse explorer who is thought to have landed in what is now Newfoundland, Canada, as well as Labrador and Nova Scotia. (In parts of Canada, the ninth of October is traditionally celebrated as Leif Eriksson Day.) Also, in A.D. 1000, Poland was established as an independent nation by a decree from Pope Otto III, leader of the Holy Roman Empire. Poland, however, officially recognizes its founding year as A.D. 966, when Christianity first arrived in the region. Hungary was also first recognized as an independent nation in A.D. 1000 but celebrates its birthday as A.D. 973, when the first ancestors of modern Hungarians migrated to the region.

It is anybody's guess what civilization will recognize as important 1,000 years from now. The only thing that seems likely, comparing our view of 1,000 years ago and the probable construction of society 1,000 years ahead, is that, because of mankind's newly found abilities to keep better records, future generations will have a significantly larger range of choices for anniversary celebrations.

The Almanac of Anniversaries is intended to be both a useful reference tool and an informative guide to historical events for which important milestones are impending. Where possible, specific dates are included.

The format of this book includes nine chapters, one for each calendar year from 1993 to 2001. Within each of these annual sections, there are twelve significant anniversary milestones: 25 years, 50 years, 75 years, 100 years, 150 years, 200 years, 250 years, 300 years, 350 years, 400 years, 450 years, and 500 years. These milestones are listed in the text from the youngest—25 years—to the oldest—500 years. Thus, for any particular calendar year until 2001, a reader may find upcoming anniversaries that will fall in that year. Under each historical year, text entries follow a chronological format, from January to December, when specific dates are available. Other entries, those without specific dates, are placed by editorial prerogative, but no hidden significance is intended.

Additional anniversaries are included within boxes. These entries are recognized in particular years based on the dates of founding, establishment, incorporation, charter, or legislation. "Birthdays and Death Days" may include names that are also covered in text entries. For "Music" anniversaries, the dates and locations of first performances are noted when applicable; other entries under this heading mark dates of publication or, in the case of recordings, the first year sold commercially. "Newspapers and Magazines" excludes publications that have ceased to exist, with a few exceptions (publications that have achieved historical note despite their demise). "Books, Poetry, and Plays" includes entries in the year of publication in the United States, with the exception of significant works created in foreign countries, especially prior to the establishment of publishing in this country. "Movies" marks cinematic features in the first year of their release.

Some of the list categories are more inclusive than others. For example, "Museums and Zoos" and "Colleges and Universities" include most of the institutions now in existence. On the other hand, "Books, Poetry, and Plays," "Music," and "Movies" contain only a sampling of the works created in specific years. The space to include everything not being available, entries were chosen by "editorial" process, using a wide variety of measurements to make the cut, including the stature of the creators, sales records, and the perspective of history. It should be noted that measurements that may seem obvious, such as the Pulitzer Prize for books or the Academy Award for movies, were generally not used to choose listings; the passage of time often eliminates or dilutes these initial honors in the perspective of cultural legend.

For occasional entries found in these brief listings, additional material may be found in text entries, especially for those names or events that have a wider effect on the public. A text entry on the birth of the *New York Times* elaborates the story of this major daily newspaper, while a listing for the *Seattle Times* ends in itself (no reflection on the quality of the latter).

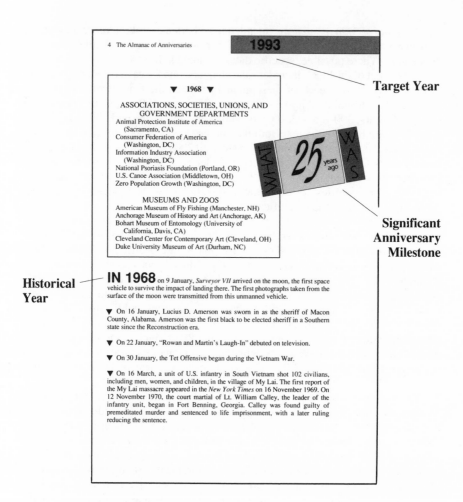

Target Year

Significant Anniversary Milestone

Historical Year

Target Year—The calendar year for each chapter listed at the top of each page.

Significant Anniversary Milestone—The anniversary milestone for each target year marked with a box indicating the number of years that have passed since the event occurred.

Historical Year—The boldfaced historical date marking the initial entry for each anniversary section. All the text entries for that historical year follow, each marked with a ▼.

Listing of Events—Additional anniversary entries listed in boxes marked by the appropriate historical date. These lists include the following categories:

▼ On 4 April, Dr. Martin Luther King, Jr., was assassinated in Memphis, Tennessee. King was 39 years old at the time, and a major leader in the civil rights movement in the United States. In 1964, King was awarded the Nobel Peace Prize.

▼ On 6 April, HemisFair 68 opened in San Antonio, Texas. This event celebrated the founding of the city in 1768.

▼ On 11 April, President Johnson signed into law the Civil Rights Act of 1968.

▼ On 23 April, student activists at Columbia University in New York City took over a school building to protest the University's involvement with military research and plans to construct a gymnasium on land requested for community use. The takeover expanded to include several other buildings and climaxed with Columbia suspending classes on 26 April. On 30 April, police moved into the occupied buildings and ended the protest, with many students injured in the process.

▼ On 25 May, the city of St. Louis celebrated the dedication of the Gateway Arch. Designed by Eero Saarinen, the Gateway Arch was chosen in 1948 as the winner in an architectural competition for the Jefferson National Expansion Memorial.

▼ On 5 June, Senator Robert Kennedy was shot by an assassin in Los Angeles. He died the following day. Kennedy was 42 years old at the time of his death and had just won the California primary for the presidential election.

▼ 1968 ▼

MUSEUMS AND ZOOS *continued*
Environmental Science Center (Houston, TX)
Gayle Planetarium (Montgomery, AL)
Headley-Whitney Museum (Lexington, KY)
Helen Allen Textile Collection Museum
    (University of Wisconsin, Madison, WI)
Louisville Zoological Gardens (Louisville, KY)
Marine World Africa USA (Vallejo, CA)
Naismith Memorial Basketball Hall of Fame
    (Springfield, MA)
Nebraska Statehood Memorial (Lincoln, NE)
Space and Rocket Center (Huntsville, AL)
Strasenburgh Planetarium (Rochester, NY)
Strong Museum (Rochester, NY)
Texas Ranger Hall of Fame and Museum (Waco, TX)
Texas Science Center (San Antonio, TX)
Tucson Botanical Gardens (Tucson, AZ)

Listing of Events

Milestone Star

Associations, Societies, Unions, and Government Departments (with location by city and state)
Museums and Zoos (with location by city and state)
Birthdays and Death Days (with dates and age at death)
Colleges and Universities (with location by city and state)
Music (with creator and date and location of first performance, if applicable)
Newspapers and Magazines (with location by city and state)
Books, Poetry, and Plays (with creator)
Movies (with director and leading actors)

Milestone Star—Some listings of events continue for more than one box. These additional boxes are indicated by milestone stars.

Calendar Locator

Target Years

		1993	1994	1995	1996	1997	1998	1999	2000	2001
	25th	1968	1969	1970	1971	1972	1973	1974	1975	1976
		p.4	p.28	p.54	p.76	p.102	p.122	p.146	p.166	p.188
	50th	1943	1944	1945	1946	1947	1948	1949	1950	1951
		p.9	p.33	p.57	p.79	p.105	p.126	p.149	p.169	p.190
	75th	1918	1919	1920	1921	1922	1923	1924	1925	1926
		p.12	p.36	p.61	p.84	p.108	p.130	p.152	p.172	p.193
	100th	1893	1894	1895	1896	1897	1898	1899	1900	1901
		p.15	p.41	p.65	p.88	p.111	p.133	p.155	p.175	p.197
	150th	1843	1844	1845	1846	1847	1848	1849	1850	1851
		p.20	p.45	p.68	p.92	p.114	p.137	p.158	p.178	p.202
	200th	1793	1794	1795	1796	1797	1798	1799	1800	1801
		p.22	p.47	p.71	p.96	p.116	p.140	p.161	p.181	p.205
	250th	1743	1744	1745	1746	1747	1748	1749	1750	1751
		p.23	p.48	p.72	p.96	p.118	p.141	p.162	p.182	p.207
	300th	1693	1694	1695	1696	1697	1698	1699	1700	1701
		p.24	p.49	p.72	p.97	p.119	p.142	p.163	p.183	p.207
	350th	1643	1644	1645	1646	1647	1648	1649	1650	1651
		p.25	p.49	p.73	p.97	p.119	p.142	p.163	p.183	p.208
	400th	1593	1594	1595	1596	1597	1598	1599	1600	1601
		p.25	p.50	p.73	p.98	p.119	p.142	p.163	p.184	p.208
	450th	1543	1544	1545	1546	1547	1548	1549	1550	1551
		p.26	p.50	p.73	p.98	p.120	p.143	p.164	p.184	p.208
	500th	1493	1494	1495	1496	1497	1498	1499	1500	1501
		p.26	p.51	p.74	p.99	p.120	p.143	p.164	p.185	p.209

Anniversary Milestones

The calender locator chart may be used to navigate this book more efficiently. It provides easy cross-referencing of upcoming calender years (1993–2001), anniversary milestones (25th–500th), and historical years (1493–1976). A reader with a particular anniversary milestone in mind, such as 100th anniversaries, may choose the appropriate milestone in the left-hand column and read across to determine all of the historical years for which 100th anniversaries will take place between 1993 and 2001. Alternatively, an upcoming year may be chosen as a starting point. Reading down the column, the reader will find all of the historical years for which major anniversary milestones will be attained between 1993 and 2001. Each historical year is accompanied by a page number for quick access to all of the events that occurred in that year.

Anniversary Glossary

Although long a dead language, Latin continues to appear in modern usage. Among the continuing uses for Latin vocabulary is the labelling of significant anniversaries. For those inclined to continue this practice, the following list contains the correct Latin equivalents of the anniversaries included in this book.

25th Anniversary	Quartocentennial
50th Anniversary	Semicentennial
75th Anniversary	Septiquinquennial
100th Anniversary	Centennial
150th Anniversary	Sesquicentennial
200th Anniversary	Bicentennial
250th Anniversary	Sesquibicentennial
300th Anniversary	Tercentennial
350th Anniversary	Sesquitercentennial
400th Anniversary	Quadricentennial
450th Anniversary	Sesquiquadricentennial
500th Anniversary	Quincentennial

Using the Index

Another useful feature included in *The Almanac* is the extensive index, which has been designed to be a major access point for the book. Each name, institution, invention, and other entry is listed separately in the index. Locations are included when they are the focus of an activity, such as the burning of Saratoga or the founding of a specific town's football team.

Conclusion

The Almanac of Anniversaries is not expected to replace historical reference works. The editorial goal is to provide a wide-ranging variety of historical events, with emphasis on the anticipation of milestones. Entries are generally designed to provide basic information and illuminating insights, without exhaustive details. For readers inspired to obtain additional information, many standard references will be useful. In the bibliography, works that were helpful in the construction of this book are listed. For many categories, including the history of invention and general history, many more titles are available than were consulted and should be considered for additional background.

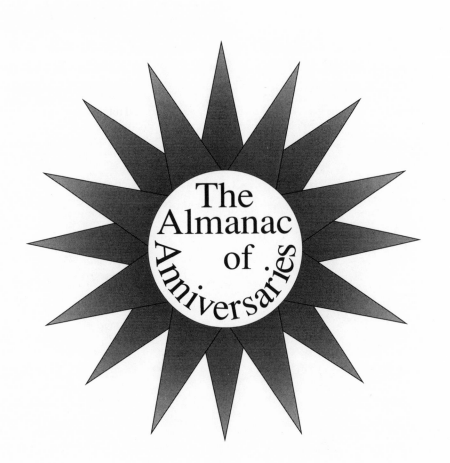

The
Almanac
of
Anniversaries

▼ 1968 ▼

ASSOCIATIONS, SOCIETIES, UNIONS, AND GOVERNMENT DEPARTMENTS

Animal Protection Institute of America
  (Sacramento, CA)
Consumer Federation of America
  (Washington, DC)
Information Industry Association
  (Washington, DC)
National Psoriasis Foundation (Portland, OR)
U.S. Canoe Association (Middletown, OH)
Zero Population Growth (Washington, DC)

MUSEUMS AND ZOOS

American Museum of Fly Fishing (Manchester, NH)
Anchorage Museum of History and Art (Anchorage, AK)
Bohart Museum of Entomology (University of
  California, Davis, CA)
Cleveland Center for Contemporary Art (Cleveland, OH)
Duke University Museum of Art (Durham, NC)

IN 1968 on 9 January, *Surveyor VII* arrived on the moon, the first space vehicle to survive the impact of landing there. The first photographs taken from the surface of the moon were transmitted from this unmanned vehicle.

▼ On 16 January, Lucius D. Amerson was sworn in as the sheriff of Macon County, Alabama. Amerson was the first black to be elected sheriff in a Southern state since the Reconstruction era.

▼ On 22 January, "Rowan and Martin's Laugh-In" debuted on television.

▼ On 30 January, the Tet Offensive began during the Vietnam War.

▼ On 16 March, a unit of U.S. infantry in South Vietnam shot 102 civilians, including men, women, and children, in the village of My Lai. The first report of the My Lai massacre appeared in the *New York Times* on 16 November 1969. On 12 November 1970, the court-martial of Lt. William Calley, the leader of the infantry unit, began in Fort Benning, Georgia. Calley was found guilty of premeditated murder and sentenced to life imprisonment, with a later ruling reducing the sentence.

▼ On 4 April, Dr. Martin Luther King, Jr., was assassinated in Memphis, Tennessee. King was 39 years old at the time, and a major leader in the civil rights movement in the United States. In 1964, King was awarded the Nobel Peace Prize.

▼ On 6 April, HemisFair 68 opened in San Antonio, Texas. This event celebrated the founding of the city in 1768.

▼ On 11 April, President Johnson signed into law the Civil Rights Act of 1968.

▼ On 23 April, student activists at Columbia University in New York City took over a school building to protest the university's involvement with military research and plans to construct a gymnasium on land requested for community use. The takeover expanded to include several other buildings and climaxed with Columbia suspending classes on 26 April. On 30 April, police moved into the occupied buildings and ended the protest, with many students injured in the process.

▼ On 25 May, the city of St. Louis celebrated the dedication of the Gateway Arch. Designed by Eero Saarinen, the Gateway Arch was chosen in 1948 as the winner in an architectural competition for the Jefferson National Expansion Memorial.

▼ On 5 June, Senator Robert Kennedy was shot by an assassin in Los Angeles. He died the following day. Kennedy was 42 years old at the time of his death and had just won the California primary for the presidential election.

▼ **1968** ▼

years ago

MUSEUMS AND ZOOS *continued*
Environmental Science Center (Houston, TX)
Gayle Planetarium (Montgomery, AL)
Headley-Whitney Museum (Lexington, KY)
Helen Allen Textile Collection Museum
    (University of Wisconsin, Madison, WI)
Louisville Zoological Gardens (Louisville, KY)
Marine World Africa USA (Vallejo, CA)
Naismith Memorial Basketball Hall of Fame
    (Springfield, MA)
Nebraska Statehood Memorial (Lincoln, NE)
Space and Rocket Center (Huntsville, AL)
Strasenburgh Planetarium (Rochester, NY)
Strong Museum (Rochester, NY)
Texas Ranger Hall of Fame and Museum (Waco, TX)
Texas Science Center (San Antonio, TX)
Tucson Botanical Gardens (Tucson, AZ)

▼ On 21 August, troops from the Soviet Union invaded Czechoslovakia to end a period of political movement toward independence.

▼ On 26 August, the Democratic Convention opened in Chicago. Delegates nominated Senator Hubert Humphrey as their presidential candidate, but a more lasting legacy was the unprecedented violence that occurred in Chicago during the event. Demonstrators who were protesting U.S. involvement in the Vietnam War clashed with police on numerous occasions, resulting in hundreds of injuries and arrests. The national media, present to cover the convention, provided first-person reports of this activity.

▼ On 5 November, Shirley Chisholm was elected to the U.S. House of Representatives. Chisholm, a Democrat representing the state of New York, was the first black woman to be elected to Congress.

▼ The Philip Morris Company introduced the first cigarette just for women, Virginia Slims.

▼   1968   ▼

COLLEGES AND UNIVERSITIES
University of Wisconsin–Green Bay (Green Bay, WI)

MUSIC
Abraham, Martin and John, by Dion
A Beautiful Morning, by the Rascals
Beggars Banquet, by the Rolling Stones
The Best of Nat "King" Cole, by Nat "King" Cole
Born To Be Wild, by Steppenwolf
Build Me Up Buttercup, by the Foundations
Can I Change My Mind, by Tyrone Davis
Cheap Thrills, by Big Brother & the Holding Company
Creedence Clearwater Revival, by Creedence
    Clearwater Revival
Crown of Creation, by the Jefferson Airplane
Cry Like a Baby, by the Box Tops
Days of Future Passed, by the Moody Blues
The Dock of the Bay, by Otis Redding
Electric Ladyland, by Jimi Hendrix
Everyday People, by Sly and the Family Stone
Goin' Out of My Head, by the Lettermen
The Graduate, by Simon & Garfunkel

25 years ago

▼ **1968** ▼

MUSIC *continued*
Greatest Hits, by the Association
Hair, by Gerome Ragni and James Rado
Harper Valley P.T.A., by Jeannie C. Riley
Hello, I Love You, by the Doors
Hey Jude, by the Beatles
Honey, by Bobby Goldsboro
In Search of the Lost Chord, by the Moody Blues
In-A-Gadda-Da-Vida, by Iron Butterfly
John Wesley Hardin, by Bob Dylan
Johnny Cash at Folsom Prison, by Johnny Cash
Lady Madonna, by the Beatles
Lady Soul, by Aretha Franklin
Little Green Apples, by O. C. Smith
Magic Carpet Ride, by Steppenwolf
Nights in White Satin, by the Moody Blues
1, 2, 3, Red Light, by the 1910 Fruitgum Company
People Got To Be Free, by the Rascals
Say a Little Prayer, by Aretha Franklin
Since You Been Gone, by Aretha Franklin
Stoned Soul Picnic, by the Fifth Dimension
Stormy, by Classics IV
Super Session, by Mike Bloomfield, Al Kooper,
   Stephen Stills

25 years ago

▼ The first space vehicle survived a trip to the moon and back. *Zond 5*, a Soviet spacecraft, was recovered after returning to earth.

▼ Widespread reports declared that Lake Erie was dead. Experts at the time offered little hope that it could be returned to a natural state, even if pollution discharge were controlled. The lake, however, did manage to recover from its precarious position.

▼ The Ringling Brothers and Barnum & Bailey Circus founded "Clown College" to attract "funsters" to their establishment and train them for work.

▼ The Intel Corporation was founded in Mountain View, California. Intel was created by Andrew Grove, Gordon Moore, and Arthur Rock to manufacture silicon chips for the computer industry.

▼ 1968 ▼

25 years ago

MUSIC *continued*

Think, by Aretha Franklin
This Guy's in Love with You, by Herb Alpert
This Magic Moment, by Jay and the Americans
Tighten Up, by Archie Bell & the Drells
Time of the Season, by the Zombies
Touch Me, by the Doors
Waiting for the Sun, by the Doors
Wheels of Fire, by Cream
White Album, by the Beatles
Who Knows Where the Time Goes, by Judy Collins
Wichita Lineman, by Glen Campbell
Yummy Yummy Yummy, by Ohio Express

NEWSPAPERS AND MAGAZINES

New York Magazine (New York, NY)
Reason (Santa Monica, CA)
Weight Watchers Magazine (New York, NY)

BOOKS, POETRY, AND PLAYS

Armies of the Night, by Norman Mailer
The Confessions of Nat Turner, by William Styron

MOVIES

Bullitt (directed by Peter Yates, with Steve McQueen)
Funny Girl (directed by William Wyler, with Omar Sharif, Barbra Streisand)
The Lion in Winter (directed by Anthony Harvey, with Katharine Hepburn, Peter O'Toole)
The Odd Couple (directed by Gene Saks, with Jack Lemmon, Walter Matthau)
Planet of the Apes (directed by Franklin Schaffner, with Charlton Heston, Roddy McDowell)
The Producers (directed by Mel Brooks, with Zero Mostel, Gene Wilder)
Rosemary's Baby (directed by Roman Polanski, with John Cassavetes, Mia Farrow)
2001: A Space Odyssey (directed by Stanley Kubrick)

▼ Manufacturers Hanover Bank was founded in New York City.

▼ Nike was founded in Beaverton, Oregon, as the first commercial manufacturer of running shoes. Originally called Blue Ribbon Sports, the company adopted its current name in 1971.

▼ Microwave Communications Inc. (MCI) was founded by Jack Goeken. MCI was created to develop a national network of microwave communication connections, a system that could be marketed as an alternative long-distance telephone network to businesses.

▼ Construction began on the World Trade Center towers in New York City.

▼ Supertankers began transporting oil.

▼ College football's Peach Bowl was held in Atlanta, Georgia. In this first game, Louisiana State University beat Florida State, 31–27.

▼ **1943** ▼

ASSOCIATIONS, SOCIETIES, UNIONS, AND GOVERNMENT DEPARTMENTS

American Academy of Allergy and
  Immunology (Milwaukee, WI)
American Helicopter Society (Alexandria, VA)
Association for Voluntary Surgical
  Contraception (New York, NY)
Educational Film Library Association
  (New York, NY)
National Savings and Loan League
  (Washington, DC)

WHAT 50 years ago WAS

IN 1943 on 5 January, George Washington Carver died at the Tuskegee Institute in Tuskegee, Alabama. Born a slave in Missouri about 1864, Carver worked his way through high school and college in Minnesota and Iowa. In 1896, Booker T. Washington brought him to the Tuskegee Institute to teach agriculture. His research in Alabama produced hundreds of products that could be made from peanuts, a crop he believed should be promoted to replace cotton. Along with his fame as a chemist, Carver is also credited with the development of the modern agricultural industry in the South.

▼   **1943**   ▼

MUSEUMS AND ZOOS
Campbell House Museum (St. Louis, MO)
Oregon Museum of Science and Industry
   (Portland, OR)

BIRTHDAYS AND DEATH DAYS
Sergei Rachmaninoff died on 28 March at age 69
Wladyslaw Sikorski died on 4 July at age 62

COLLEGES AND UNIVERSITIES
U.S. Merchant Marine Academy (Kings Point, NY)
University of Texas Health Science Center at Houston
   (Houston, TX)
University of Texas Southwestern Medical Center at
   Dallas (Dallas, TX)

MUSIC
"Black, Brown and Beige," by Duke Ellington
   (first performed on 21 January in New York, NY)
Concerto for Orchestra, by Béla Bartók
Oklahoma!, by Rogers and Hammerstein
   (first performed on 31 March in New York, NY)

▼ On 13 April, the Jefferson Memorial in Washington, D.C., was officially dedicated. The date marked the bicentennial of Thomas Jefferson's birth, 13 April 1743.

▼ On 14 June, a Supreme Court decision protected the rights of students not to salute the American flag if this action conflicted with their religious beliefs.

▼ On 10 July, Allied forces landed on Sicily. After 37 days of battle against German troops, the island was secured.

▼ On 3 September, Allied forces landed on the Italian mainland.

▼ On 17 October, the Chicago Transit Authority formally opened the Chicago subway system.

▼ On 20 November, U.S. forces landed on the island of Tarawa in the Pacific Ocean.

▼ Albert Hoffman, a Swiss chemist, discovered that a compound known as lysergic acid—a natural compound found in some kinds of plant molds—had hallucinogenic properties. He had developed a derivative of lysergic acid called lysergic acid diethylamide (LSD), which was accidentally absorbed into his skin during routine work in his laboratory. While riding his bicycle home from work, he began hallucinating and later realized what had triggered this condition.

▼ The first kidney dialysis machine was developed by Wilhelm Kolff, a Dutch physician.

▼ Streptomycin was discovered by Selman Waksman, an American microbiologist. Streptomycin proved to be the first antibiotic that was effective in fighting gram-negative bacteria. An early success for streptomycin was as the first specific treatment for tuberculosis.

▼ Tenneco was founded as the Tennessee Gas and Transmission Company by Gardiner Symonds. The company built pipelines in the South, but added other manufacturing, packaging, and services over time. In 1961, the company was renamed Tenneco after merging with the Bay Petroleum Company.

▼ Textron, Inc. was founded by Royal Little as a company producing fabrics and clothes from man-made fibers. Unsuccessful in this venture, Textron changed its fortune by becoming a conglomerate, acquiring a diversified collection of companies.

50 years ago

▼ 1943 ▼

BOOKS, POETRY, AND PLAYS
The Flies, by Jean-Paul Sartre
Here Is Your War, by Ernie Pyle
The Human Comedy, by William Saroyan
One World, by Wendell Willkie
A Tree Grows in Brooklyn, by Betty Smith
Winged Victory, by Moss Hart

MOVIES
For Whom the Bell Tolls (directed by Sam Wood,
    with Gary Cooper, Ingrid Bergman)
Phantom of the Opera (directed by Arthur Lubin,
    with Nelson Eddy)
Watch on the Rhine (directed by Herman Shumklin,
    with Betty Davis, Paul Lukas)

▼ Hazel debuted as a feature comic character in the *Saturday Evening Post*. Hazel also appeared on television as a weekly series in the 1950s. The creator was Ted Key.

▼ The aqualung was invented by Jacques Cousteau in France.

▼ American scientists and mathematicians created the world's first electronic computer. The machine, called Colossus, was designed to analyze German military codes.

▼   1918   ▼

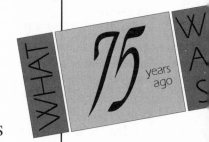

MUSEUMS AND ZOOS
Harold L. Lyon Arboretum (Honolulu, HI)
Laguna Art Museum (Laguna Beach, CA)
Phillips Collection (Washington, DC)

BIRTHDAYS AND DEATH DAYS
Claude Debussy died on 26 March at age 56
Leonard Bernstein born on 25 August
Billy Graham born on 7 November

COLLEGES AND UNIVERSITIES
Ball State University (Muncie, IN)
Eastern Nazarene College (Quincy, MA)
Jones College (Jacksonville, FL)

IN 1918 on 8 January, President Woodrow Wilson addressed the U.S.
Congress and first announced his Fourteen Points for achieving peace in the world. These points included freedom of navigation on the seas, "open covenants openly arrived at," removal of economic barriers, equal trade, reduced levels of national arms, "impartial adjustment of all colonial claims," and the formation of an organization of all nations.

▼ On 8 February, *The Stars and Stripes,* the official newspaper of the U.S. Army, published its first edition in Paris. Originally a publication for U.S. forces overseas, the paper was issued only in the United States after 1919. From 1926 to 1942, *The Stars and Stripes* was suspended; the arrival of World War II prompted its resurrection.

▼   1918   ▼

MUSIC

Classical Symphony in D Major, by Sergey
  Prokofiev (first performed on 21 April
  in St. Petersburg, Russia)
Il trittico, by Giacomo Puccini (first performed on
  14 December in New York, NY)

NEWSPAPERS AND MAGAZINES

Lion Magazine (Oak Brook, IL)

BOOKS, POETRY, AND PLAYS

The Education of Henry Adams, by Henry Brooks Adams

▼ On 31 March, the nation first observed daylight saving time. Legislation governing this change was passed by Congress on 19 March.

▼ On 13 May, the first airmail stamps appeared. The U.S. Post Office offered them in 6-, 16-, and 24-cent denominations. On 15 May, the stamps were first put to use, as airmail service began with regular delivery between Washington, D.C., and New York. Air delivery between Chicago and New York began on 1 July 1919; between New York and San Francisco it started on 20 July 1920.

▼ On 9 July, the U.S. Army established the Distinguished Service Cross as a commendation for extraordinary heroism.

▼ On 26 September, the Battle of the Meuse-Argonne began in Europe. More than 1 million American troops were involved. The battle ended with a general armistice on 11 November.

▼ On 10 October, the American Indian Church was founded in El Reno, Oklahoma. Founders included members of the Apache, Cheyenne, Comanche, Kiowa, Oto, and Ponca tribes.

▼ On 11 November, World War I came to an end with the surrender of German forces. Four days earlier, a news report from Europe was printed in some New York newspapers, incorrectly declaring the war was over on 7 November. The war was not officially over for the United States until Congress passed a joint resolution to that effect on 2 July 1921. The United States was the only nation to fail to accept the Treaty of Versailles, which was signed on 28 June 1919 but failed to get enough votes in the U.S. Senate for ratification. Final death toll from the war: 10 million.

▼ On 18 December, Robert L. Ripley, a sports cartoonist for the *New York Globe,* introduced "Believe It or Not!" This illustrated feature was syndicated nationally by the mid-1920s. Ripley's original concept focused on amazing and bizarre events in sports, but was soon expanded to include other subjects. Ripley died in 1949, but "Believe It or Not!" panels were drawn by other artists long before his death, at least from the early 1930s, and after his demise.

▼ The TASS news agency was founded in the Soviet Union. The agency was originally called ROSTA, but was renamed in 1925 as Telegrafnoie Agenstvo Soviet-skavo Soiuza. In 1992, following the dissolution of the Soviet Union, the agency was again renamed, to RITA, for Russian Intelligence Telegraph Association.

▼ Separate divisions of the Lutheran religion in the United States formed into the United Lutheran Church.

▼ The first mass spectrograph was constructed by Francis Aston, an English physicist.

▼ Alexander Graham Bell constructed the world's first hydrofoil boat.

▼ The Cleveland Symphony was established in Cleveland, Ohio.

▼ The Hertz Corporation was founded in Chicago by Walter Jacobs. Beginning with 12 Model Ts, the rental car company grew rapidly and was purchased in 1923 by John Hertz, the owner of a Chicago taxi company. In 1925, General Motors bought the business and named it the GM Hertz Drive-Ur-Self Company. John Hertz became the owner again in 1953, about the time that rental cars became a big national business. From 1918 to 1960, the founder of the company, Walter Jacobs, remained as the top employee, developing many of the concepts that made Hertz successful.

▼ The Taggert Baking Company in Indianapolis, Indiana, introduced Wonder Bread. The bread was one of the first to be sold prewrapped; the first bread wrapping machine was invented in 1914. Wonder Bread was initially promoted by giving away balloons to children.

▼ Raggedy Ann dolls were introduced during the Christmas season. Raggedy Ann was already known as the main character in a popular series of children's stories written by Johnny Gruelle.

▼ The first Kelvinator brand household refrigerator was offered to consumers. One year later, the first Frigidaire appeared.

▼ George Williamson invented the Oh Henry! candy bar in Chicago.

▼ The Teachers Insurance and Annuity Association, College Retirement Equities Fund (TIAA-CREF) was founded in New York City. Now the largest pension fund and one of the five largest life insurance companies in the United States, TIAA-CREF was created to provide college teachers with a means to save money for retirement. One of the originators of this nonprofit company was Andrew Carnegie, who used some of the wealth he generated from his steel companies to seed the concept.

▼ 1893 ▼

ASSOCIATIONS, SOCIETIES, UNIONS, AND GOVERNMENT DEPARTMENTS

Air Brake Association (Chicago, IL)
Amateur Fencers League of America (Albany, CA)
American Society for Engineering Education
   (Washington, DC)
International Association of Chiefs of Police
   (Arlington, VA)
National Association of Grocers (Reston, VA)
National Council of Jewish Women
   (New York, NY)
National Sculpture Society (New York, NY)
Pickle Packers International (St. Charles, IL)
United Boys' Brigades of America (Baltimore, MD)

WHAT 100 years ago WAS

IN 1893 on 17 January, Rutherford B. Hayes, nineteenth president of the

United States, died from heart disease at the age of 70 in Fremont, Ohio.

▼ On 4 March, Grover Cleveland was inaugurated as the twenty-fourth president of the United States, after having served an earlier term as president from 1884 to 1888. Born in 1837, Cleveland became a lawyer and practiced in Buffalo, New York. He became a Democrat, and in 1881, was elected mayor of Buffalo, then governor of the state in 1882. During Cleveland's second term as president, he was saddled with the problems brought on by the Panic of 1893 and subsequent depression, as well as a move to annex Hawaii, the move to a gold standard, and tariff debates. He lost the nomination for the election of 1896, and retired to Princeton, New Jersey, where he died on 24 June 1908.

▼ On 3 April, the first United States ambassador was appointed when Thomas Francis Bayard was named ambassador to Great Britain. Ambassadors were

▼   1893   ▼

MUSEUMS AND ZOOS

Arizona State Museum (Tucson, AZ)
Barnum Museum (Bridgeport, CT)
Bartram's Garden (Philadelphia, PA)
Dayton Museum of Natural History (Dayton, OH)
Field Museum of Natural History (Chicago, IL)
Rocky Mountain Herbarium (Laramie, WY)
St. Augustine Alligator Farm (St. Augustine, FL)
State Museum of History (Oklahoma City, OK)
Strecker Museum (Waco, TX)

BIRTHDAYS AND DEATH DAYS

Rutherford B. Hayes died on 17 January at age 70
Mary Pickford born on 8 April
Cole Porter born on 9 June
Guy de Maupassant died on 6 July at age 43
Huey Long born on 30 August
Peter Tchaikovsky died on 6 November at age 53

authorized by an Act of Congress in the Diplomatic Appropriation Act, passed on 1 March. Bayard was a former senator from Delaware and secretary of state under President Grover Cleveland. While ambassador to Great Britain, Bayard invoked criticism in the United States because of his opposition to international tariffs. He resigned his post in 1897.

▼ On 1 May, the World Columbian Exposition opened in Chicago. This fair attracted a record 12 million visitors. The event featured the introduction of the hootchy-kootchy dance by Little Egypt (the first exotic dancer), a celebration of the 400th anniversary of the discovery of America by Columbus, and the world's first major display of electric lights (supplied with alternating current from a generating system invented by Nikola Tesla, a major rival of Thomas Edison who was promoting direct current as a better source). One of the highlights of the fair was the world's largest Ferris wheel. This ride, constructed by an American engineer named George Washington Gale Ferris, was 250 feet in diameter and carried 40 passengers in each of its 36 enclosed cars. The wheel was commissioned in an attempt to match the excitement generated by the construction of the Eiffel Tower for the Paris Exposition in 1889. Although not the first such amusement ride ever built, Ferris's wheel attracted enough attention to give the ride a permanent name. Four years later, in 1897, an even larger Ferris wheel—about 300 feet in diameter—was built in London.

▼ On 16 September, a land rush began with the opening of the Cherokee Strip. Six million acres between Kansas and Oklahoma had been obtained from Cherokee tribes in 1891. More than 100,000 people participated in the land rush, attempting to gain a piece of property.

▼ In December, the first guest checked into the Waldorf Hotel in New York City. The Waldorf salad was invented here by chef Oscar Tschirky in the hotel's first year. The name of the institution was changed to the Waldorf-Astoria in 1897.

▼ At the Chicago World's Fair, the Davis Milling Company of St. Joseph, Missouri, introduced its new product, Aunt Jemima's Pancake Flour, the first ready-mix pancake product. The product was promoted by hiring Nancy Green, a black cook, to play the role of Aunt Jemima. Ongoing promotions included demonstrations across the country and a boxtop campaign selling Aunt Jemima rag dolls.

▼ The first national fly casting competition was held in Chicago at the World Exposition. The event was sponsored by the Chicago Fly Casting Club.

▼ In Chicago, Cracker Jack was first offered for sale.

▼   **1893**   ▼

100 years ago

COLLEGES AND UNIVERSITIES
American University (Washington, DC)
Aurora University (Aurora, IL)
Concordia College (St. Paul, MN)
East Stroudsburg University of Pennsylvania (East Stroudsburg, PA)
Hood College (Frederick, MD)
Lockyear College (Evansville, IN)
Maryhurst College (Maryhurst, OR)
Montana State University (Bozeman, MT)
New Mexico Highlands University (Las Vegas, NM)
Southern Connecticut State University (New Haven, CT)
University of Montana (Missoula, MT)
University of Wisconsin–Superior (Superior, WI)
Upsala College (East Orange, NJ)
Western Montana College of the University of Montana (Dillon, MT)
Western New Mexico University (Silver City, NM)
Western Washington University (Bellingham, WA)

▼   1893   ▼

MUSIC

Falstaff, by Giuseppe Verdi
   (first performed on 9 February in Milan, Italy)
Hänsel and Gretel, by Engelbert Humperdinck
   (first performed on 23 December in Munich,
   Germany)
Manon Lescaut, by Giacomo Puccini
   (first performed on 1 February in Milan, Italy)
Symphony No. 5 *(New World),* by Antonín Dvorák
   (first performed on 15 December in New York, NY)
Symphony No. 6 *(Pathétique),* by Peter Tchaikovsky
   (first performed on 28 October in St. Petersburg,
   Russia)

NEWSPAPERS AND MAGAZINES

Tampa Tribune (Tampa, FL)

BOOKS, POETRY, AND PLAYS

Mrs. Warren's Profession, by George Bernard Shaw
Salome, by Oscar Wilde
The Strange Case of Dr. Jekyll and Mr. Hyde,
   by Robert Louis Stevenson
A Woman of No Importance, by Oscar Wilde

▼ A widespread depression hit the country. In the first year, more than 70 railroads went bankrupt and fell into receivership, including the Philadelphia and Reading Railroad. Economic conditions forced the closure of 600 banks and thousands of other businesses, a situation popularly known as the Panic of 1893. The biggest blow of this period was a major collapse of the stock market on 27 June; the effects lasted until 1897.

▼ *The Psychic Mechanism of Hysterical Phenomena* was published by Sigmund Freud and Josef Breuer. The concepts presented in this book are considered to be the original basis of psychoanalysis.

▼ A gift from Marshall Field allowed establishment of the Chicago Natural History Museum. Also in this year, a pneumatic-tube message delivery system was installed in Marshall Field's department store, the first such system in a store in the United States.

▼ The first relay race was held. The race was a creation of American runners and was first demonstrated at a track meet at the University of Pennsylvania.

▼ New York State began the first traveling library in the country.

▼ The first open heart surgery was performed on the victim of a knife attack. The operation was performed by Dr. Daniel Williams.

▼ Leo Baekeland developed the Velox process, the first method of printing images in artificial light. Baekeland, a chemist, was a recent immigrant from Belgium, and used his invention to start a factory to manufacture photographic paper. In 1899, George Eastman bought Baekeland's concept for $1 million. With his financial success, Baekeland spent most of the next decade developing the first plastic material, which he named Bakelite.

▼ Whitcomb Judson, an American inventor, received a patent for a "clasp locker or unlocker for shoes." This device was the world's first zipper, but it initially attracted little attention. In 1896, the device was marketed as the Universal Fastener, but was still poorly received by consumers. Popularity for the zipper first came when the U.S. Army discovered its value just before World War I. The name was contributed accidentally by a person who admired the device's practicality, and later it was officially adopted by the company.

▼ The Mormon Temple in Salt Lake City, Utah, was dedicated. Construction of this building began in 1853 on a site personally selected by Brigham Young.

▼ The first 18-hole golf course in the United States was constructed in Wheaton, Illinois, by the Chicago Golf Club. Five years earlier, in 1888, the first U.S. golf course of any size was completed in Yonkers, New York. This course had only six holes and was named after the St. Andrew's course in Scotland.

100 years ago

▼ William Wrigley, Jr., a soap salesman, began selling Spearmint and Juicy Fruit gums. Wrigley first offered gum to his customers in 1892 as an incentive to buy his other products. The demand for the gum—originally produced by another company under the brand names Lotta Gum and Vassar—increased when he added chicle to the product. Chicle, the sap of the South American sapodilla plant, was first incorporated in chewing gum by Thomas Adams, a photographer and inventor from Staten Island, whose own brand was Adams New York Gum. Beeman's, an English gum brand, was introduced in 1894 as a treatment for heartburn.

▼ Cream of Wheat cereal was invented as a product to increase sales of wheat from a flour mill in North Dakota.

▼ Welch's Grape Juice debuted at the Chicago World's Fair. The original name of this fruit beverage was Dr. Welch's Unfermented Wine.

▼ The first version of Hires Root Beer was bottled. The beverage was first sold in 1876 as a powdered tea made from sarsaparilla root. Marketed in Philadelphia by a pharmacist named Charles Hires, the drink was changed to a concentrate by 1880 and appeared in bottled form in 1893 as Hires Herb Tea before receiving its current name.

▼ The Maytag Company was founded in Newton, Iowa, as the Parson Bandcutter and Self Feeder Company, a manufacturer of agricultural implements. The company changed its name when F. L. Maytag bought out his partners, and the first washing machine was produced in 1907.

▼ Aspirin was developed from natural plant compounds by Felix Hoffman at Bayer AG, a pharmaceutical company in Leverkusen, Germany. Aspirin was first marketed to the public in 1899 as a powder.

▼ Inland Steel was founded in Chicago, using steel-making equipment idled by the bankruptcy of the Chicago Steel Company. The first products Inland produced were farm implements.

▼ The first electric toaster was put on the market. The toaster was made by the Crompton Company of Chelmsford, England.

▼   **1843**   ▼

ASSOCIATIONS, SOCIETIES, UNIONS, AND GOVERNMENT DEPARTMENTS
B'nai B'rith International (Washington, DC)

BIRTHDAYS AND DEATH DAYS
Henry James born on 15 April
Edvard Grieg born on 15 June

COLLEGES AND UNIVERSITIES
Clarke College (Dubuque, IA)
College of the Holy Cross (Worcester, MA)
Lambuth College (Jackson, TX)

▼ **1843** ▼

MUSIC
Don Pasquale, by Gaetano Donizetti
  (first performed on 3 January in Paris, France)
Flying Dutchman, by Richard Wagner (first
  performed on 2 January in Dresden, Germany)

BOOKS, POETRY, AND PLAYS
A Christmas Carol, by Charles Dickens
Critical and Historical Essays, by Thomas Babington
  Macaulay
History of the Conquest of Mexico, by William Prescott
System of Logic, by J. S. Mill
The Wonders of the World, by Robert Sears

IN 1843 on 29 January, William McKinley was born in Niles, Ohio. After serving in the Union army during the Civil War, McKinley became a lawyer, working in private practice until 1876, when he was elected to the U.S. House of Representatives. A Republican, he served in the House until an election defeat in 1891. From 1891 to 1895, he was governor of Ohio, and in the 1896 presidential campaign he was elected over William Jennings Bryan. McKinley was the twenty-fifth president of the United States, and during his first term, he oversaw the Spanish-American War. His second term—which began with a victory in the election of 1900—ended tragically. Leon Czolgosz, a professed anarchist, shot McKinley on 6 September 1901 while the president was visiting the Pan-American Exposition in Buffalo, New York. Mortally wounded, he died on 14 September 1901 at the age of 58.

▼ Frederick Stanley founded a bolt factory in New Britain, Connecticut. The Stanley Works was the first factory in the area to use a steam engine for power, and within a decade it began producing hardware, fixtures, and tools.

▼ The word *millionaire* was first used. The term was included in a French newspaper obituary for Pierre Lorillard, a wealthy businessman who made his fortune selling tobacco and snuff.

▼ The first Tater Day was held in Benton, Kentucky. Tater Day is held annually on the first Monday in April. The festival was originally conceived as a local event to support sweet potato farmers.

▼ Nickel plating was first demonstrated by Michael Faraday.

1993

▼ John Frémont began his second expedition into the American West, leaving Missouri in May. Searching for a river expected to connect Utah's Great Salt Lake with the Pacific Ocean, Fremont's party instead demonstrated it was possible to travel overland to California.

▼ The first artificial fertilizer was produced by John Bennet Lawes in London.

▼ Thomas Hancock found a way to improve the waterproofing method for clothes developed in 1823 by Charles Macintosh, by using the same process developed by Charles Goodyear to vulcanize rubber. Hancock and Macintosh created a garment that came to be known as the mackintosh. Goodyear's discovery was known at the time, but his patent was not granted until a year later, in 1844.

▼ The sunspot cycle was first described by Samuel Schwabe, a German astronomer. Schwabe's observations indicated that the frequency of sunspots changed in a 10-year cycle (now considered to be an 11-year cycle).

▼ James Joule, an English physicist, developed the mechanical theory of heat, the beginning of the science of thermodynamics. (The term *thermodynamics* was first used in 1849 by William Thomson, later to be known as Lord Kelvin.) The initial publication to present authoritatively the first law of thermodynamics—the law of conservation of energy—was published in 1847 by Hermann von Helmholtz, a German physicist.

▼ **1793** ▼

COLLEGES AND UNIVERSITIES
Williams College (Williamstown, MA)

BOOKS, POETRY, AND PLAYS
Reineke Fuchs, by Johann Goethe
Religion within the Boundaries of Reason,
   by Immanuel Kant

WHAT 200 WAS
years ago

IN 1793 on 9 January, a French balloonist named Jean-Pierre-François Blanchard made the first major balloon ascent in the United States. He flew about 15 miles, taking off from Philadelphia and landing in New Jersey, with the flight witnessed by President George Washington. Earlier, in 1785, Blanchard and an American balloonist made the first flight across the English Channel.

▼ On 21 January, Louis XVI, King of France, was executed. His last words were, "I pray that the blood you are now going to shed may never be visited on France." On 16 October, Marie Antoinette followed him to the guillotine.

▼ On 12 February, the Fugitive Slave Act was enacted by Congress. The act specified the rights of slave owners to recover their runaway property.

▼ On 4 March, George Washington was inaugurated for his second term as president of the United States.

▼ On 25 May, in Baltimore, Maryland, the first Catholic priest was ordained in the United States.

▼ On 13 July, Jean-Paul Marat, a revolutionary journalist in France, was stabbed to death in his bathtub by Charlotte Corday.

▼ On 18 September, the cornerstone of the Capitol building was laid in Washington, D.C. The building was completed in 1830.

▼ Jabez Ricker opened an inn and stagecoach stop at Poland Springs, Maine. This location became a popular spa because of the water from the natural springs; the first Poland Springs water was bottled for sale in 1845.

▼ Alexander Mackenzie discovered the Fraser River in western Canada during an expedition through the Rocky Mountains.

▼ The French government made the Louvre Palace in Paris a public art museum.

▼ George Vancouver, an English navigator, was the first westerner to discover Vancouver Island, off the western coast of Canada.

WHAT 250 years ago WAS

▼ **1743** ▼

BIRTHDAYS AND DEATH DAYS
Thomas Jefferson born on 13 April

COLLEGES AND UNIVERSITIES
University of Delaware (Newark, DE)

MUSIC
Samson, by George Frederick Handel
(first performed on 18 February in London, England)

BOOKS, POETRY, AND PLAYS
Merope, by François Voltaire

IN 1743 on 13 April, Thomas Jefferson was born in Shadwell, Virginia.

▼ An army assembled by Georgia's Governor James Oglethorpe attacked settlements in Florida governed by Spain. This military activity, known as the War of Jenkins' Ear, was retaliation for Spanish raids into Georgia the previous year. Oglethorpe's force attacked areas around St. Augustine.

▼ The first symphony orchestra was organized in the modern style, at the court of Duke Karl Theodor in Mannheim, Germany.

▼ The first religious magazine was published in the American colonies. *Christian History* was a weekly publication that lasted until 1745.

▼   **1693**   ▼

COLLEGES AND UNIVERSITIES
College of William and Mary (Williamsburg, VA)

BOOKS, POETRY, AND PLAYS
Essay on the Present and Future Peace of Europe,
  by William Penn
Ideas on Education, by John Locke

WHAT **300** *years ago* **WAS**

IN 1693 John Ray published *Synopsis animalium quadrupedem et serpentini* (A general view of four-legged animals and snakes). This work was the first to establish the classification of animals using scientific principles.

▼ The last person was executed for witchcraft in the American colonies. A total of 20 people were hanged or pressed to death for the crime of practicing witchcraft during an epidemic of righteousness that began in Salem, Massachusetts, with the accusations of Samuel Parris, a local preacher. Also, Cotton Mather published *Wonders of the Invisible World,* a description of witchcraft activities in Salem.

▼ Edmond Halley, an English astronomer, published the first mortality tables. This work was the first statistical publication linking age with causes of death.

IN 1643 on 19 May, Connecticut, Massachusetts Bay, New Haven, and Plymouth were united as the New England Confederation. Their pact provided for a combined defense.

▼ The reign of Louis XIV of France began. He remained in power until his death in 1715.

▼ An early form of censorship was enacted by the English Parliament, affecting printers and booksellers in England and the American colonies.

▼ The mercury barometer was invented by Evangelista Torricelli, an Italian scientist considered to be the "father of hydrodynamics."

▼ The first Indian-English dictionary was written by Roger Williams of Providence, Rhode Island. The book, titled *A Key into the Language of America,* was published in England.

▼   **1593**   ▼

BOOKS, POETRY, AND PLAYS
Comedy of Errors, by William Shakespeare
Richard III, by William Shakespeare
Venus and Adonis, by William Shakespeare

IN 1593 on 30 May, Christopher Marlowe, the English poet and playwright, died in London. Marlowe was stabbed in the eye with a knife during a fight in a tavern. He had only one play published during his lifetime, *Tamburlaine the Great.* Unlike his contemporary William Shakespeare, whose works were popular during his lifetime (the same year Marlowe died, three of Shakespeare's works were published), Marlowe's acceptance came after his demise.

IN 1543

Juan Rodriguez Cabrillo, a Portuguese explorer, ventured up the California coast to what is now known as Bodega Bay. On his return trip, Cabrillo died in the Channel Islands off the coast of Santa Barbara.

▼ The first accurate text on human anatomy, *De humani corporis fabrica* (On the structure of the human body), was published by Andreas Vesalius in Belgium. Publication of this book brought accusations of body snatching against the author.

▼ Nicolaus Copernicus published *De revolutionibus orbium coelestium* (On the revolutions of celestial bodies), a book arguing that the earth and other planets must orbit around the sun. The prevailing belief at the time was that the universe, including the sun, revolved around the earth. Copernicus died on 24 May, within a few months of the book's publication. Some historical accounts report he died just as he was handed the first copy of his book, which he had delayed publishing for years because of concerns about the reaction of religious authorities.

▼ The isolated nation of Japan was first introduced to Europeans when a Chinese ship with two explorers from Portugal foundered off the shore of Kyūshū. This event also introduced modern weapons to the Japanese, as the Portuguese possessed muskets, soon duplicated by Japanese warlords.

▼ In Spain, the first Protestants were burned at the stake during the Inquisition.

IN 1493

on 25 September, Columbus left Spain for his second voyage to the New World. This expedition consisted of 17 ships and more than 1,000 men. On 3 November, the expedition reached land at Marigalante. Also, Columbus discovered Guadeloupe and Puerto Rico, and founded the first European settlement in the Americas.

▼ Spanish explorers in the Guadeloupe Islands discovered pineapple plants among the local vegetation. The first pineapples to be seen in Europe were part of the natural bounty brought back from the New World on this voyage.

▼ The first horses arrived in the New World, brought over as part of the Columbus expedition.

▼ 1969 ▼

ASSOCIATIONS, SOCIETIES, UNIONS, AND GOVERNMENT DEPARTMENTS
Friends of the Earth (Washington, DC)
National Taxpayers Union (Washington, DC)
United Transportation Union (Cleveland, OH)

MUSEUMS AND ZOOS
The Exploratorium (San Francisco, CA)
Museum of the National Center of
    Afro-American Artists (Boston, MA)
New England Aquarium (Boston, MA)
San Jose Museum of Art (San Jose, CA)
State Botanical Garden of Georgia (Athens, GA)
University Gallery (Memphis State University,
    Memphis, TN)

COLLEGES AND UNIVERSITIES
Indiana University–Purdue University at Indianapolis
    (Indianapolis, IN)
Laredo State University (Laredo, TX)

WHAT *25* years ago WAS

IN 1969 on 20 January, Richard Nixon was inaugurated as the thirty-seventh president of the United States. Born on 9 January 1913 in Yorba Linda, California, Nixon was an attorney before entering politics in 1946 as a Republican candidate for Congress.

▼ On 28 January, Union Oil's A-21 oil well began leaking into channel waters off the coast of Santa Barbara, California. The leak was closed after 12 days, leaving more than 200 miles of beaches polluted. This spill was one of the first major environmental disasters caused by oil pollution in the United States, and it inspired public awareness of environmental safety.

▼ On 4 April, in Houston, Texas, the first artificial heart was implanted. The patient lived for four days.

▼ On 15 May, police and protesters in Berkeley, California, clashed in a battle over a plot of land known as "People's Park." The park came to symbolize the political differences between the local countercultural community and the "establishment"—in this case the University of California—which wanted to use the land for a soccer field. Protesters planted trees and flowers, attempting to make the land an open park for public use, but they ended up in direct confrontation with police and the National Guard. Days of demonstrations, violence, and riots led to hundreds of arrests, many injuries, and the death of one protester who was shot with a police shotgun.

▼ On 20 July, human beings first landed on the moon. The *Apollo XI* expedition was launched on 16 July with astronauts Edwin Aldrin, Neil Armstrong, and Michael Collins. Neil Armstrong was the first to step onto the surface of the moon from the lunar module, with the statement: "That's one small step for man, one giant leap for mankind." The lunar module left the moon on 21 July, and on 24 July the astronauts returned to earth.

▼ **1969** ▼

MUSIC

The Age of Aquarius, by the Fifth Dimension
And When I Die, by Blood, Sweat & Tears
Any Day Now, by Joan Baez
Backfield in Motion, by Mel and Tim
The Ballad of John and Yoko, by the Beatles
The Band, by the Band
Bayou Country, by Creedence Clearwater Revival
Best of Cream, by Cream
Blind Faith, by Blind Faith
Chicago Transit Authority, by Chicago
Crosby, Stills & Nash,
    by Crosby, Stills & Nash
Didn't I, by the Delfonics
Donovan's Greatest Hits, by Donovan
Don't Cry Daddy, by Elvis Presley
Galveston, by Glen Campbell
Get Back, by the Beatles
Give Me Just a Little More Time,
    by Chairmen of the Board
Goodbye, by Cream
Green River, by Creedence Clearwater Revival
Hair, by the Cowsills
Holly Holy, by Neil Diamond
Honky Tonk Women, by the Rolling Stones
Hot Buttered Soul, by Isaac Hayes

25
years ago

▼ On 9 August, the discovery of five bodies in the home of Sharon Tate marked the beginning of the investigation and successful prosecution of Charles Manson and five of his followers. The trials were concluded in 1971.

▼ On 15 August, the Woodstock Music and Art Fair opened on Max Yasgur's farm outside Bethel, New York. More than 500,000 people arrived over the next four days to participate in this event, marking a significant point in the development of the popular music and alternative life-style scene in the United States.

▼ On 24 September, the trial of the Chicago Eight began. The accused were eight alleged ringleaders of the violent demonstrations that occurred during the Democratic National Convention in 1968. Of the eight defendants, one—Bobby Seale, a Black Panther—was found guilty of contempt of court early in the trial (some reports thus referred to the group as the Chicago Seven). Five of the defendants—Rennie Davis, David Dellinger, Tom Hayden, Abbie Hoffman, and Jerry Rubin—were found guilty of violating the antiriot provision of the Civil Rights Act of 1968.

▼   **1969**   ▼

MUSIC *continued*
I Got Dem Ol' Kozmic Blues Again Mama,
    by Janis Joplin
In the Court of the Crimson King, by King Crimson
In the Ghetto, by Elvis Presley
It's Your Thing, by the Isley Brothers
Jingle Jangle, by the Archies
Joe Cocker!, by Joe Cocker
Laughing, by the Guess Who
Leaving on a Jet Plane, by Peter, Paul, and Mary
Let It Bleed, by the Rolling Stones
Nashville Skyline, by Bob Dylan
Oh Happy Day, by the Edwin Hawkins Singers
On the Threshold of a Dream, by the Moody Blues
One, by Three Dog Night
Only the Strong Survive, by Jerry Butler
Put a Little Love in Your Heart, by Jackie DeShannon
Raindrops Keep Fallin' on My Head, by B. J. Thomas
Rainy Night in Georgia, by Brook Benton
Retrospective, by Buffalo Springfield
The Soft Parade, by the Doors
Something, by the Beatles

▼ 1969 ▼

MUSIC *continued*
Spinning Wheel, by Blood, Sweat & Tears
Spirit in the Sky, by Norman Greenbaum
Stand Up, by Jethro Tull
Sugar, Sugar, by the Archies
Suspicious Minds, by Elvis Presley
Sweet Caroline, by Neil Diamond
These Eyes, by the Guess Who
Through the Past, Darkly, by the Rolling Stones
To Our Children's Children's Children, by the Moody
　Blues
Tommy, by the Who
Touching You Touching Me, by Neil Diamond
Volunteers, by the Jefferson Airplane
Warm, by Herb Alpert & the Tijuana Brass
Whole Lotta Love, by Led Zeppelin
Willie and the Poor Boys, by Creedence Clearwater
　Revival
With a Little Help from My Friends, by Joe Cocker
Yellow Submarine, by the Beatles
You've Made Me So Very Happy, by Blood, Sweat & Tears

25 years ago

▼ On 20 November, Native American activists invaded Alcatraz Island in San Francisco Bay, the site of the abandoned Alcatraz Federal Prison. The Indians occupied the island to demonstrate their right to reclaim native lands. After 19 months, on 11 June 1971, the activists surrendered to federal marshals.

▼ On 1 December, the first drawing in a resurrected draft lottery was held; the draft lottery had last been used in 1942. The Selective Service System switched to the lottery system on 26 November, when President Nixon signed a bill authorizing a change from the previous system. In the drawing, the first date picked was 14 September. Although the system was intended to be completely random, an analysis later indicated that entrants with birthdays late in the year were picked more often than those with birthdates early in the year.

▼ On 2 December, a Boeing 747 was put into service for the first time, flying from Seattle to New York City.

▼ All-male Princeton University began admitting women for the first time. In the first year, 130 women were admitted to the school.

▼   **1969**   ▼

NEWSPAPERS AND MAGAZINES
Circus Magazine (New York, NY)
Dog Fancy (San Diego, CA)
Family Health (New York, NY)
Fly Fisherman (Harrisburg, PA)
Interview (New York, NY)
Metropolitan Home (New York, NY)
Off-Road (Los Angeles, CA)
Penthouse (New York, NY)

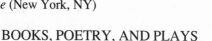

BOOKS, POETRY, AND PLAYS
Ada, by Vladimir Nabokov
Airport, by Arthur Hailey
Couples, by John Updike
The Money Game, by Adam Smith
Myra Breckenridge, by Gore Vidal
Slaughterhouse Five, by Kurt Vonnegut

MOVIES
Bob and Carol and Ted and Alice (directed by Paul
    Mazursky)
Butch Cassidy and the Sundance Kid (directed by George
    Roy Hill, with Paul Newman, Robert Redford)
Easy Rider (directed by Dennis Hopper, with Peter
    Fonda, Dennis Hopper)
Hello, Dolly! (directed by Gene Kelly, with Walter
    Matthau, Barbra Streisand)
Midnight Cowboy (directed by John Schlesinger, with
    Dustin Hoffman, Jon Voight)
The Prime of Miss Jean Brodie (directed by Ronald
    Neame, with Maggie Smith)
True Grit (directed by Henry Hathaway, with John Wayne)
The Wild Bunch (directed by Sam Peckinpah)

▼ The scanning electron microscope was perfected.

▼ DHL Worldwide Express was founded in Redwood City, California. Originally
a company that provided document delivery service to Hawaii from West Coast
cities, DHL eventually began providing worldwide delivery and competing in the
overnight package delivery industry.

▼ The first Wendy's hamburger store opened. David Thomas created this fast-food concept, naming the restaurant after his daughter. The first store was located in Columbus, Ohio.

▼ A group of dedicated health food fans established Celestial Seasonings in Boulder, Colorado, to sell herbal teas.

▼ Storage Technology Corporation was founded in Louisville, Colorado, to develop and manufacture magnetic tape drives for computers.

▼ **1944** ▼

ASSOCIATIONS, SOCIETIES, UNIONS, AND GOVERNMENT DEPARTMENTS

American Veterans of World War II, Korea and Vietnam (Lanham, MD)

International Chemical Workers Union (Akron, OH)

National Association of Schools of Art and Design (Reston, VA)

National Association of Teachers of Singing (Jacksonville, FL)

National Council on Alcoholism (New York, NY)

National Science Teachers Association (Washington, DC)

National Society of Arts and Letters (Washington, DC)

North American Association of Ventriloquists (Littleton, CO)

Society for the Advancement of Material and Process Engineering (Covina, CA)

Society of Chartered Property and Casualty Underwriters (Malvern, PA)

Sports Car Club of America (Englewood, CO)

United Negro College Fund (New York, NY)

WHAT 50 years ago WAS

IN 1944 on 22 January, U.S. forces landed at Anzio, Italy.

▼ On 8 May, the first eye bank was opened to provide replacement corneas. The eye bank was at New York Hospital in New York City.

▼   1944   ▼

MUSEUMS AND ZOOS
Cumberland Museum (Nashville, TN)
Cumberland Science Museum (Nashville, TN)
National Museum of Transport (St. Louis, MO)

BIRTHDAYS AND DEATH DAYS
Edvard Munch died on 23 January at age 80
Stephen Leacock died on 28 March at age 74
Wendell Willkie died on 8 October at age 52

COLLEGES AND UNIVERSITIES
Fashion Institute of Technology (New York, NY)
Fresno Pacific College (Fresno, CA)

MUSIC
Appalachian Spring, by Aaron Copland
Concerto for Orchestra, by Béla Bartók (first performed
  on 1 December in New York, NY)

▼ On 18 May, after months of failed assaults, Allied forces pushed German units out of Cassino, Italy.

▼ On 5 June, Allied forces entered Rome after German units moved out of the city.

▼ On 6 June, Allied forces landed in Europe in Normandy, France, on what was known as D-Day.

▼ On 6 July, in Hartford, Connecticut, one of the worst fires in circus history hit the Ringling Brothers and Barnum and Bailey Circus during a performance. In the rush to escape the flames, 167 people were killed.

▼ On 20 July, U.S. forces landed on Guam. After 20 days of fighting against defending Japanese troops, the island was conquered on 9 August.

▼ On 25 August, German forces holding Paris surrendered to advancing Allied units, freeing the city.

▼ On 7 September, the German military launched the first V-2 rocket at London. The first recorded impact of a V-2 was on 8 September, landing at 6:40 P.M. and killing two people near London. On 27 March 1945, the last V-2 rocket hit near Orpington, Kent, at 4:54 P.M., killing one person. More than 4,300 rockets were launched, with 1,115 known hits and 2,855 fatalities.

▼ On 20 October, U.S. forces landed on Leyte in the Philippines. Manila was reached on 7 February, and the country was declared liberated from the Japanese by General MacArthur on 5 July. Losses to American forces were about 12,000; Japanese losses topped 400,000.

▼ On 16 December, the Battle of the Bulge began with an attack by German forces in Belgium.

▼   1944   ▼

NEWSPAPERS AND MAGAZINES
Beacon and Alabama Citizen (Mobile, AL)
Campus Life (Wheaton, IL)
Seventeen (New York, NY)
Sports Car (Tustin, CA)

BOOKS, POETRY, AND PLAYS
Forever Amber, by Kathleen Winson
The Glass Menagerie, by Tennessee Williams
No Exit, by Jean-Paul Sartre
Strange Fruit, by Lillian Smith

MOVIES
Arsenic and Old Lace (directed by Frank Capra, with Cary Grant)
Double Indemnity (directed by Billy Wilder, with Barbara Stanwyck)
Gaslight (directed by George Cukor, with Ingrid Bergman, Charles Boyer)
Lifeboat (directed by Alfred Hitchcock, with Tallulah Bankhead, William Bendix)
Meet Me in St. Louis (directed by Vincente Minnelli, with Margaret O'Brien, Judy Garland)
Murder, My Sweet (directed by Edward Dmytryk, with Dick Powell)
To Have and Have Not (directed by Howard Hawks, with Laureen Bacall, Humphrey Bogart)

50 years ago

▼ On 24 December, Glenn Miller died in a plane crash while flying from France to England. A major recording star and leader of the most popular band in the United States, Miller directed U.S. armed forces bands during World War II.

▼ The first tetracycline compound was discovered by a U.S. Army medical team. The initial compound was aureomycin, which proved to be a potent antibiotic.

▼ Congress passed the Servicemen's Readjustment Act, often referred to as the GI Bill. This legislation created a system of hospitals and rehabilitation programs, and provided financial aid to veterans. The financial aid packages included home mortgages at low-interest rates and support for advanced education.

▼ Paul Harvey began broadcasting the news on radio from Chicago.

▼ Little Lulu debuted in animated short features produced by Paramount. Little Lulu originated as a character for comics in the *Saturday Evening Post,* created by Marjorie Henderson. Also, Pepe le Pew, an animated skunk of French ancestry, first appeared in "The Odor-able Kitty," produced by Warner Brothers. In 1949, Pepe was awarded an Oscar.

▼ General Electric introduced an unusual silicone product that was then called "bouncing putty." The product remained a curiosity until 1949, when Peter Hodgson, a freelance advertising writer, discovered the material and came up with the product Silly Putty. Sales were already brisk when an article appeared in a 1950 edition of the *New Yorker,* triggering the first post–World War II product fad.

▼   1919   ▼

ASSOCIATIONS, SOCIETIES, UNIONS, AND GOVERNMENT DEPARTMENTS
Aerospace Industries Association of America
    (Washington, DC)
Agricultural History Society (Washington, DC)
Alpha Zeta Omega (Montvale, NJ)
American Classical League (Oxford, OH)
American Council of Learned Societies (New York, NY)
American Defense Preparedness Association (Arlington, VA)
American Farm Bureau Federation (Park Ridge, IL)
American Legion (Indianapolis, IN)
American Meteorological Society (Boston, MA)
American Petroleum Institute (Washington, DC)

▼ 1919 ▼

ASSOCIATIONS, SOCIETIES, UNIONS, AND GOVERNMENT DEPARTMENTS *continued*

American Welding Society (Miami, FL)
Associated Actors and Artists of America (New York, NY)
    Cosmopolitan International (Overland Park, KS)
    Institute of International Education (New York, NY)
    International Association of Fairs and Expositions
        (Springfield, MO)
    International Order of DeMolay (Kansas City, MO)
    Junior Achievement (Stamford, CT)
    Magazine Publishers Association (New York, NY)
National Association of Accountants (Montvale, NJ)
National Federation of Business and Professional
    Women's Clubs (Washington, DC)
National Restaurant Association (Washington, DC)
National Soft Drink Association (Washington, DC)
National Sojourners (Alexandria, VA)
Optimist International (St. Louis, MO)

years ago

IN 1919 on 6 January, Theodore Roosevelt, twenty-sixth president of the United States, died from inflammatory rheumatism at Oyster Bay, New York, at the age of 60. His last words: "Please put out the light."

▼ On 15 January, a huge holding tank containing more than 2 million gallons of molasses burst open in Boston. A sea of molasses oozed through a large area of the city, hitting buildings and people with a wall of sticky goo up to 30 feet high. Twenty-one people died in this event, known as the Great Boston Molasses Flood.

▼ On 29 January, the Eighteenth Amendment of the U.S. Constitution was ratified, putting prohibition into effect throughout the country. Prohibition lasted for 14 years, until it was repealed with the passage of the Twenty-First Amendment in 1933. To date, the Eighteenth Amendment has been the only one ever repealed.

▼ On 3 March, the first international airmail route was initiated, from Seattle, Washington, to Victoria, British Columbia.

▼ On 15 March, the American Legion was founded during a meeting of former U.S. military personnel in Paris. The anniversary of the American Legion is

1994

celebrated on 16 September, the date in 1919 when the U.S. Congress issued a charter to the group.

▼ On 29 May, during a total eclipse of the sun, Einstein's general theory of relativity was put to the test for the first time. Measurements of starlight indicated the effects of gravity, as predicted by Einstein.

▼ In June, Harcourt Brace Jovanovich, a book publishing company, was founded in New York City by Alfred Harcourt, Donald Brace, and Will Howe. The original name of the business was Harcourt, Brace & Howe, changing to Harcourt, Brace & Company shortly thereafter when Will Howe left the company. In 1960, the name was changed to Harcourt, Brace & World after the acquisition of the World Book Company. The current name was taken in 1970.

▼ On 11 October, the first in-flight meals were served on a commercial passenger airliner. The lucky passengers were aboard a British-owned Handley Page Transport on a flight from London to Paris.

▼ On 10 November, the first Book Week was observed in the United States.

▼ On 20 November, the municipal airport in Tucson, Arizona, opened. This was the first municipal airport in the United States.

▼   1919   ▼

MUSEUMS AND ZOOS
Daughters of the Republic of Texas Museum
   (Austin, TX)
Dayton Art Institute (Dayton, OH)
Huntington Library (San Marino, CA)
International Institute of Metropolitan Detroit
   (Detroit, MI)
Islesford Historical Museum (Bar Harbor, ME)
Missouri State Museum (Jefferson City, MO)
Oregon Trail Museum (Gering, NE)

BIRTHDAYS AND DEATH DAYS
Theodore Roosevelt died on 5 January at age 61
Margot Fonteyn born on 18 May
Edmund Hillary born on 20 July
Andrew Carnegie died on 11 August at age 84
Pierre Auguste Renoir died on 3 December at age 78

▼ **1919** ▼

COLLEGES AND UNIVERSITIES
Babson College (Babson Park, MA)
Bemidji State University (Bemidji, MN)
John Brown University (Siloam Springs, AR)
New School for Social Research (New York, NY)
University of California at Los Angeles
(Los Angeles, CA)

NEWSPAPERS AND MAGAZINES
American Legion Magazine (Indianapolis, IN)
True Story (New York, NY)

BOOKS, POETRY, AND PLAYS
The American Language, by H. L. Mencken
Winesburg, Ohio, by Sherwood Anderson

MOVIES
The Cabinet of Dr. Caligari (directed by Robert Wiene,
with Werner Krauss, Conrad Veidt)

▼ The Radio Corporation of America (RCA) was founded as a cooperative effort of General Electric, Westinghouse, and American Telephone & Telegraph. On 1 July 1920, the companies signed a joint patent agreement allowing the purchase of the rights to build radio equipment from Marconi in England.

▼ Bernarr Macfadden founded *True Story* magazine in New York City. *True Story* was the first magazine in the confession genre; its motto: Truth is stranger than fiction. Macfadden's first publishing venture was *Physical Culture,* which he founded in 1898. This magazine promoted his theory of health, based on the concept of "physcultopathy." Macfadden publications included *True Romances, Dream World, True Detective Mystery Magazine,* and *Photoplay,* among others, as well as ten daily newspapers in various cities.

▼ The National Football League (NFL) was founded with 11 teams participating. The original name of the organization was the American Professional Football Association, with teams from Akron (Ohio), Canton (Ohio), Cleveland (Ohio), Chicago (Illinois), Dayton (Ohio), Decatur (Illinois), Hammond (Indiana), Massilon (Ohio), Muncie (Indiana), Rochester (Illinois), and Rock Island (Illinois).

1994

▼ The Hobart Company began selling the first Kitchen Aid food mixers.

▼ The Foster Grant Company was established in Leominster, Massachusetts, to manufacture combs. Foster Grant was one of the pioneers in making plastic products using new injection molding equipment.

75 years ago

▼ The Los Angeles Philharmonic orchestra was established in Los Angeles, California.

▼ Joe Johnson founded the Snap-On Tool Company to market his invention, tools with interchangeable handles. The company was incorporated in 1920 and published its first catalog in 1923. The trademark Snap-On Tool vans were developed in 1945 to allow salesmen to take their products to customers.

▼ Horace Moses established the Junior Achievement organization, a group that provides realistic business training for high school students.

▼ The ConAgra company was founded in Omaha, Nebraska, with the merger of four flour mills. The company's original name was Nebraska Consolidated Mills; ConAgra was adopted as the official company name in 1971.

▼ Rockwell International was founded in Oshkosh, Wisconsin, as Rockwell-Standard, a manufacturer of axles for trucks. The founders, Willard Rockwell and his son, Willard Rockwell, Jr., acquired many other businesses, including North American Aviation, a major aerospace company.

▼ The Reynolds Metals Company was founded by R. S. Reynolds under the name U.S. Foil. Located in Louisville, Kentucky, Reynolds got the idea for manufacturing tin and aluminum foil while working for his uncle, R. J. Reynolds, the owner of a major tobacco company. His observation: increased demand for cigarettes during World War I was curtailed by the short supply of the foil used in cigarette packages.

▼ The Green Bay Packers professional football team was founded in Green Bay, Wisconsin. Created by George Calhoun and Curly Lambeau, the team was originally sponsored by the Indian Packing Company, which also inspired the team name. In 1921, the Packers became part of the National Football League. Vince Lombardi was hired as coach in 1959.

▼ Oliver Smith, a California inventor, created the mechanical rabbit used as a lure in dog racing.

▼ The Electrolux vacuum cleaner company was founded in Sweden. One of the first lightweight vacuums, Electrolux pioneered the concept of door-to-door sales.

▼ The Cummins Engine Company was founded in Columbus, Indiana, by Clessie Cummins. Cummins was employed as a chauffeur when he built his first diesel engine, and the company was financed by his boss, a local banker.

▼ Conrad Hilton, along with L. M. Drown and Jay Powers, purchased his first hotel, an aging structure in Cisco, Texas. The Hilton chain was established primarily through the rehabilitation of older hotels, and became one of the major chains by franchising its name to many different hotel owners.

▼ United Artists was founded as a film production company. Original founders included Douglas Fairbanks, Mary Pickford, and Charlie Chaplin.

▼ The first coast-to-coast telephone links were established in the United States.

▼ The Bauhaus was founded in Weimar, Germany. This influential design school was established by Walter Gropius.

▼ 1894 ▼

ASSOCIATIONS, SOCIETIES, UNIONS, AND GOVERNMENT DEPARTMENTS
American Society of Heating, Refrigeration and Air Conditioning Engineers (Alexandria, VA)
Civitan International (Birmingham, AL)
Jockey Club (New York, NY)
Knights of Ak-Sar-Ben (Omaha, NE)
National Civic League (New York, NY)
National Municipal League (New York, NY)
United Daughters of the Confederacy (Richmond, VA)
U.S. Golf Association (Far Hills, NJ)

IN 1894 on 8 March, the first dog licensing law in the United States was passed in New York. The legislation called for a $2 annual fee for a dog license, and unlicensed dogs were destroyed if they were not claimed within 48 hours.

1994

▼ **1894** ▼

MUSEUMS AND ZOOS
Denver Art Museum (Denver, CO)
Iowa State Museum (Des Moines, IA)
Lowell Observatory (Flagstaff, AZ)
Nantucket Historical Museum (Nantucket, MA)
Port of History Museum (Philadelphia, PA)
Seneca Park Zoo (Rochester, NY)

BIRTHDAYS AND DEATH DAYS
Harold Macmillan born on 10 February
Nikita Khrushchev born on 17 April
Aldous Huxley born on 26 July
Hermann Helmholtz died on 8 September at age 73
Oliver Wendell Holmes died on 7 October at age 85
Robert Louis Stevenson died on 3 December at age 44
James Thurber born on 8 December

▼ On 26 June, a national railway strike began. Originating with a strike by workers at the Pullman Company in May, this major union activity was focused on Chicago. Strike breakers and private security hired by railroad companies were involved in numerous clashes with strikers, and city, state, and U.S. troops were eventually involved as President Cleveland and Congress stepped in to prevent disruption of rail-delivered mail. The strike ended on 3 August with more than $3 million in property damage, several deaths, and hundreds of injuries.

▼ On 8 August, the U.S. government recognized the Republic of Hawaii. The republic had been formed after a failed revolution led by Queen Liliuokalani, on 17 January 1893.

▼ On 22 December, the U.S. Golf Association was created. The first official competition sponsored by this group was also held in this year.

▼ William Kellogg and Dr. John Kellogg, brothers working at a health spa in Battle Creek, Michigan, invented the first flaked breakfast cereal. Their cereal was the result of a mistake; a batch of wheat dough mixed for hot cereal was left too long without cooking and instead of wasting it, they toasted it. This produced a unique food, sold as Granose Flakes, that was soon a popular item. The Kellogg brothers were slow to capitalize on their discovery, with many other companies rushing in before them to manufacture and market the new form of cereal. The Kellogg Company did, however, become a major player in the cereal industry, creating products such as Bran Flakes, All-Bran, Rice Krispies, and Special K, among others. Their most popular creation, Kellogg's Corn Flakes, was introduced in 1898.

▼ George Haskell and William Bosworth began a partnership to distribute dairy goods, eggs, and produce in Beatrice, Nebraska. The business soon became the Beatrice Creamery, and expanded to Lincoln and other cities. Acquisition of other companies beginning after World War II turned Beatrice into a major food processing business.

▼ The Reebok company got its start with the invention of a running shoe by Joseph W. Foster in England. The shoe's success led to the founding of JW Foster and Sons, which made shoes for competitive runners, including the British running team that won the 1924 Olympics. Reebok—a company founded by the grandsons of Joseph Foster—bought up JW Foster and Sons in 1958.

▼ The first children's division of a public library opened at the Denver Public Library in Denver, Colorado.

▼ **1894** ▼

COLLEGES AND UNIVERSITIES
Concordia Teachers College (Seward, NE)
Fitchburg State College (Fitchburg, MA)
Goshen College (Goshen, IN)
Lewis-Clark State College (Lewiston, ID)
Louisiana Tech University (Ruston, LA)
Morningside College (Sioux City, IA)
North Adams State College (North Adams, MA)
Southwestern Adventist College (Keene, TX)
Thomas College (Waterville, ME)
University of Lowell (Lowell, MA)
University of Tulsa (Tulsa, OK)
University of Wisconsin–Stevens Point
(Stevens Point, WI)

MUSIC
Guntrum, by Richard Strauss
Prelude to the Afternoon of a Faun, by Claude Debussy
(first performed on 23 December in Paris, France)
Resurrection Symphony, by Gustav Mahler
Thaïs, by Jules Massenet (first performed on 16 March
in Paris, France)

1994

▼ The Ralston Purina Company was founded in St. Louis, Missouri, by William H. Danforth. The original company name was the Robinson-Danforth Commission Company. In 1898, the company introduced a new cereal named Purina, with an endorsement from Everett Ralston, a leading proponent of whole grains in the human diet. Ralston's name was added to the cereal and the company in 1902, when the business was renamed Ralston Purina.

▼ Augustus Sachett invented plasterboard in New York City. Plasterboard, also known as wallboard or gypsum board, was one of the building products that helped develop mass production of commercial and residential buildings.

▼ Two English scientists discovered argon, an inert gas that comprises about 1 percent of the earth's atmosphere. William Ramsay and John Strutt are credited with finding this gas, which is used in some types of fluorescent lights and welding applications. Their discovery was announced on 13 August; in 1904 the two were awarded Nobel Prizes for their work.

▼ Lowell Observatory opened in Flagstaff, Arizona. Established by Percival Lowell, an amateur astronomer from Boston, the first major work carried out by this observatory was a comprehensive study of the planet Mars. Lowell established a professional reputation as an astronomer and went on to teach at the Massachusetts Institute of Technology. He was one of the first scientists to speculate on the existence of a planet beyond the orbit of Neptune because of unexplained variations in the orbit of Uranus. His theory was confirmed when Pluto was first recognized in 1930. Lowell died in 1916 while conducting research at the Flagstaff facility.

▼ Selchow & Righter introduced Parcheesi, a board game inspired by an ancient game of Indian royalty. Within a few years, Parcheesi was the most popular game in the country. Among the fans of this pastime were Thomas Edison, President Calvin Coolidge, and Clara Bow.

▼   **1894**   ▼

NEWSPAPERS AND MAGAZINES
American Mathematical Monthly (Washington, DC)
Billboard (Los Angeles, CA)
Daily Racing Form (Hightstown, NJ)
Oklahoma City Oklahoman (Oklahoma City, OK)

BOOKS, POETRY, AND PLAYS
Arms and the Man, by George Bernard Shaw
The Jungle Book, by Rudyard Kipling

▼   **1844**   ▼

ASSOCIATIONS, SOCIETIES, UNIONS, AND GOVERNMENT DEPARTMENTS

American Psychiatric Association
(Washington, DC)

MUSEUMS AND ZOOS

Museum and Library of Maryland History
(Baltimore, MD)

BIRTHDAYS AND DEATH DAYS

Nicolay Rimsky-Korsakov born on 18 March
Paul Verlaine born on 30 March
Anatole France born on 16 April
John Dalton died on 27 July at age 77
Friedrich Nietzsche born on 15 October

IN 1844

on 24 May, Samuel Morse demonstrated the practicality of the telegraph with a message sent on the first telegraph line, which stretched from Washington, D.C., to Baltimore, Maryland. Morse, working the telegraph key in a room in the Supreme Court building, sent the message, "What hath God wrought?" The patent for the telegraph was granted in 1843, but the demonstration was not possible until a special bill was passed by Congress, allowing an expenditure of $30,000 to construct a test line between the two cities. When the bill was finally passed after many delays and problems, Morse heard the news from the daughter of the Commissioner of Patents, and allowed her to chose what the text of the first message would be. The words were from the book of Numbers in the Old Testament. The same day, the first telegraphic news was wired to Baltimore from Washington, allowing the *Baltimore Patriot* to report: "One o'clock—There has just been made a motion in the House to go into committee of the whole on the Oregon question. Rejected—ayes, 79; nays, 86."

▼ On 15 June, a patent was issued for vulcanized rubber. Invented by Charles Goodyear, this material was discovered five years earlier when the inventor accidentally mixed and heated raw rubber and sulphur.

▼ On 27 June, Joseph Smith was killed in Carthage, Illinois. The founder of the Mormon religion, Smith, along with his brother, was attacked by an angry mob while they were being held in the local jail.

▼ On 15 September, the Mesabi iron range was discovered in the region west of Lake Superior. The discoverer was William Burt, a government surveyor who unearthed iron deposits in an attempt to find out what was causing his compass to give erratic readings.

▼ The Orvis Company published their first fishing equipment catalog.

▼ Nitrous oxide was first used as an anesthetic by dentists. Also referred to as laughing gas, it had been discovered in 1772 by Joseph Priestly, an English minister with a strong interest in science. As early as 1800, a report by Humphry Davy, an English doctor, described the unusual effect of the gas on humans who inhaled it. He suggested it might have some use as an anesthetic, but initially the gas was used as a form of amusement.

▼ The Young Men's Christian Association (YMCA) was founded in England. The first American chapter opened in Boston in 1851.

▼ *The Pencil of Nature* was published, the first book to include photographic illustrations.

▼   1844   ▼

COLLEGES AND UNIVERSITIES
Hillsdale College (Hillsdale, MI)
Olivet College (Olivet, MI)
State University of New York at Albany (Albany, NY)
University of Mississippi (University, MS)

MUSIC
Sonata in B Minor, by Frédéric Chopin
Violin Concerto in E Minor, by Felix Mendelssohn

NEWSPAPERS AND MAGAZINES
American Journal of Psychiatry (Washington, DC)
The Citizen (Ottawa, Ontario, Canada)
Republican and American (Waterbury, CT)

▼ **1794** ▼

BIRTHDAYS AND DEATH DAYS
Edward Gibbon died on 16 January at age 57
Antoine Lavoisier died on 8 May at age 50
John Roebuck died on 17 July at age 76

COLLEGES AND UNIVERSITIES
Bowdoin College (Brunswick, ME)
University of Tennessee (Knoxville, TN)

MUSIC
Symphony No. 101 (*Clock* Symphony),
  by Franz Joseph Haydn (first performed
  on 3 May in London, England)

NEWSPAPERS AND MAGAZINES
Intelligencer Journal (Lancaster, PA)
Rutland Herald (Rutland, VT)

BOOKS, POETRY, AND PLAYS
The Age of Reason, by Thomas Paine
The Fall of Robespierre, by Samuel Taylor Coleridge
Letters Concerning the Aesthetic Education of Mankind,
  by Friedrich von Schiller

IN 1794 on 14 March, a patent was granted for the cotton gin. Invented

by Eli Whitney in 1793, it allowed a huge increase in the amount of cotton that could be prepared for weaving. Whitney made little profit from his invention, as it was quickly appropriated by others, but was more successful financially with his development of mass production through interchangeable parts, produced by standardizing industrial processes. According to one source, Whitney got the idea by observing his wife Henrietta—later referred to as "Nutty Grandma" by their descendants—while she cracked walnuts for hours at a time with repetitive motions of her rocking chair.

▼ On 27 March, President Washington signed the legislation that created the U.S. Navy. This is the earliest date that officially marks its existence; on 3 May 1798, the Department of the Navy was established by an Act of Congress. The Navy had previously been administered as part of the War Department. The first secretary of the Navy was Benjamin Stoddert, appointed on 21 May 1798.

▼ On 10 June, Richard Allen established the Bethel African Methodist Episcopal (A.M.E.) Church in Philadelphia. The A.M.E. Church was the first major religious body created by African Americans in the United States. On 29 July, the church was dedicated a member of the Methodist Episcopal Church organization.

▼ In July, the Whisky Rebellion began in western Pennsylvania, led by citizens who were outraged at the federal excise tax on whiskey, which had been enacted in 1791. President Washington ordered action by the militia on 7 August, calling out almost 13,000 troops from Maryland, New Jersey, Pennsylvania, and Virginia. The rebellion was under control by the middle of November, after 200 arrests.

▼ Benjamin Franklin published his *Autobiography*. Since Franklin was already famous in the United States, his book was a bestseller in its time. The personal history covered his life through 1759; additional material that covered the rest of his life was added to a later release, published in 1867 after his death.

▼ Noah Webster founded a daily newspaper in New York City, *American Minerva*. After many changes of ownership and title, the paper was merged with the *New York Sun* in 1923.

▼ One of the toll roads in the country, the Philadelphia-Lancaster Turnpike, was opened. The road was 61 miles long and paved with macadam, a form of crushed rock.

▼ The U.S. government signed a treaty with the Oneida, Tuscarora, and Stockbridge tribes. It was the first to provide for educational opportunities for Indians.

▼ The first explanation for the origin of meteors was offered by Ernst Chladni, a German physicist.

▼ The first maximum-minimum thermometer was invented by Daniel Rutherford.

IN 1744 the first organized mapping survey of a country was begun in France by Cesar-Francois Cassini.

▼ Sotheby's auction house in London, England, had its beginning with an auction for a book collection, which sold for 826 pounds. The company was originally owned by Samuel Baker; the first Sotheby at the company was Baker's nephew John Sotheby, who took over in 1767.

▼ The first official cricket match was played in England, with a team from Kent competing against an All England team.

IN 1694 on 21 April the Maryland Toleration Act was passed, marking a major step in the development of religious tolerance in the American colonies. Among its provisions, the act stated that no one "professing to believe in Jesus Christ shall, from henceforth, be any ways troubled, molested, or discountenanced for, or in respect of, his or her religion, nor in the free exercise thereof within this province."

▼ On 27 July, the Bank of England was founded in London.

▼ The Ancient Mystical Order Rosicrucis, or Rosicrucian Order, was founded. The first lodge was located in Philadelphia, Pennsylvania.

▼   1644   ▼

BOOKS, POETRY, AND PLAYS
Areopagitica, by John Milton
Principia Philosophiae, by René Descartes

IN 1644 the village of New York constructed a stone wall across the upper boundary of the town in order to protect the citizens against Indian attacks. The wall was later removed to make room for a new street, which was named Wall Street.

▼ The Ming dynasty in China came to an end with the death of Emperor Chongzhen. The emperor killed himself after the city of Beijing was conquered by Li Dzucheng, a former bandit and self-proclaimed rebel.

▼   **1594**   ▼

BOOKS, POETRY, AND PLAYS
Taming of the Shrew, by William Shakespeare
Titus Andronicus, by William Shakespeare

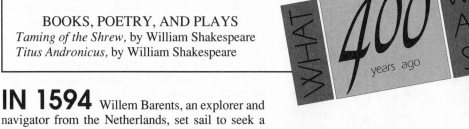

IN 1594 Willem Barents, an explorer and navigator from the Netherlands, set sail to seek a navigable link from the Atlantic Ocean to the Pacific Ocean, the so-called Northwest Passage. This quest was unsuccessful, but along the way Barents discovered many of the islands and features of the Arctic. Although some explorers did eventually find effective routes, ice packs foiled all attempted passages until 14 September 1969, when the SS *Manhattan,* a tanker, broke through on a voyage from Chester, Pennsylvania, to Point Barrow, Alaska.

▼   The Dutch East India Company was established to create trade in spices from India and the New World. The company was formed after the port of Lisbon banned spice trade with the Dutch and the English. The first expedition to India set out four years later in 1598.

▼   The concept of logarithms, one of the most important foundations of modern mathematics, was invented by John Napier, a Scottish mathematician. Napier outlined his discovery in treatises that were published in 1614 and 1619. A later invention used to simplify logarithm calculations was a series of rods thereafter known as Napier's bones; this was an early version of the slide rule.

IN 1544 Spanish explorers first brought tomatoes to Italy from South America. The Aztecs were known to have developed a yellow tomato they called *tomatl*; in Italy, the fruit was called *pomodoro,* "the golden apple." For at least 100 years, the tomato was not grown for food, but as an ornamental plant and a remedy for skin diseases. Appreciation of tomatoes as food did not come until the 1700s in Europe and the mid-1800s in the United States.

▼   Sebastian Münster, a German cartographer, published the first major book on world geography. This book, *Cosmographia,* followed an earlier text in which he had translated the work of Ptolemy, the Greek mathematician and astronomer. Ptolemy's original book, *Geographia,* was one of the first collections of maps, which were created using woodcuts.

IN 1494 on 5 May, Columbus discovered Jamaica during his second voyage to the New World.

▼ On 7 June, the Treaty of Tordesillas was enacted. This pact between Spain and Portugal ceded land claims to the two countries dependent on whether they were west or east of a north-south line situated about 1,000 miles west of the Azores. Spain got the western pieces; Portugal got those to the east.

▼ Luca Pacioli, an Italian mathematician, published *Summa de arithmetica geometria proportioni et proportionalita,* the first algebra book to be printed in multiple copies.

▼ The first mill designed specifically for the production of paper was built in England. The earliest known use of paper was around A.D. 100 in China; the earliest reported paper mills in Europe date to the 1300s. The invention of the printing press in the mid-1400s created an instant demand for larger quantities of paper. Paper mills operated with hand labor to make one sheet at a time until 1798, when Nicola-Louis Robert, a French inventor, created a machine to make paper in continuous lengths.

1995

▼ 1970 ▼

ASSOCIATIONS, SOCIETIES, UNIONS, AND GOVERNMENT DEPARTMENTS
American Aging Association (Omaha, NE)
Association of American Publishers
(New York, NY)
Environmental Protection Agency
(U.S. government)
Gray Panthers (Philadelphia, PA)
International Society of Certified Electronics
Technicians (Fort Worth, TX)
National Highway Traffic Safety Administration
(U.S. Department of Transportation)
National Oceanic and Atmospheric Administration
(U.S. Department of Commerce)
Occupational Safety and Health Administration
(U.S. Department of Labor)

WHAT *25 years ago* *WAS*

IN 1970 on 5 March, after the United States, the Soviet Union, and other countries had ratified it, the nuclear nonproliferation treaty went into effect, limiting the development of nuclear weapons.

▼ On 22 April, the first Earth Day was held to educate people about dangers to the environment. Programs and activities were held at more than 2,000 colleges and 10,000 high schools. On the same day, at a convention of the Daughters of the American Revolution in Washington, D.C., a resolution was passed declaring Earth Day to be un-American.

▼ On 4 May, National Guardsmen at an antiwar rally at Kent State University in Ohio opened fire, killing four demonstrators. On 8 November 1974, a federal judge acquitted eight guardsmen who had been charged with the killings.

▼ On 15 May, police at an antiwar rally at Jackson State College in Mississippi opened fire, killing two demonstrators.

▼ Ted Turner founded the Turner Communications Corporation in Atlanta, Georgia, with the purchase of a local television station. The station developed into the largest independent TV outlet in the Southern states, and led to the creation of WTBS, which was marketed to cable television systems around the country. In 1980, Turner originated the Cable News Network (CNN), the first 24-hour news service.

▼ The John Hancock Center Building in Chicago was completed. The same year, construction began on Chicago's Sears Tower.

▼ The first waterbeds went on sale. This mattress concept was invented by Charles Hall, a furniture designer in California, who spent several years experimenting with methods of making a liquid-filled bed. Hall began in 1968 with experiments using liquid starch; in 1971, his invention was patented.

▼ The first industrial lasers were introduced.

▼ 1970 ▼

MUSEUMS AND ZOOS
Huntsville Museum of Art (Huntsville, AL)
Science Museum of Virginia (Richmond, VA)
Science Museum of Western Virginia (Roanoke, VA)
Sea World of Ohio (Aurora, OH)
Western Museum of Mining and Industry
  (Colorado Springs, CO)

MUSIC
Abraxas, by Santana
All Things Must Pass, by George Harrison
American Beauty, by the Grateful Dead
American Woman, by the Guess Who
Band of Gypsies, by Jimi Hendrix
Bitches Brew, by Miles Davis
Bridge over Troubled Water, by Simon & Garfunkel
Chicago II, by Chicago
Close to You, by the Carpenters
Cosmo's Factory, by Creedence Clearwater Revival
Cracklin' Rosie, by Neil Diamond
Déjà Vu, by Crosby, Stills, Nash & Young
Get Yer Ya-Ya's Out!, by the Rolling Stones
Hello, I'm Johnny Cash, by Johnny Cash
Instant Karma, by John Lennon
John Barleycorn Must Die, by Traffic
Knock Three Times, by Tony Orlando and Dawn
Ladies of the Canyon, by Joni Mitchell
Layla, by Derek and the Dominos
Let It Be, by the Beatles
Lonely Days, by the Bee Gees

25
years ago

1995

▼ The first videocassette recorder (VCR) was developed, a design by Phillips.

▼ Arthur June, an inventor in Florida, began selling the first Nautilus body-building machines.

▼ Floppy discs for computer systems were introduced.

▼ 1970 ▼

MUSIC *continued*
Mad Dogs and Englishmen, by Joe Cocker
Mama Told Me, by Three Dog Night
Moondance, by Van Morrison
Morrison Hotel, by the Doors
My Sweet Lord, by George Harrison
Okie from Muskogee, by Merle Haggard
A Question of Balance, by the Moody Blues
Rose Garden, by Lynn Anderson
Self Portrait, by Bob Dylan
Snowbird, by Anne Murray
Stage Fright, by the Band
Turn Back the Hands of Time, by Tyrone Davis
Whales & Nightingales, by Judy Collins
The Wonder of You, by Elvis Presley
Workingman's Dead, by the Grateful Dead

NEWSPAPERS AND MAGAZINES
Mother Earth News (Hendersonville, NC)
National Lampoon (New York, NY)
New Woman (New York, NY)
Sail (Charlestown, MA)
Smithsonian Magazine (Washington, DC)

BOOKS, POETRY, AND PLAYS
Everything You Always Wanted To Know about Sex,
   by Dr. David Reuben
The French Lieutenant's Woman, by John Fowles
The Godfather, by Mario Puzo
The Greening of America, by Charles Reich
Islands in the Stream, by Ernest Hemingway

▼ **1970** ▼

BOOKS, POETRY, AND PLAYS
continued
Jonathan Livingston Seagull, by Richard Bach
Love Story, by Erich Segal
Portnoy's Complaint, by Philip Roth
The Promise, by Chaim Potok
Rich Man, Poor Man, by Irwin Shaw
The Selling of the President, by Joe McGinniss
Sexual Politics, by Kate Millett

MOVIES
Catch-22 (directed by Mike Nichols, with Alan Arkin)
Cotton Comes to Harlem (directed by Ossie Davis)
Five Easy Pieces (directed by Bob Rafelson, with Jack
   Nicholson)
M*A*S*H (directed by Robert Altman, with Elliott
   Gould, Donald Sutherland)
Patton (directed by Franklin Schaffner, with Karl
   Malden, George C. Scott)

IN 1945 on 9 February, U.S. forces landed on Iwo Jima. The raising of

the U.S. flag on Mount Suribachi—the inspiration for a monument, a movie, and

a Pulitzer Prize–winning photograph—occurred on February 23. The island was conquered on 16 March. The U.S. Marine Corps lost 4,000 men in the battle; Japanese losses topped 20,000.

▼ On 9 March, the most destructive air raid in history took place over Tokyo, Japan, during World War II. The U.S. Army Air Corps destroyed more than 16 square miles of the city in a nighttime incendiary bomb attack, using 334 B-29 bombers to drop 2,000 tons of explosives. More than 250,000 buildings were destroyed, with an official death count on the ground of 83,793.

▼ On 1 April, U.S. forces landed on Okinawa. The island was conquered on 21 June with a surrender by Japanese forces. Losses for the United States were 16,646 men; the Japanese lost more than 100,000 troops.

▼   1945   ▼

ASSOCIATIONS, SOCIETIES, UNIONS, AND GOVERNMENT DEPARTMENTS

Children's Book Council (New York, NY)
Federation of American Scientists (Washington, DC)
Financial Analysts Federation (Charlottesville, VA)
Future Homemakers of America (Reston, VA)
Girls Clubs of America (New York, NY)
Institution of Navigation (Washington, DC)
National Fisheries Institute (Washington, DC)
National Multiple Sclerosis Society (New York, NY)
National Society of Public Accountants
   (Alexandria, VA)
Office and Professional Employees International Union
   (New York, NY)
Society of American Soil Conservation (Ankeny, IA)
Utility Workers Union of America (Washington, DC)

MUSEUMS AND ZOOS

Morris County Historical Society (Morristown, NJ)
Shore Line Trolley Museum (East Haven, CT)

▼ On 12 April, President Franklin D. Roosevelt died in Warm Springs, Georgia, at the age of 63, during his fourth term in office. The president had been in ill health for some time, although official reports from the White House indicated no problem until March, when the White House physician requested Roosevelt go to Warm Springs for treatment at a national center for infantile paralysis. During an afternoon session with an artist, he suffered a cerebral hemorrhage. His last words were, "I have a terrific headache." Vice President Truman was sworn in as president on the same day.

▼ On 24 April, representatives from 50 nations met in San Francisco at the first United Nations Conference. On 26 June, the United Nations charter was signed, formalizing this institution. The U.S. Senate voted to ratify the charter on 28 July. United Nations Day, marking the founding of this organization, is officially recognized as 24 October, also the date in 1949 when the United Nations building was dedicated.

▼ On 7 May, Germany signed surrender papers in Reims, France, ending World War II in Europe.

▼ On 6 July, the United States Medal of Freedom was established to recognize heroism or commendable service by civilians.

▼ On 16 July, outside of Alamogordo, New Mexico, the era of atomic weapons was officially begun at 5:30 in the morning with the explosion of the first atomic bomb.

▼ On 6 August, the *Enola Gay,* an American B-29 bomber, dropped an atom bomb on Hiroshima, Japan. The first atom bomb was based on uranium-235. Estimates of deaths caused by this bomb range from 45,000 to 133,000.

▼ On 9 August, an American B-29 bomber dropped an atom bomb on Nagasaki, Japan. This weapon, the second atom bomb, was based on plutonium. Estimates of deaths range from 24,000 to 74,000.

▼ On 14 August, Japan surrendered, ending World War II in the Pacific. Official surrender ceremonies took place aboard the USS *Missouri* in Tokyo Bay on 2 September. In some states, 14 August is recognized as V-J Day (Victory over Japan Day).

▼   **1945**   ▼

BIRTHDAYS AND DEATH DAYS
Franklin Delano Roosevelt died on 12 April at age 63
Benito Mussolini died on 28 April at age 61
Adolf Hitler died on 30 April at age 56
Béla Bartók died on 26 September at age 64
George Patton died on 21 December at age 60
Theodore Dreiser died on 28 December at age 74

COLLEGES AND UNIVERSITIES
Berklee College of Music (Boston, MA)
Indiana University at Kokomo (Kokomo, IN)
Roosevelt University (Chicago, IL)
University of Calgary (Alberta, Canada)

MUSIC
Carousel, by Richard Rogers and Oscar Hammerstein
(first performed on 19 April in New York, NY)
White Christmas, by Bing Crosby
Peter Grimes, by Benjamin Britten

▼   1945   ▼

NEWSPAPERS AND MAGAZINES
Cats Magazine (Port Orange, FL)
Outdoor Sports and Recreation (St. Paul, MN)

BOOKS, POETRY, AND PLAYS
Black Boy, by Richard Wright
Captain from Castile, by Samuel Shellabarger
The Egg and I, by Betty MacDonald

MOVIES
The Corn Is Green (directed by Irving Rapper, with
   Bette Davis, John Dall)
The Picture of Dorian Gray (directed by Albert Lewin,
   with George Sanders)
They Were Expendable (directed by John Ford, with
   Robert Montgomery, John Wayne)

▼ In November, *Ebony* magazine debuted in Chicago. Founded by John Johnson, *Ebony* was the first major "slick paper" magazine written for and marketed to blacks.

▼ Slinkies were first offered for sale. Invented by Richard James, a mechanical engineer in Philadelphia, the product was an almost instant hit, but production problems delayed national distribution until the early 1950s.

▼ The first Eddie Bauer catalog was published, featuring a range of products for outdoor sportsmen. Eddie Bauer originally went into business in Seattle in 1921, opening a shop to restring tennis rackets. In 1936, he obtained patents for goose-down jackets and sleeping bags.

▼ The first precooked, frozen dinners were served to passengers on an airline flight.

▼ The first commercial Volkswagen Beetle was produced at the Volkswagen factory in Wolfsburg, Germany. The factory was built in 1937 to produce vehicles for the German military.

▼ Mattel was founded in Los Angeles by Harold Matson and Ruth and Elliott Handler. The company was created to make toy furniture from excess picture frame wood; Elliott Handler ran a picture framing business at the time. Mattel was already successful when Ruth Handler created the Barbie doll in 1959.

▼ Tupperware was developed by Earl Tupper, an inventor in Massachusetts and a former chemist at Du Pont. These sealable containers were used to create a unique, in-home marketing strategy, the Tupperware party, which Tupper introduced in 1951.

▼ Paramount Studios produced the first animated Casper cartoon, titled "The Friendly Ghost." After years of popularity, Casper's star faded and he disappeared in the 1960s, but not before starting a successful career in comic books. Casper later reappeared as an animated feature on television.

▼ Urban water supplies in some cities in the United States were fluoridated for the first time to prevent tooth decay. The first city to adopt fluoride as an additive was Grand Rapids, Michigan, which began adding the compound on 25 January.

▼ 1920 ▼

ASSOCIATIONS, SOCIETIES, UNIONS, AND GOVERNMENT DEPARTMENTS

American Association of Community and
   Junior Colleges (Washington, DC)
American Association of Law Libraries
   (Chicago, IL)
American Civil Liberties Union (New York, NY)
American Society of Association Executives
   (Washington, DC)
Child Welfare League of America
   (Washington, DC)
Disabled American Veterans (Cold Spring, KY)
Federal Bar Association (Washington, DC)
League of Women Voters of the U.S. (Washington, DC)
Military Order of the World Wars (Alexandria, VA)
National Association of Bank Women (Chicago, IL)
National Association of Mutual Savings Banks
   (New York, NY)
National Council of Teachers of Mathematics (Reston, VA)
National Federation of State High School Associations
   (Kansas City, MO)
National Health Council (New York, NY)

WHAT WAS 75 years ago

IN 1920 on 10 January, the League of Nations was founded. The organization established the basic framework upon which the United Nations was formed.

1995

▼ On 5 June, Congress passed the Merchant Marine Act, establishing a shipping system with ships owned by the government.

▼ On 26 August, the Nineteenth Amendment to the U.S. Constitution was ratified, giving women the right to vote. Tennessee was the last state to vote for this change. The first national election in which women could participate was in November. After the Amendment was ratified, Carrie Chapman Catt, the president of the National American Woman Suffrage Association, stated, "The ratification of the amendment is more than a victory for us. In the hour of victory there is but one regret and that is that every man and woman in the nation does not share our joy. Today there are those yet too blinded by prejudice to recognize the justice and inevitability of woman suffrage." Indeed, speaking for the opposition, Mary Kilbreth, the president of the National Association Opposed to Woman Suffrage, commented, "If the amendment has really been passed, it means that a blow has been struck at representative government, and that the balance of power between the Federal Government and the States has been destroyed."

▼ On 2 November, the age of radio began with the first regular broadcast from station KDKA in East Pittsburgh, Pennsylvania. The first program was election coverage of the presidential race between Warren Harding and James Cox. The number of radio sets in the United States in 1920 was estimated to be less than 5,000. In 1922, the first commercials were heard during broadcasts from WEAF in New York City.

▼ 1920 ▼

MUSEUMS AND ZOOS
Cleveland Museum of Natural History (Cleveland, OH)
Frick Collection (New York, NY)
Mission Houses Museum (Honolulu, HI)
Robert Bebb Herbarium (University of Oklahoma, Norman, OK)
Roosevelt Zoo (Minot, ND)

BIRTHDAYS AND DEATH DAYS
Robert Peary died on 19 February at age 64

MUSIC
La Valse, by Maurice Ravel

NEWSPAPERS AND MAGAZINES
Architectural Digest (Los Angeles, CA)
Senior Scholastic (New York, NY)

years ago

▼ **1920** ▼

BOOKS, POETRY, AND PLAYS
Beyond the Horizon, by Eugene O'Neill
The Emperor Jones, by Eugene O'Neill
Main Street, by Sinclair Lewis
This Side of Paradise, by F. Scott Fitzgerald

MOVIES
The Mark of Zorro (directed by Fred Niblo, with Douglas Fairbanks)

▼ On 16 November, the first letter was mailed using a postage meter. Arthur Pitney, a clerk in a wallpaper store, had designed the first postage meter in 1901, but found little acceptance for his invention; the post office did not allow it to be used for first class mail. In 1920, in collaboration with Walter Bowes, legislation was passed by Congress permitting postage meters for first class mail. During the same year the Pitney Bowes company was founded in Stamford, Connecticut.

▼ Allied Signal was founded in Morristown, New Jersey, as the Allied Chemical Company. When founded with the merger of five existing chemical companies, Allied was the third largest chemical company in the United States.

▼ C. L. Griggs, from Price's Branch, Missouri, created a soft drink he called "Bib-Label Lithiated Lemon-Lime Soda." The name was later changed to 7-Up.

▼ Earle Dickson invented the first self-sticking adhesive bandage in New Brunswick, New Jersey. The Johnson & Johnson Company, where he worked, trademarked this creation under the name Band-Aid. The first Band-Aid products were sheets 3 inches by 18 inches; customers cut a piece off whenever they needed a bandage. Precut sizes were introduced in 1924. One early promotion by the company was to provide free samples to butchers.

▼ Donald Douglas founded the McDonnell Douglas Corporation in Los Angeles. The company was originally the Davis-Douglas Company, formed to design and build an airplane that could fly coast-to-coast nonstop. The first commercial success for the renamed Douglas Company was the DC-3, a major advance for the airline industry in the United States. In 1967, Douglas merged with McDonnell Aircraft of St. Louis, Missouri (founded in 1939).

1995

▼ The Occidental Petroleum Corporation was founded as an oil exploration company in California. In 1956, Dr. Armand Hammer invested in the company and helped it gain international drilling rights.

▼ Simon Barry, a restaurant owner in Portland, Oregon, invented the first soft ice cream maker.

▼ ITT was founded as a manufacturer of telephones and telephone switching equipment. Originally known as the International Telephone and Telegraph Corporation, ITT sold the last of its telecommunications branches in 1987. Most of the company's business is now in insurance, hotels, and industrial equipment.

▼ Rubbermaid was founded in Wooster, Ohio. The company was originally known as the Wooster Rubber Company, a manufacturer of balloons, but moved into household products in 1934 with the introduction of a rubber dustpan. The company's name was changed in 1957.

▼ Emanuel Haldeman-Julius began publishing "Little Blue Books" in Girard, Kansas. Haldeman-Julius, a socialist and "free thinker," was born Emanuel Julius; he added his wife's maiden name after their marriage. The inexpensive mini-books—usually no more than 64 pages long and selling for 5 to 25 cents— eventually numbered in the thousands. They included classic works, unusual collections of trivia, socialist tracts, and self-help titles. Authors included H. G. Wells, Bertrand Russell, Upton Sinclair, and Will Durant. More than 3 million copies were sold; publication continued until Haldeman-Julius died in 1951.

▼ The original Chicago Bears professional football team was founded in Chicago, Illinois, as the Decatur Staleys. Chicago Bears became the official name of the team in 1922.

▼ The first live radio broadcast of a college football game was carried by WTAW in College Station, Texas. The game was a matchup between the University of Texas and Texas A&M University.

▼ The first measurement was made of the diameter of a star. Albert Michelson used a new device, the stellar interferometer, to measure the star Betelgeuse.

▼ The American Civil Liberties Union was founded. Organizers included Jane Addams, Helen Keller, and Norman Thomas.

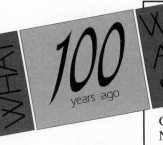

▼   **1895**   ▼

ASSOCIATIONS, SOCIETIES, UNIONS, AND GOVERNMENT DEPARTMENTS

American Bowling Congress (Greendale, WI)
Commercial Law League of America (Chicago, IL)
National Medical Association (Washington, DC)
National Society of the Children of the American Revolution (Washington, DC)
Sons of Norway (Minneapolis, MN)

MUSEUMS AND ZOOS

Georgia State Museum of Science and Industry (Atlanta, GA)
New Jersey State Museum (Trenton, NJ)
New York Zoological Park (Bronx, NY)
Wyoming State Museum (Cheyenne, WY)

IN 1895 on 11 June, Charles Duryea became the first American to receive a patent in the United States for a gasoline-powered automobile. Duryea's car was first driven in September 1893 in Springfield, Massachusetts. The vehicle was jointly developed by Charles and his brother Frank, although Charles is historically credited with the invention. In 1894, a U.S. patent had been granted to Karl Benz, a German, for his motorized vehicle, invented in Germany. Also on 11 June in France, the world's first gasoline-powered automobile race was held. The race covered a round-trip course from Paris to Bordeaux, a total distance of 732 miles, and the winner was a Peugeot. Back in the States, the first automobile race was also held, a round-trip competition from Chicago to Evanston, Illinois, and back. Frank Duryea, driving the Duryea creation, won this race, beating an entry made by Karl Benz.

▼   On 31 August, according to some sources, the first football game was played with a professional, paid player.

▼   On 9 September, the American Bowling Congress was established to standardize rules and specifications for equipment.

1995

▼ On 8 November, X rays were discovered by Wilhelm Röntgen, a German physicist. His discovery was announced in 1896 to the scientific community, which heralded the discovery of a previously unknown form of energy. One of the first experiments that Röntgen performed with the new rays was photographing the bone structure of his hand. Within a few years, doctors in many countries began to put X rays to active use in diagnosing medical problems and studying the human body. In 1901, the first year that Nobel Prizes were offered, Röntgen received the first Nobel Prize for medicine.

▼ The Washington Arch in Greenwich Village, New York City, was completed. It was designed by Stanford White.

▼ Volleyball was invented by William Morgan, an instructor at the Young Men's Christian Association in Holyoke, Massachusetts. Official rules were first published in 1900. Morgan's original game—called Mignonette for unknown reasons—used a basketball, but this was soon replaced by a special ball created by the Spalding Company. At its inception, volleyball required nine players per side; the rules were changed after World War I to six players per side.

▼   1895   ▼

BIRTHDAYS AND DEATH DAYS
Oscar Hammerstein born on 12 July
Louis Pasteur died on 28 September at age 73
Paul Hindemith born on 16 November

COLLEGES AND UNIVERSITIES
Bluefield State College (Bluefield, WV)
Eastern Illinois University (Charleston, IL)
Fort Valley State College (Fort Valley, GA)
Graceland College (Lamoni, IA)
Montana College of Mineral Science and Technology
    (Butte, MT)
Northern Illinois University (De Kalb, IL)
Palmer College of Chiropractic (Davenport, IA)
Southeastern Massachussetts University
    (North Dartmouth, MA)
University of Texas at Arlington (Arlington, TX)
West Virginia Institute of Technology
    (Montgomery, WV)
Wichita State University (Wichita, KS)
Wingate College (Wingate, NC)

▼ 1895 ▼

MUSIC
Till Eulenspiegel's Merry Pranks, by Richard Strauss (first performed on 5 November in Cologne, Germany)

NEWSPAPERS AND MAGAZINES
Atlantic City Press (Atlantic City, NJ)
Bridgeport Telegram (Bridgeport, CT)
Denver Post (Denver, CO)
Field and Stream (New York, NY)
Fort Worth Star Telegram (Fort Worth, TX)
Sierra (San Francisco, CA)
Stockton Record (Stockton, CA)
Terre Haute Tribune and Star (Terre Haute, IN)

BOOKS, POETRY, AND PLAYS
Confessions, by Paul Verlaine
The Importance of Being Earnest, by Oscar Wilde
Poems, by W. B. Yeats
Quo Vadis, by Henryk Sienkiewicz
The Red Badge of Courage, by Stephen Crane
Studies in Hysteria, by Sigmund Freud

▼ The San Francisco Symphony was established in San Francisco, California.

▼ The Harris Corporation was founded in Niles, Ohio. The company was established by Alfred and Charles Harris, inventors and brothers, and was engaged in the development of printing presses. Decades of growth and diversification led to a much larger company, which, in 1983, got out of the printing equipment industry in favor of other products.

▼ The University of Chicago founded Yerkes Observatory in Lake Geneva, Wisconsin. The observatory was finished and began conducting research in 1897. This facility was made possible by a gift from Charles Tyson Yerkes, a prominent financier who made his fortune in the streetcar industry in Chicago. Yerkes donated funds to the university in 1892 so that the observatory could be built. The donation came at the peak of Yerkes's financial success, from which he rapidly fell, dying almost broke in London in 1905.

▼ The existence of helium was discovered by William Ramsay, a British chemist who had participated in the discovery of argon in 1894.

▼ The first pizza restaurant opened in New York City. Located on Spring Street, the pizzeria was run by Italian immigrants.

▼ Charles Post, an ex-employee of the newly formed Kellogg cereal company in Battle Creek, Michigan, developed Grape-Nuts as his own ready-to-eat breakfast food. Post also was responsible for creating Postum, a cereal-based coffee substitute. Natural products were his major focus, part of his interest in holistic health and spiritual healing. This interest, however, could not keep his own problems in check; Post committed suicide in 1914.

▼ The Kennedy Biscuit Works in Cambridge, Massachusetts, began selling Fig Newtons. These fig-based cookies were named after the local town of Newton, and they were the first product to be made with a newly developed extruding machine.

▼   **1845**   ▼

MUSEUMS AND ZOOS
New Jersey Historical Society (Newark, NJ)

BIRTHDAYS AND DEATH DAYS
Elihu Root born on 15 February
Wilhelm Röntgen born on 27 March
Andrew Jackson died on 18 June at age 78
Sarah Bernhardt born on 23 October

COLLEGES AND UNIVERSITIES
Baylor University (Waco, TX)
Limestone College (Gaffney, SC)
U.S. Naval Academy (Annapolis, MD)
University of Mary Hardin-Baylor (Belton, TX)
Wittenberg University (Springfield, OH)

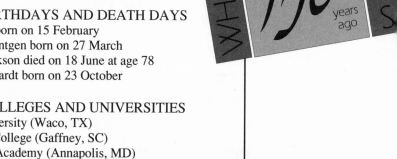

WHAT *150* WAS years ago

IN 1845 in January, the first clipper ship was launched in New York City.

Christened the *Rainbow,* the ship's unique design was created by John Griffiths, an American marine architect. His research was the first to prove that ships with narrow bows and sides with negative curvature would move through the water faster than the prevailing designs—ships with wide, blunt bows. The *Rainbow,* a three-master of 750 tons, made her first run to China in 92 days and returned in 88 days, a remarkable speed for the time. The *Rainbow* inspired the building of the second clipper, the *Sea Witch,* and influenced other shipbuilders to change their designs. This opened the era of the clipper ship, which lasted until steam-powered vessels took over in the 1870s.

▼ On 29 January, Edgar Allan Poe's poem, "The Raven," was first published in the *New York Evening Mirror.* Poe signed the poem with the pseudonym Quarles, but the immediate positive response to his work prompted him to use his real name when it was rerun in the same paper. Poe was working as a staff writer on the *Evening Mirror* at the time. The same year, his successful debut as a poet resulted in the publication of his first book, *The Raven and Other Poems.* It was a bestseller in its time.

▼ On 3 March, Florida became the twenty-seventh state. The state was named in 1513 by Ponce de León, a Spanish explorer, when he first set foot on shore, calling the land *Pascua Florida* or "feast of flowers." *Pascua* refers to the Easter period; de León arrived during the first week of April. Originally a Spanish territory, Florida was ceded to the United States in 1819, and 3 March is its official Admission Day. The first governor of Florida was William D. Moseley, a Democrat who served from 1845 to 1849.

▼ On 4 March, James K. Polk was inaugurated as the eleventh president of the United States. Polk was 49 when he was elected, making him the youngest U.S. president up to that time. He served only one term, dying shortly after leaving office in 1849.

▼ On 11 March, John Chapman died near Fort Wayne, Indiana. Better known as Johnny Appleseed, Chapman was born in about 1774 in Massachusetts. He was known for his widespread travels, during which he planted thousands of apple trees. His epitaph states he was a " . . . patron saint of American orchards and Soldier of Peace." After his death, General Sam Houston addressed Chapman's life and work in a speech in the U.S. Senate in Washington, D.C., saying " . . . He has left a place that can never be filled. Farewell, dear old eccentric heart. Your labor has been a labor of love, and generations yet unborn will rise up and call you blessed." Johnny Appleseed Day is celebrated on 11 March.

▼ **1845** ▼

MUSIC
Tannhäuser, by Richard Wagner (first performed on 19 October in Dresden, Germany)

BOOKS, POETRY, AND PLAYS
The Count of Monte Cristo, by Alexandre Dumas
Cromwell, by Thomas Carlyle
"The Raven," by Edgar Allan Poe
The Raven and Other Poems, by Edgar Allan Poe
Sybil, by Benjamin Disraeli

150 years ago

▼ On 8 June, Andrew Jackson, seventh president of the United States, died from the effects of consumption at the Hermitage in Nashville, Tennessee, at the age of 78. His last words were, "I hope to meet each of you in heaven. Be good children, all of you, and strive to be ready when the change comes."

▼ On 28 August, the first edition of *Scientific American* was published. The magazine was a weekly until 1921, when it switched to monthly publication. The original publisher was Rufus Porter, who sold the magazine after six months to Orson Munn, Salem Wales, and Alfred Beach. Beach, who had previous experience working on the *New York Sun* (owned by his father), was responsible for focusing the magazine on inventions since he was an inventor himself. He patented a pneumatic mail delivery system, a cable railway, and a typewriter. Articles in the early editions of the *Scientific American* were written mostly by amateur scientists.

▼ On 10 October, the United States Naval Academy officially opened in Annapolis, Maryland. Originally known as the Naval School, the academy operated out of Fort Severn until a campus was built. The name was changed in 1850. In 1861, the academy was moved to Newport, Rhode Island, because of the Civil War; in 1865, it returned to Annapolis.

▼ On 29 December, Texas was admitted to the Union as the twenty-eighth state. Although Alonso Álvarez de Piñeda was known to have explored the state's Gulf Coast as early as 1519, the first settlement by westerners was an outpost established by Spanish explorers in 1682 (now El Paso). Both France and Spain claimed ownership of the Texas territory at various times, and in 1821 it was declared part of Mexico. Colonists from the United States began establishing their own settlements in the early 1800s, leading to an uprising against Mexican rule in 1835. Texans declared independence from Mexico on 2 March 1836, but did not become part of the United States until 1845. The state is named after a Native American word, *texia,* meaning "friends." The state's Admission Day is marked on 29 December. The first governor of Texas was Anson Jones, a Democrat, who served from 1844 (predating statehood) to 1846.

▼ John Brunswick began making billiard tables.

▼ The first self-rising flour was offered to the public. It was developed in England by Henry Jones.

▼ The first telegraph cable was laid under the English Channel. This was the first linking of two countries across a body of water, initiating an era of rapidly developing undersea communications.

▼ Mechanically produced carpeting became possible with the invention of the powered loom by Erastus Bigelow. The inventor, living in West Boylston, Massachusetts, founded the Bigelow Carpet Mills.

▼ Rudolph Virchow, a German doctor, published the first description of leukemia.

▼ A major famine began in Ireland with the failure of the potato crop due to blight. Within two years, more than one million people died from starvation and another two million emigrated to other countries.

▼ Mark Cross opened a store to sell fine leather goods in New York City.

▼ 1795 ▼

BIRTHDAYS AND DEATH DAYS
James Boswell died on 19 May at age 56
John Keats born on 31 October
James K. Polk born on 2 November
Thomas Carlyle born on 4 December

COLLEGES AND UNIVERSITIES
Union College (Schenectady, NY)
University of North Carolina at Chapel Hill
   (Chapel Hill, NC)

MUSIC
Symphony No. 104 (*London* Symphony), by Franz Joseph
   Haydn (first performed on 4 May in London, England)

IN 1795 on 13 February, the University of North Carolina opened in the town of Chapel Hill. This institution was the first state university to be founded in the United States.

▼ On 2 November, James Polk was born in Pineville, North Carolina. He became a lawyer, member of the House of Representatives from Tennessee, and Governor of Tennessee from 1839 to 1841. He was elected the eleventh president of the United States in 1844 as a Democrat dark-horse candidate supporting the annexation of Texas by the United States. While Polk was president, war was declared with Mexico; the victory gave the United States control of Texas, California, and most of the southwestern territory. Polk served one term as president. He moved to Nashville, Tennessee, in 1849 and died on 15 June of that year.

▼ The British navy began requiring its sailors to receive regular rations of lime juice. In 1753, James Lind first announced the ability of juice from some citrus fruits to prevent scurvy, a major health problem in the navy. His discovery was first made in 1747; the first outbreak of scurvy dates to the first long ocean voyage—the exploration of Vasco da Gama in 1497.

▼ Jacob Beam began distilling bourbon in Clermont, Kentucky. This type of liquor was originally called bourbon whiskey; it was distinct from other whiskeys because it was made primarily from corn. The first use of the term *bourbon* on a label was in 1848.

▼ The metric system became the official system of measurement in France.

IN 1745 on 28 November, Saratoga, New

York, was burned by a combined group of French and Indian raiders. Hostilities in the American colonies between English and French forces occurred while King George's War was being waged in Europe.

▼ Russian fur traders established the first settlement on Attu in the Aleutian Islands.

▼ Two scientists independently invented the Leyden jar, the first device capable of storing static electricity. Pieter van Musschenbroek, a Dutch physicist, and Ewald Georg von Kleist, a German physicist, share this discovery. Both scientists learned about the power of their electrical devices the same way—by getting an electrical shock accidentally. The device was referred to as a Leyden jar because van Musschenbroek held a position at the University of Leyden. In 1799, 53 years later, Alessandro Volta succeeded in creating the first device that could actually generate an electric current—the first battery. The announcement of this discovery was published on 20 March 1800.

▼ 1695 ▼

BOOKS, POETRY, AND PLAYS
Love for Love, by William Congreve

IN 1695 the first paid street cleaners were
employed by the city of New York.

▼ Epsom salt was discovered by Nehemiah Grew. This compound, magnesium sulfate, occurs naturally in some types of groundwater. Grew named his salt after the place it was discovered—Epsom Springs, a natural springs with water used for medicinal purposes, located southwest of London, England.

IN 1645 on 14 July, French Canadians and their allies signed a treaty with Chief Kiotsaton of the Iroquois. The pact was known as Montmagny's Peace.

▼ Otto von Guericke, a German physicist, invented the first efficient air pump. It was used to create vacuums, with which von Guericke proved the concept that sound cannot travel though a vacuum, a theory originally proposed by Aristotle.

▼ **1595** ▼

BOOKS, POETRY, AND PLAYS
Amoretti, by Edmund Spenser
Love's Labor Lost, by William Shakespeare
Romeo and Juliet, by William Shakespeare

IN 1595 Sir Walter Raleigh, already an established explorer, sailed from England with four ships and a force of 150 men on a quest for gold in the Amazon.

IN 1545 Geronimo Cardano, an Italian mathematician, published *Ars magna* (Great art), a book believed to be the first true book of mathematics. The text included explanations of complex numbers, negative numbers, and cube roots.

▼ Ambrolise Pare, a French surgeon, published the first report outlining methods of modern surgery.

▼ The Council of Trent convened in Trent, Italy. This meeting of officials of the Catholic Church introduced many reforms into the traditional religious practices of this body.

IN 1495 the governing body of the Holy
Roman Empire—the Diet of Worms—enacted the "Ewiger Landfriede" (perpetual public peace). Worms was the site of more than 100 meetings of the Diet, among them an assembly in 1521 that included a personal appearance by Martin Luther. He was called before the leaders of the Empire to defend his radical interpretation of Christianity.

▼ The first recorded cases of syphilis were reported in Naples, Italy. This sexually transmitted disease initially appeared among soldiers in the army of Charles VIII of France, then occupying the city. An unappreciated affliction, the disease was originally referred to as Neapolitan disease or French disease, depending on the nationality of the victim.

▼   **1971**   ▼

ASSOCIATIONS, SOCIETIES, UNIONS, AND GOVERNMENT DEPARTMENTS
U.S. Hang Gliding Association
   (Pearblossom, CA)

MUSEUMS AND ZOOS
Fullerton Museum Center (Fullerton, CA)
Pacific Asia Museum (Pasadena, CA)
Sedgwick County Zoo and Botanical Garden
   (Wichita, KS)
Walt Disney World/Epcot Center
   (Lake Buena Vista, FL)

COLLEGES AND UNIVERSITIES
University of the Virgin Islands (St. Thomas, VI)

MUSIC
American Pie, by Don McLean
Bark, by the Jefferson Airplane
Blessed Are..., by Joan Baez
Blue, by Joni Mitchell
Brand New Key, by Melanie
Carpenters, by the Carpenters
Cherish, by David Cassidy
Chicago at Carnegie Hall, by Chicago
Chicago III, by Chicago

IN 1971 on 1 January, advertising for cigarettes on radio and television was no longer allowed.

▼ On 1 May, Amtrak began operating as a passenger train service.

▼ On 22 May, the Lyndon Baines Johnson Library-Museum was dedicated at the University of Texas in Austin.

▼ On 13 June, the *New York Times* began publishing a report secretly furnished by Dr. Daniel Ellsberg, an official with the Defense Department. The Pentagon Papers, the secret report of the United States policy in Vietnam, was a major factor in the antiwar effort.

▼ On 1 July, the Post Office Department was officially replaced with the U.S. Postal Service. The new organization was granted independence from most government control.

▼ On 5 July, 18-year-olds were granted voting rights when the Twenty-Sixth Amendment to the U.S. Constitution was signed into law by President Nixon. On 30 June, Ohio became the thirty-eighth and final state needed to ratify the amendment.

▼ On 20 August, the first pocket calculator was introduced by Texas Instruments. This first model, the Pocketronic, sold for $149 and weighed about 2.5 pounds; within one year, prices dropped to about $50.

25 years ago

▼ 1971 ▼

MUSIC *continued*
Coal Miner's Daughter, by Loretta Lynn
Day after Day, by Badfinger
Don't Let the Green Grass Fool You,
    by Wilson Pickett
Emerson, Lake & Palmer, by Emerson, Lake & Palmer
Every Good Boy Deserves Favor, by the Moody Blues
Every Picture Tells a Story, by Rod Stewart
4 Way Street, by Crosby, Stills, Nash & Young
Go Away Little Girl, by Donny Osmond
Gypsys, Tramps and Thieves, by Cher
How Can You Mend a Broken Heart, by the Bee Gees
If I Could Only Remember My Name, by David Crosby
Imagine, by John Lennon
It's Too Late, by Carole King
Jackson Browne, by Jackson Browne
Joy to the World, by Three Dog Night
Killer, by Alice Cooper
Kiss an Angel Good Morning, by Charley Pride
Love It to Death, by Alice Cooper
The Low Spark of High Heeled Boys, by Traffic
Master of Reality, by Black Sabbath
Me and Bobby McGee, by Janis Joplin
The Night They Drove Old Dixie Down, by Joan Baez
A Nod Is as Good as a Wink to a Blind Horse, by Faces
Paranoid, by Black Sabbath
Pearl, by Janis Joplin

▼ 1971 ▼

MUSIC *continued*
Proud Mary, by Ike and Tina Turner
Put Your Hand in the Hand, by Ocean
Rainbow Bridge, by Jimi Hendrix
She's a Lady, by Tom Jones
Sticky Fingers, by the Rolling Stones
Take Me Home, Country Roads, by John Denver
Tapestry, by Carole King
Tarkus, by Emerson, Lake & Palmer
Tupelo Honey, by Van Morrison
Uncle Albert, by Paul McCartney
Without You, by Nilsson
You've Got a Friend, by James Taylor

NEWSPAPERS AND MAGAZINES
East West Journal (Boston, MA)
Easyriders (Agoura, CA)
Forum (New York, NY)
Safari (Tucson, AZ)
Travel and Leisure (New York, NY)

BOOKS, POETRY, AND PLAYS
The Bell Jar, by Sylvia Plath
Bury My Heart at Wounded Knee, by Dee Brown
Day of the Jackal, by Frederick Forsyth
Pentagon Papers, by Neil Sheehan et al.

MOVIES
A Clockwork Orange (directed by Stanley Kubrick, with
     Malcolm McDowell)
Dirty Harry (directed by Don Siegel, with Clint Eastwood)
Fiddler on the Roof (directed by Norman Jewison,
     with Topol)
The French Connection (directed by William Friedkin,
     with Gene Hackman)
Klute (directed by Alan Pakula, with Jane Fonda,
     Donald Sutherland)
The Last Picture Show (directed by Peter Bogdanovich,
     with Sybil Shepard)
Straw Dogs (directed by Sam Peckinpah)

▼ On 8 September, the Kennedy Center for the Performing Arts in Washington, D.C., opened. The first performance was the public debut of the *Mass* by Leonard Bernstein.

▼ On 9 September, prisoners at the Attica State Correctional Facility in New York State began a riot. The riot was ended by a mass assault of law enforcement officers on 13 September, resulting in the deaths of 43 people, including 9 hostages (five deaths, due to injuries sustained during the violence, occurred after the riot was over).

▼ On 13 November, *Mariner 9* became the first man-made object to orbit a planet other than earth. The spacecraft transmitted more than 7,000 photographs of the surface of Mars. A Soviet spacecraft, the *Mars 2,* arrived at Mars two weeks later, on 27 November.

▼ Intel introduced the first microprocessor computer chips for sale.

▼ Fred Smith, a Vietnam veteran with the U.S. Marines, founded Federal Express in Memphis, Tennessee. According to company lore, the original idea for the overnight package delivery system came from a class paper Smith wrote while studying at Yale University; the paper received a passing grade of C. In its early years, Federal Express had difficulty attracting customers, and according to more company lore, the founder once flew to Las Vegas and won $27,000 at blackjack to cover a company payroll after being turned down for a bank loan.

▼ 1946 ▼

ASSOCIATIONS, SOCIETIES, UNIONS, AND GOVERNMENT DEPARTMENTS
Aaron Burr Association (Winston-Salem, NC)
Air Force Association (Arlington, VA)
American Association for Gifted Children
 (New York, NY)
American Society for Quality Control
 (Milwaukee, WI)
Armed Forces Communications and Electronics
 Association (Fairfax, VA)
Atomic Energy Commission (U.S. government)

IN 1946 on 1 January, the first baby boomer was born. Arriving one second after midnight, the pioneer baby was Kathleen Casey Wilkens, born in Philadelphia.

1996

▼ On 10 January, the first meeting of the United Nations was held. Since it had no permanent base until 1952, the organization held its first meeting in London.

▼ On 4 July, the Philippines became an independent nation.

▼ On 5 July, the first bikini was introduced to the public at a Paris fashion show. Created by Louis Reard, the two-piece garment was named after the Bikini Atoll in the South Pacific, the site only a few days earlier of highly publicized test explosions of atomic bombs by the U.S. military. Made of cotton with a newsprint pattern, the first bikini was modeled by Micheline Barnardi, a French dancer.

▼ On 25 July, the last reported public lynching in the United States occurred in Walton County, Georgia. The incident began with the alleged nonfatal stabbing of a white man by Roger Malcolm, a local black farm worker. Released from jail on bail, Malcolm was being driven to work by his employer when their vehicle was stopped by a group of about 25 men. Malcolm was taken from the car, along with his wife, her brother, and her brother's wife, and shot to death. Although none of the attackers wore masks, no identification was ever made of the perpetrators, and a grand jury failed to issue any indictments. This incident received major coverage in the national press, and along with other incidents of lynching in the South, helped motivate President Truman and the U.S. Attorney General to attempt to improve the legal process affecting civil rights.

▼ On 1 August, the Atomic Energy Commission was established by President Truman.

▼   1946   ▼

ASSOCIATIONS, SOCIETIES, UNIONS, AND GOVERNMENT DEPARTMENTS *continued*

Bureau of Land Management (U.S. Department of the Interior)
Guide Dog Foundation for the Blind (Smithtown, NY)
National Basketball Association (NBA) (New York, NY)
National Business Education Association (Reston, VA)
National Cartoonists Society (Brooklyn, NY)
National Skeet Shooting Association (San Antonio, TX)
Public Relations Society of America (New York, NY)

▼   **1946**   ▼

MUSEUMS AND ZOOS
Bar Harbor Historical Society (Bar Harbor, ME)
Museum of Peoples and Cultures (Provo, UT)
Museum of the Historical Society of Early
    American Decoration (New York, NY)
National Air and Space Museum
    (Washington, DC)
Norton Art Gallery (Shreveport, LA)
PT Boat Museum (Memphis, TN)
Queens Botanical Garden (Flushing, NY)
Scalamandre Museum of Textiles (New York, NY)
Southwest Museum of Science and Technology
    (Dallas, TX)
Springfield Art Museum (Springfield, MO)
Susan B. Anthony Memorial (Rochester, NY)
University of Michigan Museum of Art (Ann Arbor, MI)
Walt Whitman Association (Camden, NJ)

years ago

▼ On 4 November, the United Nations established UNESCO, the United Nations Educational, Scientific, and Cultural Organization.

▼ On 12 November, the first drive-up banking facility was opened in Chicago, Illinois, by the Exchange National Bank of Chicago.

▼ On 13 November, weather manipulation by cloud seeding was first attempted, and with positive results: a snowstorm was created in western Massachusetts. Vincent Schaefer, a physicist, used dry ice pellets dropped from an airplane to generate the precipitation.

▼ The Los Angeles Rams professional football team was founded with a move of the Cleveland Rams to California.

▼ Chip and Dale, animated cartoon chipmunks created by the Walt Disney Studio, first appeared in a Pluto animated feature titled "Squatter's Rights." Chip 'n' Dale features were produced until the close of the 1950s, after which the chipmunks continued to appear in other Disney programs, including television shows. Also in 1946, Foghorn Leghorn debuted in a Warner Brother's cartoon titled "Walky Talky Hawky." Heckle and Jeckle, a pair of mischievous birds, first appeared in 1946 in "The Talking Magpies," an animated feature by Paul Terry.

▼ Radioactive carbon 14 was first used to establish the age of objects.

1996

▼ **1946** ▼

BIRTHDAYS AND DEATH DAYS
Gertrude Stein died on 29 July at age 72
Damon Runyon died on 10 December at age 62

COLLEGES AND UNIVERSITIES
Anna Maria College (Paxton, MA)
Claremont McKenna College (Claremont, CA)
Franciscan University of Steubenville (Steubenville, OH)
King's College (Wilkes-Barre, PA)
Lake Superior State University (Sault Sainte Marie, MI)
Le Moyne College (Syracuse, NY)
LeTourneau University (Longview, TX)
Mississippi Valley State University (Itta Bena, MS)
New England College (Henniker, NH)
Ohio University at Chillicothe (Chillicothe, OH)
Ohio University at Zanesville (Zanesville, OH)
Portland State University (Portland, OR)
Rutgers, State University of New Jersey, Newark
   College of Arts and Sciences (Newark, NJ)
State University of New York at Binghamton
   (Binghamton, NY)
Tennessee Temple University (Chattanooga, TN)
University of Connecticut at Hartford (West Hartford, CT)
University of North Carolina at Charlotte (Charlotte, NC)
Utica of Syracuse University (Utica, NY)

▼ The first nonspecialized electronic computer was finished by John Eckart and John Mauchly. The machine was known as the Electronic Numerical Integrator and Computer, or ENIAC, and was located in Philadelphia. ENIAC weighed 30 tons and was 1,500 feet square at its base.

▼ The U.S. government established the Argonne National Laboratory outside Chicago, Illinois. The laboratory was created to be a center of research and development for atomic power.

▼ The Boston Celtics professional basketball team was founded in Boston by Walter Brown, whose Irish heritage influenced the choice of team name. In 1950, Red Auerbach was hired as head coach, and the team won its first NBA title in 1956.

▼ The first Gator Bowl was held in Jacksonville, Florida. In this first game, Wake Forest beat South Carolina, 26-14.

▼ Akio Morita, Massaru Ibuka, and Ibuka's father-in-law founded the Sony Corporation in Tokyo. Sony's first name was Tokyo Telecommunications Engineering, and the company developed products that were based on electronics, including radios and tape recorders. In 1957, the first pocket-sized transistor radio was created by the company, the first official Sony product; the name was chosen by combining syllables from dictionary entries. The success of the transistor radio prompted the company to adopt Sony as a name in 1958.

▼ Warren Avis founded the Avis rental car company. The first outlet was at the Detroit airport; Avis had been the owner of a car dealership in the city. Avis was the first rental car company to locate at airports rather than downtown centers.

▼ 1946 ▼

MUSIC
Annie Get Your Gun, by Irving Berlin (first performed
on 16 May in New York, NY)

NEWSPAPERS AND MAGAZINES
Anchorage News (Anchorage, AK)
Arizona Sun (Flagstaff, AZ)
Highlights for Children (Columbus, OH)
Sport Magazine (New York, NY)
Workbench (Kansas City, MO)

BOOKS, POETRY, AND PLAYS
All the King's Men, by Robert Penn Warren
The Foxes of Harrow, by Frank Yerby
The Iceman Cometh, by Eugene O'Neill
Member of the Wedding, by Carson McCullers

MOVIES
The Best Years of Our Lives (directed by William
Wyler, with Myrna Loy, Fredric March)
The Big Sleep (directed by Howard Hawks, with Lauren
Bacall, Humphrey Bogart)
It's a Wonderful Life (directed by Frank Capra, with
Donna Reed, James Stewart)
The Postman Always Rings Twice (directed by Tay
Garnett, with John Garfield, Lana Turner)
The Razor's Edge (directed by Edmund Goulding, with
Tyrone Power, Gene Tierney)

50 years ago

▼ Frederick Mellinger founded Frederick's of Hollywood in Hollywood, California. This lingerie store soon branched into mail-order sales.

▼ W. Russell Kelly created the temporary office service business with the founding of a business offering secretarial and clerical services in Detroit. The company was local until 1954, when outlets were established in other cities. The original company name, Russell Kelly Office Service, was changed to Kelly Girl Service because of the demand for "Kelly girls."

▼ Proctor & Gamble introduced Tide, the product of more than 20 years of research.

▼ Airborne Express was founded in Seattle. The company started as an air freight business and entered the overnight package delivery industry in 1980.

▼ Estée Lauder founded her cosmetic company. The founder's first product was Super-Rich All Purpose Cream, which she formulated at home and sold through beauty salons until 1946, when her market expanded to department stores.

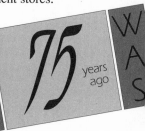

▼   1921   ▼

ASSOCIATIONS, SOCIETIES, UNIONS, AND GOVERNMENT DEPARTMENTS

Alpha Tau Delta (Thousand Oaks, CA)
American Foundation for the Blind (New York, NY)
American Institute of Steel Construction (Chicago, IL)
American Physical Therapy Association (Alexandria, VA)
Association of Junior Leagues (New York, NY)
Automotive Booster Clubs International
    (Arlington Heights, IL)
International Order of Job's Daughters (Omaha, NE)
International Pilot Club (Macon, GA)
National Association of Retired Federal Employees
    (Washington, DC)
National Cosmetology Association (St. Louis, MO)
National Hairdressers and Cosmetologists Association
    (St. Louis, MO)
Polish Army Veterans Association of America
    (New York, NY)
Science Service (Washington, DC)
Service Employees International Union (Washington, DC)
Soroptomist International of the Americas (Philadelphia, PA)
U.S. Olympic Committee (Colorado Springs, CO)

IN 1921

IN 1921 on 4 March, Warren Harding was inaugurated as the twenty-ninth president of the United States. Two years later, on 2 August 1923, he died from apoplexy in San Francisco. Vice President Calvin Coolidge succeeded him as president on 3 August 1923. Harding was a Republican from Ohio, where he was elected to the State Senate in 1898. After a failed attempt to be elected governor, he ran successfully for the U.S. Senate in 1914. He was considered a dark-horse candidate for the presidential nomination in 1920; as the Republican nominee his major campaign slogan was "a return to normalcy," a sentiment widely supported by a nation recovering from the effects of World War I. During his term in office, Harding was distinguished mainly by his distance from political activity. Allegations of corruption were increasing, particularly regarding the Teapot Dome Scandal, when he died suddenly during a trip to the western states.

▼ On 5 May, Coco Chanel introduced Chanel No. 5, now one of the most recognized brand names in the perfume industry. The name "No. 5" was chosen because this digit was Chanel's lucky number; she also planned the product's introduction for the fifth day of the fifth month.

▼ On 10 June, the General Accounting Office (GAO) was established by an Act of Congress. Part of the Budget and Accounting Act, the GAO was created as an auditing office for government transactions.

▼ 1921 ▼

MUSEUMS AND ZOOS
Edgar Allan Poe Museum (Richmond, VA)
Houston Zoological Gardens (Houston, TX)
Jackson Zoological Gardens (Jackson, MA)
Museum of Paleontology (University of California, Berkeley, CA)
San Francisco Museum of Modern Art (San Francisco, CA)
Slater Mill (Pawtucket, RI)
Union Pacific Historical Museum (Omaha, NE)

BIRTHDAYS AND DEATH DAYS
Camille Saint-Saëns died on 16 December at age 86

COLLEGES AND UNIVERSITIES
Rutgers, State University of New Jersey, Cook College (New Brunswick, NJ)

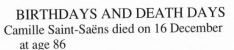

years ago

1996

▼ 1921 ▼

MUSIC
The Love for Three Oranges, by Sergey Prokofiev (first performed on 30 December in Chicago, IL)
Piano Concerto No. 3, by Sergey Prokofiev (first performed on 16 December in Chicago, IL)

NEWSPAPERS AND MAGAZINES
Barron's Weekly (New York, NY)
Child Life (Indianapolis, IN)
National Catholic Register (Los Angeles, CA)

BOOKS, POETRY, AND PLAYS
The Circle, by W. Somerset Maugham

MOVIES
The Kid (directed by Charlie Chaplin, with Charlie Chaplin)
The Sheik (directed by George Melford, with Rudolph Valentino)

▼ On 21 July, a new era of military technology began with the successful sinking of the captured German battleship *Ostfriesland* by aerial bombardment. Led by General William "Billy" Mitchell, this was a demonstration of the power and versatility of airplanes in battle. The event was staged in waters off Hampton Roads, Virginia. Mitchell was later demoted to Colonel, and after making derogatory public comments about the War Department and Navy Department, he was court-martialed on 28 October 1925. Found guilty, he resigned from the U.S. Army. A few years later, he warned about the potential of an air attack by Japanese bombers on Hawaii.

▼ Lead additives were discovered to prevent pinging, or engine knock, in gasoline-powered engines.

▼ The Royce Hailey's Pig Stand, a barbecue restaurant in Dallas, Texas, opened a new era in dining with the introduction of drive-in service.

▼ The first experiments began with insulin as a treatment for diabetes. Two doctors, Sir Frederick Banting from Canada and John Macleod from Scotland, discovered insulin and received the Nobel Prize in 1923 for this important breakthrough.

▼ The jewelry industry was introduced to the first cultured pearls.

▼ Billy Ingram opened the first White Castle restaurant in Wichita, Kansas. This establishment grew into a major chain within a few years.

▼ The magnetron was invented. This specialized vacuum tube produced microwaves.

▼ The lie detector was invented by John Larson, a medical student.

▼ Ink blots were introduced as a psychological testing device by Hermann Rorschach.

▼ The first Miss America contest was held. Originally intended as a publicity gimmick for the resort town of Atlantic City, New Jersey, the first pageant featured eight women representing cities instead of states. Competition was based on popularity and a bathing suit contest, during which even the orchestra wore swimsuits. The first Miss America was Margaret Gorman, a 16-year-old from Washington, D.C. The contest was generally well received in its early years, although some in the media criticized it from the first for exploiting sexual attractiveness over intelligence. In 1935, pageant organizers finally added a talent competition.

▼ Gold Medal Flour introduced a new promotional creation—a fictitious cook by the name of Betty Crocker. This concept was developed to encourage more women to write the company for recipes and advice.

▼ The public was first offered Eskimo Pies. On 24 January 1922, a patent was granted for this ice cream novelty, invented by Christian Nelson, the owner of an ice cream store in Onawa, Iowa.

▼ Land O'Lakes was founded as a cooperative of dairy farms in Minnesota. The company's logo, a stylized young Indian woman, was created in 1924.

▼ The first aerial crop dusting was initiated by the Ohio Agricultural Experiment Station. The first dusting used powdered lead arsenate to attack leaf caterpillars infesting catalpa trees.

▼ The British government changed the political stature of Ireland, creating the independent country of Ireland and retaining Northern Ireland as part of Great Britain.

▼ The first Kotex sanitary napkins were made available commercially by the Kimberly-Clark Company.

▼   1896   ▼

ASSOCIATIONS, SOCIETIES, UNIONS, AND GOVERNMENT DEPARTMENTS

American Federation of Musicians of the United States
 and Canada (New York, NY)
American Foundrymen's Society
 (Des Plaines, IL)
American Guild of Organists (New York, NY)
American Nurses' Association (Kansas City, MO)
International Union of Operating Engineers
 (Washington, DC)
Jewish War Veterans of the U.S.A.
 (Washington, DC)
National Association of Credit Management
 (New York, NY)
National Fire Protection Association (Quincy, MA)
The Order of the Founders and Patriots of America
 (Irving, TX)
Sons of Confederate Veterans (Hattiesburg, MS)

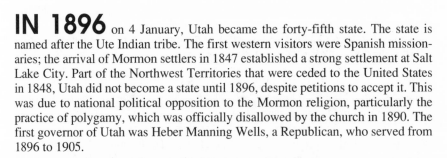

IN 1896 on 4 January, Utah became the forty-fifth state. The state is named after the Ute Indian tribe. The first western visitors were Spanish missionaries; the arrival of Mormon settlers in 1847 established a strong settlement at Salt Lake City. Part of the Northwest Territories that were ceded to the United States in 1848, Utah did not become a state until 1896, despite petitions to accept it. This was due to national political opposition to the Mormon religion, particularly the practice of polygamy, which was officially disallowed by the church in 1890. The first governor of Utah was Heber Manning Wells, a Republican, who served from 1896 to 1905.

▼ On 4 January, the first actor's union in the United States was chartered in New York City. The Actors' National Protective Union was formed under the authority of the American Federation of Labor, and it later merged with other unions, becoming the Associated Actors and Artists of America in 1919.

▼ On 29 January, X-ray treatment for breast cancer was performed for the first time.

▼ On 1 March, Antoine Henri Becquerel, a French physicist, observed previously unknown rays coming from a sample of uranium. This turned out to be the discovery of radiation.

▼ On 6 April, the Olympic Games were resurrected in Athens, Greece. A total of 12 events were held, with the American team winning 9 of them.

▼ On 17 April, the first state accountancy law in the United States was signed into law in New York. The law was created to regulate the work of certified public accountants, and included the appointment of a Board of Certified Public Accountant Examiners.

▼ On 23 April, the first public demonstration of motion pictures was held in New York City. The films shown were *The Execution of Mary, Queen of Scots* (a 30-second film) and *The Kiss* (a close-up of a kiss), both by Thomas Edison. The films were made with Edison's new invention, the Vitascope, and included some hand-tinted color films. A report in the *New York Times* remarked about a filmed dance sequence: "Every movement was as natural as if living dancers were working their way toward salary day." The article also reported in anticipation the next Edison filming project: a railroad wreck to be staged with two locomotives running into each other.

▼ On 4 June, Henry Ford's first automobile was driven.

▼ 1896 ▼

MUSEUMS AND ZOOS

Carnegie Museum of Art (Pittsburgh, PA)
Carnegie Museum of Natural History
   (Pittsburgh, PA)
De Young Memorial Museum (San Francisco, CA)
Denver Zoological Gardens (Denver, CO)
Everson Museum of Art (Syracuse, NY)
Manchester Historic Association (Manchester, NH)
New York Aquarium (Brooklyn, NY)
Roger Williams Park Museum of Natural History
   (Providence, RI)
South Carolina Confederate Museum (Columbia, SC)
Worcester Art Museum (Worcester, MA)

BIRTHDAYS AND DEATH DAYS

Paul Verlaine died on 8 January at age 51
John Dos Passos born on 14 January
Harriet Beecher Stowe died on 1 July at age 85
Anton Bruckner died on 11 October at age 72
Alfred Nobel died on 10 December at age 63

▼   1896   ▼

COLLEGES AND UNIVERSITIES

Adelphi University (Garden City, NY)
Clarkson University (Potsdam, NY)
Delaware Valley College of Science and Agriculture
(Doylestown, PA)
Grand View College (Des Moines, IA)
Oakwood College (Huntsville, AL)
Parsons School of Design (New York, NY)
University of Montevallo (Montevallo, AL)

MUSIC

Also sprach Zarathustra, by Richard Strauss
La Bohème, by Giacomo Puccini (first performed on 1
February in Turin, Italy)

NEWSPAPERS AND MAGAZINES

House Beautiful (New York, NY)
Journal of Physical Chemistry (Washington, DC)
Seattle Times (Seattle, WA)

BOOKS, POETRY, AND PLAYS

The Seagull, by Anton Chekhov

▼ On 17 August, gold was discovered in the Yukon Territory of Canada. It was discovered by three prospectors in Bonanza Creek near its confluence with the Klondike River. The discovery resulted in a gold rush that lasted from 1897 to 1898, bringing more than 100,000 eager fortune hunters to the region. The date is recognized as Klondike Gold Discovery Day.

▼ On 17 August, the first person was killed by an automobile near the Crystal Palace in London. The victim was Mrs. Bridget Driscoll, an onlooker during a public demonstration of early autos; she panicked and ran into the path of the vehicle, which crushed her skull.

▼ On 7 September, the first automobile race on a race track was held in Cranston, Rhode Island, during the state fair. Eight cars—two electric and six gasoline-powered—competed in front of more than 40,000 spectators. The winning vehicle was an electric Riker, running at about 24 miles per hour.

▼ On 1 October, the U.S. government established the rural free postal delivery system.

▼ The concept of the intelligence test was developed by Alfred Binet. Binet was the psychology laboratory director at Sorbonne University in Paris.

▼ Christiaan Eijkman, a Dutch doctor, discovered that beriberi, a disease prevalent in the East Indies, was caused by a deficiency of thiamine. This was the second disease to be identified and treated through dietary manipulation, the first being scurvy. Eijkman was awarded a Nobel Prize in 1929.

▼ Carlisle & Finch began making the first electric toy trains.

▼ Lick Observatory in California published the first photographic atlas of the lunar surface.

▼ The first medical diagnosis with an X ray in the United States occurred at Columbia University.

▼ Pieter Zeeman, a Dutch physics student, discovered the Zeeman effect, changes in the visible spectrum produced by a light source when affected by a magnetic field. Zeeman's work earned him a Nobel Prize in 1902, shared with Hendrik Lorentz, his teacher.

▼ The Tabulating Machine Company was founded by Herman Hollerith. The name was later changed to the International Business Machine Company, or IBM, in 1924. Hollerith, a statistician with experience in mechanical engineering, worked at the U.S. Patent Office while he experimented with various means of automating the tabulation of data. His invention, a device that could read holes punched in cards, was used in 1890 during the census. By 1900, the system was in widespread use in many countries and was a significant contribution to the development of data analysis.

▼ Chop suey was invented by Li-Hung-Chang, the chef for the Chinese ambassador to the United States.

▼ The first comic features appeared in a newspaper. The *New York World* published "The Yellow Kid," created by R. F. Outcault.

▼ Book matches produced by the Diamond Match Company were the first matchbooks to include advertising. Matchbooks were originally developed and patented in 1892 by Joshua Pusey, a Pennsylvanian, but it was not until 1896 that the Diamond Match Company in Barberton, Ohio, received an order for 10 million matchbooks imprinted with a local brewery's name.

▼ Enzymes were first identified by Eduard Buchner, a German chemist. Buchner discovered that biochemical reactions were created by extracts from live yeast cells. The Nobel Prize was awarded to Buchner in 1907.

▼ The *New Orleans Picayune* became the first daily newspaper to run an advice column. The feature was written by Dorothy Dix, a pseudonym for Elizabeth Gilmer.

100 years ago

▼ The science of acoustics was formed by the work of Wallace Sabine, an American physicist. Sabine established this field while trying to eliminate a reverberation problem in a lecture room at Harvard University.

▼ Hockey was first played in organized games in the United States.

▼ Sears, Roebuck, and Company published its first mail-order catalog. The company had been founded in Chicago in 1891 by Richard W. Sears.

▼ The first Broadway Department Store was opened by Arthur Letts. Located in Los Angeles at Fourth and Broadway, the store expanded with branches in Hollywood and Pasadena, and it merged with the Hale Brothers Stores in 1951. Currently, the Broadway stores are part of the Carter Hawley Hale Stores Corporation.

▼ Thomas Sperry and Shelly Hutchinson established a company to sell trading stamps—known as S&H Green Stamps—to stores as an incentive for their customers.

▼ Leo Hirschfield, a candy-store owner in New York City, made some chocolate candies for his daughter, Tootsie. Tootsie and her friends found the confection appealing, and Hirschfield soon began selling the goodies—named Tootsie Rolls— for a penny each in his store, first wrapping them individually.

▼   **1846**   ▼

ASSOCIATIONS, SOCIETIES, UNIONS, AND GOVERNMENT DEPARTMENTS
United Order of True Sisters (New York, NY)

MUSEUMS AND ZOOS
National Museum of American Art (Washington, DC)
National Museum of American History (Washington, DC)
National Museum of Natural History (Washington, DC)
State Historical Museum of Wisconsin (Madison, WI)

IN 1846 on 13 April, the Pennsylvania Railroad was officially chartered.

▼ On 15 June, the Oregon Treaty was signed by Congress. The treaty, made with England, established the northern border of Oregon as the 49th parallel and defined territory that would eventually become the states of Idaho, Montana, Oregon, Washington, and Wyoming.

▼ 1846 ▼

BIRTHDAYS AND DEATH DAYS
George Westinghouse born on 6 October
Georg Friedrich List died on 30 November at age 57

COLLEGES AND UNIVERSITIES
Beloit College (Beloit, WI)
Bucknell University (Lewisburg, PA)
Carroll College (Waukesha, WI)
Grinnell College (Grinnell, IA)
Mount Union College (Alliance, OH)
Northeastern Oklahoma State University (Tahlequah, OK)
Saint Vincent College (Latrobe, PA)
State University of New York at Buffalo (Buffalo, NY)
Taylor University (Upland, IN)

▼ On 19 June, in Hoboken, New Jersey, the first official baseball game was held. This was the first game for which records were kept: New York Nine, 6; Knickerbockers, 1. Also in this record was the first fine in baseball history: 6 cents levied against the New York Nine pitcher for cursing at the umpire.

▼ On 10 September, the first sewing machine was patented by Elias Howe. In 1851, another patent was issued to Isaac Singer, who was sued by Howe for copying part of his design. Howe won the case and a $15,000 settlement from Singer, but Singer's company achieved the ultimate victory with the successful marketing and commercialization of this device.

▼ On 23 September, Neptune was discovered by John Galle, a German astronomer. The existence of Neptune had first been proposed a year earlier by other astronomers, based on known irregularities in the orbit of Uranus.

▼ On 28 December, Iowa became the twenty-ninth state. The state's name is believed to come from a Dakota Indian word meaning "sleeping one." The first western settlers were French explorers, and the area was considered French territory until the Louisiana Purchase in 1803, when it was ceded to the United States. The first governor was Ansel Briggs, a Democrat, who served from 1846 to 1850.

▼ The McCormick Harvesting Machine Company was opened in Chicago to manufacture the implement that Cyrus McCormick had invented in 1831. The factory was established by Cyrus and his two brothers, who had just moved to the city from Rockbridge County, Virginia. The McCormick brothers were second-generation inventors—their father had struggled for years to perfect a mechanical reaper, an accomplishment that was eventually achieved by Cyrus. In Chicago, production of reapers included many advances and improvements in the original design, as well as ongoing legal battles with competitors. After Cyrus died in 1884, the company was run by his wife, Nancy. In 1902, it merged with other companies to form International Harvester, a company that developed and built agricultural equipment, tractors, and trucks. The International Harvester name was retired in 1986, when the company was renamed Navistar International.

▼ T. T. Pond established a business in Utica, New York, to make herbal medicines from witch hazel. In 1907, the company first offered Cold Cream as a facial product.

▼ Ether was first used as an anesthetic during a public demonstration in Boston of the removal of a wen from a patient's neck. The patient, Gilbert Abbot, reported he felt no pain. In a test the month before, ether was first used successfully for a tooth extraction by William Morton, a dentist in the same city. Morton convinced Dr. John Warren of ether's value and was there to administer it during the first operation, which Dr. Warren performed. Ether's anesthetic properties had first been reported in 1841, but the first use of the word *anesthesia* occurred after the Boston operation, in a letter written by Oliver Wendell Holmes. Also in 1846, chloroform was first used as an anesthetic, given to women during childbirth.

▼ The first psychology lab in the United States was opened. Granville Hall established this experimental facility at Johns Hopkins University in Baltimore, Maryland.

▼ A. T. Cross began manufacturing fine writing pens in Rhode Island.

▼   1846   ▼

MUSIC
The Damnation of Faust, by Hector Berlioz
   (first performed on 6 December in Paris, France)
Polonaise-Fantasie, by Frédéric Chopin
Symphony No. 2, by Robert Schumann

NEWSPAPERS AND MAGAZINES
Town and Country (New York, NY)

BOOKS, POETRY, AND PLAYS
The Book of Nonsense, by Edward Lear
La mare au diable, by George Sand

▼ Isaac D. Baker and Charles Scribner founded Baker & Scribner, a book publishing company, in Boston. In 1878, the company's name was changed to Charles Scribner's Sons.

▼ The first rotary printing press was patented by Richard Hoe. This innovation in press design was the first to discard the moving flat plate, incorporating for the first time numerous impression cylinders. The major advantage of the rotary press was speed: the first model came to be known as the lightning press. Capable of producing many thousands of impressions per hour, Hoe's invention revolutionized the newspaper industry, making this medium the first to truly be available to the masses. In 1847, the *Philadelphia Public Ledger* became the first newspaper to adapt to the new system. Hoe also later developed the first high-speed folding machines for newspapers and contributed to the development of the web press, printers that were fed by continuous rolls of paper.

▼ The Mead Corporation was founded in Dayton, Ohio, to manufacture paper for printers.

▼ The Smithsonian Institution was established in Washington, D.C., the result of an endowment from James Smithson in 1829. Smithson, the illegitimate son of an English duke, desired that his bequest be used to establish an institution in the United States "for the increase and diffusion of knowledge among men." The will Smithson wrote originally left the bequest to be controlled by his heirs, but as none were around to do so, the funds came to the United States government. Smithson had never visited this country, but apparently was in sympathy with its rebellious nature; his own illegitimate stature made him an outcast in England. Despite Smithson's gift, the first reaction of the U.S. government was to refuse the money for a variety of legal and political reasons. After years of public debate, sometimes vicious, a bill was passed by Congress on 10 August, establishing the Smithsonian Institution. However, in the interim, the original money had been invested in state bonds that had shrunk considerably in value, requiring the government to find additional funds. Although the passage of the bill allowed the construction of the original institution building, the Castle, arguments continued about the real purpose of the endowment. The first secretary of the Smithsonian, Joseph Henry, remarked during one of these debates: " . . . the money was not given to the United States exclusively for its own benefit but for the good of man—given in trust for a special object."

▼ Norbert Rillieux received the first patent issued for an efficient refining process for sugar. Rillieux, a black American educated in Paris, lived most of his life in France because of racial discrimination in his home state of Louisiana.

▼ Trinity Church in New York City was completed and dedicated on 21 May.

▼ 1796 ▼

BIRTHDAYS AND DEATH DAYS
Jean Corot born on 26 July
Robert Burns died on 31 July at age 37

MUSIC
Emperor Quartet, by Franz Joseph Haydn

BOOKS, POETRY, AND PLAYS
Regicide Peace, by Edmund Burke
Wilhelm Meister's Apprenticeship, by Johann Goethe

IN 1796 on 1 June, Tennessee became the sixteenth state of the Union.
The first governor was John Sevier, who served until 1801. Tennessee is known as
the Volunteer State, a nickname commemorating volunteer soldiers from the state
who fought in the battle of New Orleans during the War of 1812. The state flag was
officially adopted on 17 April 1905. Tennessee was the last territory to be granted
statehood in the eighteenth century.

▼ The United States Department of State began collecting copies of publications
as required by the copyright law of 1790.

▼ The first American cookbook was published. The book, *American Cookery:
Adapted to This Country and All Grades of Life,* was written by Amelia Simmons.

▼ Ballet dancers in London first performed with toe shoes.

▼ Edward Jenner first used a vaccine to inoculate people against smallpox, using
a preparation made from cowpox. Although Jenner is usually considered the father
of immunology, experiments with inoculation against smallpox were recorded as
early as 1701. Four years later, in 1800, Dr. Benjamin Waterhouse was the first to
use the vaccine in the United States.

IN 1746 on 4 February, Tadeusz Kosci-
uszko was born. This Polish-American fought with
the American colonists during the Revolutionary War
and later returned to Poland, where, in 1794, he led an
unsuccessful rebellion against the Prussian and Russian domination of the country. The date is recognized
as Kosciuszko Day in some regions of the United
States.

▼ **1746** ▼

COLLEGES AND UNIVERSITIES
Princeton University (Princeton, NJ)

MUSIC
Judas Maccabeus, by George Frederick Handel

▼ The English Parliament banned the wearing of tartan patterns, a reaction to continuing rebellion in Scotland, especially the escape of "Bonnie" Prince Charles to France. The ban was lifted 36 years later, in 1782.

▼ The first medical description of a duodenal ulcer was published, the work of George Hamberger, a German doctor.

IN 1696 the power of the microscope was first made known to science

with the publication of *Arcana naturae* (Mysteries of nature), by Anton van Leeuwenhoek, a Dutch scientist who created the first microscope sometime before 1673.

▼ The Marquis Antoine de l'Hospital, a French mathematician, published the first known book of calculus, *Analyse des infiniments petits* (Analysis of infinitesimals).

IN 1646 the Taj Mahal was completed in Agra, India. The emperor Shah

Jahan commissioned a Turkish architect to build this ornate structure as a mausoleum for his deceased wife. Construction began in 1630 and involved more than 20,000 laborers and craftsman from many countries.

▼ The magic lantern was invented by Athanasius Kirchner in Germany. Kirchner's invention allowed images to be projected onto flat surfaces.

▼ Smoking was banned in towns in Massachusetts as a precaution against fire.

1996

▼ **1596** ▼

BOOKS, POETRY, AND PLAYS
Midsummer Night's Dream, by William
Shakespeare
Richard II, by William Shakespeare

WHAT 400 WAS years ago

IN 1596 on 28 January, Sir Francis Drake, the English explorer, died from
a plague off the coast of Panama. At the time, Drake was on a voyage of discovery
and conquest against the Spanish in the West Indies.

▼ Ludolf van Ceulen, a Dutch mathematician, succeeded in figuring the value of
pi to 20 decimal places, the first significant calculation for pi since Archimedes
determined it to be 3.142.

▼ The first self-contained whaling ship was built by François Zaburu, a Basque
sailor. The ship design improved on existing whaling vessels by adding equipment
to boil down whale blubber into oil, a process previously requiring shore-based
facilities.

▼ The first math book listing trigonometric tables was published.

IN 1546 the first use of the word *fossil* was
recorded in a book published by Georgius Agricola,
a German. *De natura fossilium* (About the nature of
digging) used the word to describe anything that was
found in the ground.

WHAT 450 WAS years ago

▼ A book by the Italian scientist Hieronymus Girolamo first established the theory that diseases
might be transmitted from one person to another by
tiny, self-replicating life-forms. The book, *De con-
tagione et contagiosis morbis* (On contagion and contagious diseases), postulated
that disease could be spread by direct contact, by clothes or soiled linen, and through
the air. In this work Girolamo is credited with having first recorded a scientific
description of the nature of the transmission of disease as well as with having first
described typhus. Earlier, in 1530, he used rhyme to write *Syphilis sive morbus
Gallicus* (Syphilis or the French disease), which referred to the first European
outbreak of syphilis.

IN 1496 the government of Poland created the "Magna Carta of Poland," officially known as the Statute of Piotrków. This edict promoted extensive rights for the privileged classes while diminishing the rights of peasants. Over a period of years, the lower classes of Poland were gradually turned into the equivalent of property to be owned by the higher classes.

▼ The native people of the Canary Islands—the Guanches—were finally defeated by Spanish invaders. During a long history of trade and control by Romans, Arabs, Italians, French, and Portuguese, they had remained unconquered. A tribe with roots in North Africa, the Guanches were decimated by the Spanish and soon died out completely.

▼   1972   ▼

ASSOCIATIONS, SOCIETIES, UNIONS, AND GOVERNMENT DEPARTMENTS
American Public Health Association (Washington, DC)

MUSEUMS AND ZOOS
Alexandria Zoological Park (Alexandria, VA)
Kimball Art Museum (Fort Worth, TX)
Montgomery Zoo (Montgomery, AL)
San Diego Wild Animal Park (Escondido, CA)
Wildlife Safari (Winston, OR)

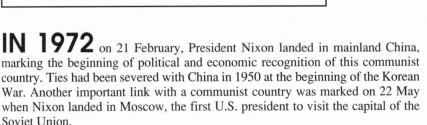

MUSIC
Amazing Grace, by Aretha Franklin
Baby Don't Get Hooked on Me, by Mac Davis
Bare Trees, by Fleetwood Mac
Burning Love, by Elvis Presley
Chicago V, by Chicago
Colors of the Day, by Judy Collins
The Cover of Rolling Stone, by Dr. Hook
Crocodile Rock, by Elton John
Eat a Peach, by the Allman Brothers Band
Everybody Plays the Fool, by the Main Ingredient
Exile on Main Street, by the Rolling Stones
The First Time Ever I Saw Your Face, by Roberta Flack

IN 1972 on 21 February, President Nixon landed in mainland China, marking the beginning of political and economic recognition of this communist country. Ties had been severed with China in 1950 at the beginning of the Korean War. Another important link with a communist country was marked on 22 May when Nixon landed in Moscow, the first U.S. president to visit the capital of the Soviet Union.

▼ On 2 May, an era ended at the Federal Bureau of Investigation with the death of J. Edgar Hoover. Hoover was the only director ever to head the FBI, and was 77 years old when he died.

▼ On 3 June, in Cincinnati, Ohio, Sally Priesand became the first woman in the United States and only the second woman in Judaic history to be ordained as a rabbi.

▼ On 17 June, the Watergate era began with the arrest of five burglars at the headquarters of the Democratic Party in Washington, D.C. The burglars and two former White House aides were indicted by a federal grand jury on 15 September. On 17 May 1973, the Senate Select Committee on Presidential Campaign Activities opened hearings about the Watergate incident. Articles of impeachment against the president were accepted by the House Judiciary Committee on 30 July 1974, and on 9 August 1974, Nixon resigned from office.

▼ On 29 June, the U.S. Supreme Court declared that the death penalty was unconstitutional because it was a form of "cruel and unusual punishment."

▼ On 11 September, service began on the Bay Area Rapid Transit System in San Francisco and the nearby East Bay.

▼ Seymour Cray founded Cray Research, Inc. in Chippewa Falls, Wisconsin. Cray was earlier one of the founders of Control Data Corporation, which he left in order to design supercomputers.

▼ 1972 ▼

MUSIC *continued*
For the Roses, by Joni Mitchell
Freddie's Dead, by Curtis Mayfield
Get on the Good Foot, by James Brown
The Happiest Girl in the Whole U.S.A., by Donna Fargo
Heart of Gold, by Neil Young
 History of Eric Clapton, by Eric Clapton
 A Horse with No Name, by America
 I Am Woman, by Helen Reddy
 Let's Stay Together, by Al Green
 Live, by the J. Geils Band
 Long Cool Woman, by the Hollies
 Long John Silver, by the Jefferson Airplane
Look What You Done for Me, by Al Green
Machine Head, by Deep Purple
Mardi Gras, by Creedence Clearwater Revival
My Ding-A-Ling, by Chuck Berry
The Night the Lights Went Out in Georgia,
 by Vicki Lawrence
Pictures at an Exhibition, by Emerson, Lake & Palmer
The Rise and Fall of Ziggy Stardust, by David Bowie
Rock of Ages, by the Band
Rockin' Pneumonia, by Johnny Rivers

25 years ago

▼ Nolan Bushnell founded the Atari Corporation in Sunnyvale, California. Atari's initial product was Pong, the first computer game.

▼ Prime Computer was founded in Natick, Massachusetts. The company was one of the first to develop and market minicomputers.

▼ In England, the first CAT scanner was introduced. The device, formally known as a computerized axial tomography scanner, was developed by physicists Godfrey Hounsfield, an Englishman, and Allan Cormack, an American. The CAT scan arrived in the United States in 1973.

▼ *Landsat I* was launched. This satellite was the first specialized platform to study earth resources.

▼ **1972** ▼

MUSIC *continued*
School's Out, by Alice Cooper
Seventh Sojourn, by the Moody Blues
A Song for You, by the Carpenters
Song Sung Blue, by Neil Diamond
Stop and Smell the Roses, by Mac Davis
Superfly, by Curtis Mayfield
Sylvia's Mother, by Dr. Hook
Thick as a Brick, by Jethro Tull
Toulouse Street, by the Doobie Brothers
Will the Circle Be Unbroken, by the Nitty Gritty Dirt Band
The World Is a Ghetto, by War
You Don't Mess Around with Jim, by Jim Croce
Your Mama Don't Dance, by Loggins & Messina
You're So Vain, by Carly Simon

NEWSPAPERS AND MAGAZINES
Cuisine (New York, NY)
Money (New York, NY)
Ms. (New York, NY)
Oui (New York, NY)
W (New York, NY)

BOOKS, POETRY, AND PLAYS
The Boys of Summer, by Roger Kahn
I'm O.K., You're O.K., by Dr. Thomas Harris
The Winds of War, by Herman Wouk

▼ **1972** ▼

MOVIES

Blazing Saddles (directed by Mel Brooks, with Cleavon Little, Gene Wilder)

Cabaret (directed by Bob Fosse, with Joel Grey, Liza Minnelli)

Deep Throat (with Linda Lovelace)

Deliverance (directed by John Boorman, with Burt Reynolds, Jon Voight)

The Godfather (directed by Francis Ford Coppola, with Marlon Brando, Al Pacino)

Harold and Maude (directed by Hal Ashby, with Bud Cort, Ruth Gordon)

Play It Again Sam (directed by Herbert Rossi, with Woody Allen, Diane Keaton)

The Poseidon Adventure (directed by Ronald Neame, with Ernest Borgnine, Gene Hackman)

Sleuth (directed by Joseph Mankiewicz, with Michael Caine, Laurence Olivier)

▼ The first Victoria's Secret stores were opened by The Limited, an established chain of clothing stores, to sell lingerie.

▼ The Instamatic camera was first marketed by Kodak.

▼ Hacky Sack was invented by John Stalberger in Oregon. The Hacky Sack was a small weighted bag, about the size of a golf ball, created to improve coordination and increase leg strength. The bag is kicked into the air with the foot.

▼ **1947** ▼

ASSOCIATIONS, SOCIETIES, UNIONS, AND GOVERNMENT DEPARTMENTS

Central Intelligence Agency (U.S. government)

Department of Defense (U.S. government)

Department of the Air Force (U.S. Department of Defense)

IN 1947 on 25 July, federal legislation created the Department of Defense, under the control of a secretary of defense. The first person appointed to this post was James Forrestal.

▼ On 27 December, the "Howdy Doody Show" debuted on television. Broadcast on NBC, Howdy Doody was on the air until 1960. Howdy Doody himself did not appear until the third show, as construction of the puppet was delayed. Unfortunately for the original model, the popularity of the show created a legal dispute between the network and the puppet's designer. A decision was made to switch designs, giving Howdy a new look. The changeover was accomplished by having the original puppet appear with its face bandaged until a new model could be created. On 8 June 1948, the Howdy that is now a cultural institution in the United States appeared for the first time.

▼ The Xerox Corporation began in Rochester, New York. Chester Carlson, an inventor, succeeded in developing the process of xerography—originally called electrophotography—in 1938, but it was not until 1947 that the Haloid Company, a manufacturer of photographic paper, began to design a machine that could use the process to duplicate documents. The first copier was on the market in 1949, but the first commercial success was with a model introduced in 1950.

▼ The LTV Corporation was founded by James Ling in Dallas, Texas. Ling, a high school dropout and Navy veteran, started the Ling Electric Company in 1947, adding Temco Electronics and Chance-Vought Aircraft. The initials of the three firms were combined to form LTV.

▼ 1947 ▼

MUSEUMS AND ZOOS
Charles Allis Art Museum (Milwaukee, WI)
Finch Arboretum (Spokane, WA)
Honolulu Zoo (Honolulu, HI)
Nature Museum (Charlotte, NC)
Old Court House Museum (Vicksburg, MA)
Plimoth Plantation (Plymouth, MA)

BIRTHDAYS AND DEATH DAYS
Henry Ford died on 7 April at age 82
Ettore Bugatti died on 21 August at age 65
Fiorello La Guardia died on 20 September at age 64
Max Planck died on 4 October at age 89

▼ **1947** ▼

COLLEGES AND UNIVERSITIES
California State University (Los Angeles, CA)
California State University (Sacramento, CA)
College of Santa Fe (Santa Fe, NM)
Daemen College (Amherst, NY)
Madonna College (Livonia, MI)
Merrimack College (North Andover, MA)
Oregon Institute of Technology (Klamath Falls, OR)
School of Visual Arts (New York, NY)
Texas Southern University (Houston, TX)
University of Maryland University College
  (College Park, MD)
University of North Carolina at Wilmington
  (Wilmington, NC)

MUSIC
Brigadoon, by Alan Lerner and Frederick Loewe (first
  performed on 13 March in New York, NY)

▼ The Dead Sea Scrolls were discovered at Khirbat Qumran near the northwest
shore of the Dead Sea. Eleven caves at this site yielded ancient documents dating
to the third century B.C. Many of them were biblical, including numerous psalms
and the Hebrew Old Testament.

▼ The first tubeless tires were put on the market by B. F. Goodrich. In the first
few years, the tubeless concept was not well received by the motoring public, and
it took a concerted advertising campaign promoting a "self-sealing" feature to
convince people to begin changing their attitudes.

▼ Percy Spencer, an engineer at Raytheon, developed the concept of microwave
ovens. He got the idea that microwaves could be used for cooking in 1945 as he
was standing near equipment that was generating microwave signals for communications; the energy melted a candy bar that was in his pocket. The first test of the
concept was the successful bombardment of popcorn.

▼ Anthony Rossi founded Tropicana Products in Florida as a provider of citrus juices.

▼ Dennis Gabor, an English physicist, developed the concept of holography,
although holographic images were not created until later. The Nobel Prize was
awarded to Gabor in 1971.

1997

▼ 1947 ▼

NEWSPAPERS AND MAGAZINES
Air Force Times (Washington, DC)
American Motorcyclist (Westerville, OH)
Changing Times (Washington, DC)
Road and Track (Newport Beach, CA)

BOOKS, POETRY, AND PLAYS
The Age of Anxiety, by W. H. Auden
Gentleman's Agreement, by Laura Hobson
A Streetcar Named Desire, by Tennessee Williams

MOVIES
Gentleman's Agreement (directed by Elia Kazan,
   with Dorothy McGuire, Gregory Peck)

▼ Jackie Robinson was signed to play professional baseball with the Brooklyn Dodgers. Robinson was the first black to be allowed into professional baseball in the United States. His first game as a professional was an exhibition game between the Dodgers and the Yankees, held on 11 April.

▼ The first National Hockey League (NHL) All-Star Game was held in Toronto, Ontario.

▼ United Fruit introduced Chiquita brand bananas.

▼ 1922 ▼

ASSOCIATIONS, SOCIETIES, UNIONS, AND GOVERNMENT DEPARTMENTS
Alpha Alpha Gamma (St. Louis, MO)
American Society of Clinical Pathologists (Chicago, IL)
American Society of Newspaper Editors (Reston, VA)
Association of Governing Boards (Washington, DC)
Business-Professional Advertising Association (Edison, NJ)
Izaak Walton League of America (Arlington, VA)
National Association of American Business Clubs
   (High Point, NC)

IN 1922 in February, De Witt Wallace and Lila Wallace founded

Reader's Digest in Chappaqua, New York (publication later moved to Pleasantville, New York). The magazine concept was originally rejected by several publishing companies, prompting Wallace to start the periodical on his own with the help of his wife. The first edition stated the publication's purpose was to print articles " . . . from leading magazines—each article of enduring value and interest, in condensed and compact form." The first year, there were only 1,500 subscribers, but by the end of the decade, the number increased to more than 200,000. The first foreign-language edition was published in 1938.

▼ On 30 May, the Lincoln Memorial in Washington, D.C., was officially dedicated.

▼ **1922** ▼

ASSOCIATIONS, SOCIETIES, UNIONS, AND GOVERNMENT DEPARTMENTS
continued
National Association of Broadcasters (Washington, DC)
Reserve Officers Association of the U.S.
   (Washington, DC)

MUSEUMS AND ZOOS
Akron Art Museum (Akron, OH)
Beardsley Zoological Gardens (Bridgeport, CT)
Dallas Historical Society Museum (Dallas, TX)
Fort Western Museum (Augusta, ME)
   Honolulu Academy of Arts (Honolulu, HI)
   Oakland Zoo (Oakland, CA)
   St. Louis County Historical Society (Duluth, MN)

BIRTHDAYS AND DEATH DAYS
Ernest Shackleton died on 5 January at age 48
Kingsley Amis born on 16 April
Alexander Graham Bell died on 1 August at age 75
Marcel Proust died on 15 November at age 51

COLLEGES AND UNIVERSITIES
Central Bible College (Springfield, MO)
Midwestern State University (Wichita Falls, TX)

75 years ago

▼   1922   ▼

NEWSPAPERS AND MAGAZINES
American Horticulturist (Alexandria, VA)
Elks Magazine (Chicago, IL)
Outdoor America (Arlington, VA)
True Confessions (New York, NY)

BOOKS, POETRY, AND PLAYS
Anna Christie, by Eugene O'Neill
The Beautiful and the Damned, by F. Scott Fitzgerald
Etiquette, by Emily Post
Hairy Ape, by Eugene O'Neill
The Waste Land, by T. S. Eliot

MOVIES
Nanook of the North (directed by Robert Flaherty)
Nosferatu (directed by Frederich Marnau, with Max Schreck)
Robin Hood (directed by Allan Dwan, with Douglas
   Fairbanks)

▼ On 27 June, the first Newbery Medal was presented. Sponsored by the American Library Association, the annual Newbery Medal is presented to the winner of a competition for the most important American children's book published in the preceding year. In 1922, the first award went to *The Story of Mankind,* by Hendrik van Loon.

▼ On 6 November, a telegraphed message from archaeologist Howard Carter announced the discovery of the tomb of Tutankhamen in Egypt. Carter and his crew entered the final burial room on 17 February 1923, discovering the undisturbed golden shrine that contained the mummified remains of King Tut, as he came to be known. An article in the *New York Times* commented, "This has been, perhaps, the most extraordinary day in the whole history of Egyptian excavation."

▼ On 15 November, the discovery of white corpuscles in the blood was announced by the Rockefeller Institute.

▼ The first issue of *Better Homes and Gardens* was published in Des Moines, Iowa. The original name of the magazine was *Fruit, Garden, and Home,* with a subscription price of 35 cents for 12 monthly issues. The name was changed in 1924.

▼ Philip Smith purchased a large movie theater in Boston to initiate the General Cinema Corporation as a business. General Cinema is responsible for creating the first drive-in theater, the first mall cinemas, and the first multiscreen cinema operation.

▼ The first planned shopping center in the United States opened in Kansas City, Missouri. Country Club Plaza was designed to be primarily accessible by automobile.

▼ An ad agency working on the Listerine mouthwash account invented a new health term: *halitosis.*

▼ George Mecherle, a retired farmer, founded State Farm Insurance in Bloomington, Illinois. Mecherle's inspiration was to provide lower cost automotive insurance to car owners who lived in rural areas; existing policies charged rural drivers the same rate as city drivers. The first sales outlets for State Farm were local chapters of the Farm Bureau; State Farm sales agencies were opened beginning in 1949.

▼ The Chock Full O'Nuts coffee shop chain was born with the opening of a nut stand in Times Square in New York City.

▼ *Ulysses,* by James Joyce, was published in Paris, but official U.S. government objections delayed publication in this country until 1933.

▼ Vitamin E was discovered by Herbert Evans and K. J. Scott, and vitamin D was discovered by Elmer McCollum.

▼ 1897 ▼

ASSOCIATIONS, SOCIETIES, UNIONS, AND GOVERNMENT DEPARTMENTS

Chess League of America (Warrenville, IL)
Customs Brokers and Forwarders Association of
    America (New York, NY)
General Society of Mayflower Descendants (Plymouth, MA)
Iron Castings Society (Des Plaines, IL)
National Association of Manufacturers (Washington, DC)
National Congress of Parents and Teachers (PTA)
    (Chicago, IL)
Zionist Organization of America (New York, NY)

IN 1897 on 17 February, the National Congress of Mothers was formed in Washington, D.C., to provide communication and progressive action for parents and teachers. In 1924, the group's name was changed to the National Congress of Parents and Teachers, now known as the PTA.

▼ On 4 March, William McKinley was inaugurated as the twenty-fifth president of the United States. During his term in office, he dealt with the involvement of the United States in the Spanish-American War.

▼   **1897**   ▼

MUSEUMS AND ZOOS

Arlington Historical Society (Arlington, MA)
Audubon Naturalist Society (Chevy Chase, MD)
Cooper-Hewitt Museum (New York, NY)
General Grant Memorial (New York, NY)
Grand Army of the Republic Memorial Museum
    (Chicago, IL)
John Adams and John Quincy Adams Birthplaces
    (Quincy, MA)
Mayflower Society Museum (Plymouth, MA)
Montgomery County Historical Society (Dayton, OH)
Nashville Parthenon (Nashville, TN)
St. Paul's Como Zoo (St. Paul, MN)
Utah State Historical Society Museum (Salt Lake City, UT)

BIRTHDAYS AND DEATH DAYS

Johannes Brahms died on 3 April at age 63

▼   On 23 September, the first celebration of Frontier Day was held in Cheyenne, Wyoming. The celebration, now extended to a week, is still marked by an annual rodeo and western exposition.

▼   The first Boston Marathon was held in Boston, Massachusetts. The race has been held annually since that year.

▼   The Dow Chemical Company was founded by Herbert Henry Dow in Midland, Michigan. Dow developed methods for extracting chemicals from underground deposits of brine, and he began his company by manufacturing chlorine bleach, bromine, chloroform, ethylene, and magnesium. The onset of World War I and the resulting embargo of chemical imports from Germany—then a major supplier of chemical products—gave Dow a major boost in business.

▼   K mart had its humble beginnings in a single store in Memphis, Tennessee. Based on the concept of low-cost "dime" items, the store was opened by Sebastian Kresge and J. G. McCrory. It had expanded to 150 locations by 1916, when the name S. S. Kresge was adopted. The president of Kresge's in 1962 was Harry Cunningham, who opened the first K mart outlet that year in Detroit, Michigan. The almost immediate success of the K mart concept led the company to change its name in 1977.

▼   Boston became the first city in the United States to have a working subway system.

▼ A widespread strike led by the United Mine Workers affected coal mines in Ohio, Pennsylvania, and West Virginia. The strike was a success for the union, resulting in the establishment of an eight-hour workday.

▼ The "Katzenjammer Kids" debuted on the comic pages of newspapers. The Kids also starred in films, being featured in animated cartoons as early as 1916. The comic strip was renamed "Hans and Fritz" and "The Captain and the Kids" in later years.

▼ The first oscilloscope was developed by Karl Braun, a German physicist.

▼ The first speedometer for vehicles was invented by J. Jones.

▼ The California Almond Growers Exchange was founded in California by 71 growers. Almonds had recently become popular because of their use in the confectionary industry.

▼ Eduard Buchner, a German biologist, accidentally discovered that an extract made from yeast could turn sugar into alcohol. That accidental observation began the science of biochemistry.

▼ 1897 ▼

COLLEGES AND UNIVERSITIES
Bradley University (Peoria, IL)
Lincoln Memorial University (Harrogate, TN)
San Diego State University (San Diego, CA)
San Francisco State University (San Francisco, CA)
Southern Utah State College (Cedar City, UT)
Trinity College (Deerfield, IL)
Trinity College (Washington, DC)

MUSIC
"The Stars and Stripes Forever," by John Philip Sousa

NEWSPAPERS AND MAGAZINES
Barre-Montpelier Times-Argus (Barre, VT)
Winston-Salem Journal (Winston-Salem, NC)

BOOKS, POETRY, AND PLAYS
Cyrano de Bergerac, by Edmond Rostand
The Devil's Disciple, by George Bernard Shaw
In His Steps, by Charles Monroe Sheldon
Le Jardin d'Epicure, by Anatole France
Resurrection, by Leo Tolstoy

▼ Joseph Thomson discovered the electron. In 1899, he succeeded in measuring its charge for the first time.

▼ Edwin S. Votey received a patent for the Pianola player piano.

▼ Ronald Ross, an English doctor, discovered that malaria was carried by the anopheles mosquito. Subsequently, the first programs were established to limit the spread of malaria and other insect-born diseases by controlling mosquito breeding and screening areas used by humans. Ross was awarded a Nobel Prize in 1902.

▼ J. M. Smucker established the Smucker's Company in Ohio to sell cider. In subsequent years, jams and jellies were added to the product list.

▼ The ice cream sundae was born at the Red Cross Pharmacy in Ithaca, New York. Because local laws prevented the sale of soda water on Sundays, the pharmacy's soda fountain created sundaes as a way to sell ice cream to customers craving the newly popular ice cream sodas.

▼ The first gasoline-powered lawn mowers were produced. Companies in both the United States and Germany received the credit: the Coldwell Lawn Mower Company in Newbury, New York, and the Benz Company in Stuttgart, Germany.

▼ The Campbell company developed the first soup condensing and canning process.

▼   1847   ▼

ASSOCIATIONS, SOCIETIES, UNIONS, AND GOVERNMENT DEPARTMENTS
American Medical Association (Chicago, IL)
American Society for the Advancement of Science
(Boston, MA)

MUSEUMS AND ZOOS
Concordia Historical Institute (St. Louis, MO)

BIRTHDAYS AND DEATH DAYS
Alexander Graham Bell born on 3 March
Paul von Hindenburg born on 2 October

COLLEGES AND UNIVERSITIES
Carthage College (Kenosha, WI)
City College of City University of New York
(New York, NY)

▼   1847   ▼

COLLEGES AND UNIVERSITIES
continued
College of Mount Saint Vincent (Riverdale, NY)
Earlham College (Richmond, IN)
Lawrence University (Appleton, WI)
Otterbein College (Westerville, OH)
Rockford College (Rockford, IL)
Saint Francis College (Loretto, PA)
Saint Xavier College (Chicago, IL)
University of Iowa (Iowa City, IA)

150 years ago

IN 1847 on 3 March, Alexander Graham Bell was born in Edinburgh, Scotland. Bell was a noted authority on acoustics and speech, and a quest to improve the quality of life for deaf people brought him to the United States in 1871. Working with electrical apparatus, he conducted research into methods of improving sound transmissions; on 3 June 1875, he succeeded with the first known demonstration of a telephone, although the spoken message was not clear. After receiving a patent for his invention, Bell made the now-famous transmission to his assistant, Mr. Watson, on 10 March 1876. Other inventors contributed to this breakthrough, and some individuals and companies sued Bell because of his product's similarity to their own creations. Eventually, Bell's patent rights were confirmed in court. Wealth from his invention allowed Bell to experiment with other technologies, leading to more inventions. Bell died on 2 August 1922 in Nova Scotia.

▼ On 9 March, the first major amphibious landing by the U.S. Army occurred during the Mexican War. The U.S. force, led by General Winfield Scott, landed 10,000 men on the shore south of the city of Vera Cruz. A successful operation, the action led to the surrender of Vera Cruz on 27 March.

▼ On 7 May, doctors and representatives of established medical societies and medical schools established the American Medical Association (AMA). The AMA was founded in Philadelphia with Dr. Jonathan Knight as the first president.

▼ On 1 July, the first adhesive postage stamps were put on sale by the U.S. Post Office. This date is recognized as American Stamp Day. The first two adhesive stamps issued were a five-cent stamp with a portrait of Benjamin Franklin and a ten-cent stamp with a portrait of George Washington.

▼ 1847 ▼

MUSIC
Minute Waltz, by Frédéric Chopin

NEWSPAPERS AND MAGAZINES
Chicago Tribune (Chicago, IL)

BOOKS, POETRY, AND PLAYS
Jane Eyre, by Charlotte Brontë
The Princess, by Alfred Tennyson
Wuthering Heights, by Emily Brontë

▼ The Philip Morris Company was founded as a single tobacco shop in London. Philip Morris, the proprietor, originally imported all of his wares, but he established a bigger business with the introduction of his own brands. The company received a decree in 1901, making it the royal tobacconist, and began selling cigarettes in the United States in 1902. In 1929, the company began cigarette production in the United States at a plant in Richmond, Virginia.

▼ Salt Lake City was founded in Utah territory by the Mormons. The first settlers arrived in the Salt Lake valley on or about 24 July after a long and arduous trek from a temporary settlement in Nauvoo, Illinois. Brigham Young, the new leader of the Mormons after the murder of Joseph Smith, arrived on 24 July. Since 1849, a date on or near 24 July has been recognized in Utah as Pioneer Day.

▼ The Italian scientist Ascanio Sobrero discovered nitroglycerin, an explosive so powerful he spent little additional time experimenting with it. About 20 years later, in 1866, Swedish chemist Alfred Nobel found a way to make nitroglycerin easier to handle. His new product, dynamite, was a major commercial success and made him a very rich man. It was his fortune, originally made possible by Ascanio Sobrero, that was bequeathed after his death to the establishment of the Nobel Prize awards.

▼ 1797 ▼

ASSOCIATIONS, SOCIETIES, UNIONS, AND GOVERNMENT DEPARTMENTS
General Grand Chapter of Masons
(Lexington, KY)

IN 1797 on 4 March, John Adams was inaugurated as the second president

of the United States. He was born in Quincy (originally known as Braintree), Massachusetts, on 19 October 1735. An early supporter of American independence, Adams was a delegate to the Continental Congress and served in the first U.S. Congress. In 1789, he was elected as the first vice president, a post he held for the next eight years under President George Washington. As second-in-command, he stated, "My country has in its wisdom contrived for me the most insignificant office that ever the invention of man contrived or his imagination conceived." After being elected president in 1796, Adams helped avoid a war with France, although he lost much popular and political support for his efforts. He was defeated by Thomas Jefferson in the presidential election of 1800. Adams died on 4 July 1826, on the 50th anniversary of the signing of the Declaration of Independence. Thomas Jefferson also died the same day.

200 years ago

▼   1797   ▼

MUSEUMS AND ZOOS
Maryland Science Center (Baltimore, MD)
Mission San Juan Bautista (San Juan Bautista, CA)
San Fernando Mission (Mission Hills, CA)
USS *Constitution* (Charlestown, MA)

BIRTHDAYS AND DEATH DAYS
Franz Schubert born on 31 January
Horace Walpole died on 2 March at age 80
Edmund Burke died on 8 July at age 68
Mary Wollstonecraft Shelley born on 30 August
Heinrich Heine born on 13 December

COLLEGES AND UNIVERSITIES
Hartwick College (Oneonta, NY)

NEWSPAPERS AND MAGAZINES
J. Gruber's Hagerstown Town & Country Almanac
(Hagerstown, MD)

BOOKS, POETRY, AND PLAYS
Hermann und Dorothea, by Johann Goethe

▼ On 15 May, the first special session of the U.S. Congress was held at the request of President John Adams. The reason for this precedent-setting event was worsening relations between the United States and France, peaking with the expulsion of an American diplomat from France. The crisis led to attacks on merchant and naval ships from both countries, but war was never declared. The situation calmed down by 1800, but lingering political dissatisfaction from the situation cost Adams the next presidential election.

▼ On 24 June, the first patent was granted for a cast-iron plow. Inventor Charles Newbold, from Burlington County, New Jersey, designed this revolutionary agricultural implement to improve the efficiency of plowing, but farmers were initially reluctant to use it because of a widespread belief that the iron would release poisons into the soil.

▼ On 21 October, the USS *Constitution* was launched in Boston. Still afloat and the oldest commissioned vessel in the U.S. Navy (which at the time was part of the War Department), the *Constitution* was nicknamed Old Ironsides because the ship's planking was so strong that cannonballs would often bounce off the sides instead of penetrating through them.

▼ Albany became the new capital of New York. Formerly, the capital had been New York City.

▼ French balloonist André-Jacques Garnerin became the first human being to use a parachute successfully. Earlier experiments had demonstrated its potential: in 1785, a dog was successfully dropped from a balloon using a parachute. Garnerin's parachute was about 23 feet in diameter and attached to a central wooden staff.

▼ Louis-Nicolas Vauquelin, a French chemist, discovered the metal chromium.

▼ The top hat was designed by John Etherington, a London hatter.

IN 1747 the first conclusive cures for scurvy were demonstrated by James Lind, a naval doctor from Scotland. Lind experimented with citrus and various other compounds, including vinegar and cider, to prove that the effects of scurvy, later shown to be caused by a lack of vitamin C, could be reversed.

▼ The New York Bar Association was formed as the first organization of lawyers in the American colonies.

IN 1697 Peter the Great became the first ruler of Russia to leave the country. He traveled to Europe and England, observing their activities, social practices, and industrial advances with which he intended to modernize his own country.

▼ The Treaty of Ryswick was signed between England and France. The treaty's provisions reversed the territorial conquests made during King William's War, with Newfoundland transferred to English rule.

IN 1647 on 11 November, the first compulsory school law in this country was passed in Massachusetts. This act required towns with more than 50 inhabitants to provide teachers and schooling for children. Known as the Old Deluder Law, the text begins, "It being one chief project of the old deluder, Satan, to keep men from the knowledge of the Scriptures, as in former times by keeping them in an unknown tongue, . . . that learning may not be buried in the grave of our fathers in the church and commonwealth. . . . "

▼ The first cases of yellow fever in the Americas were reported. The disease was carried from Africa by slaves brought to Barbados.

▼ The first map of the moon was published by Johannes Hevelius.

▼ The Society of Friends of Truth was founded by George Fox and other religious reformers in northwest England. This group later became known as the Quakers.

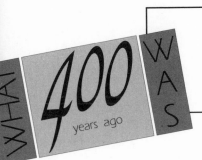

▼ **1597** ▼

BOOKS, POETRY, AND PLAYS
King John, by William Shakespeare
The Merchant of Venice, by William Shakespeare

IN 1597 Andrea Libau, a German alchemist, published the first major book of chemistry.

IN 1547 in Russia, Ivan IV became the first

ruler officially to be titled Czar. The reign of this man marked the beginning of the Romanov line of royalty.

▼ Brittany was added to the royal domain of the French king, Henri II. Fifteen years earlier, in 1532, the independent duchy of Brittany was annexed to France with the signing of the Treaty of Plessis-Mace.

IN 1497 on 24 June, explorer John Cabot

(also known as Giovanni Caboto) discovered Newfoundland, originally called Prima Vista. This date is recognized as Discovery Day in Newfoundland (celebrated on the Monday closest to this date).

▼ On 8 July, Vasco da Gama, an explorer and navigator from Portugal, set sail for a voyage around the horn of Africa, the first such trip by a European. De Gama arrived in Calicut, India, on 20 May 1498.

▼ An observation by Nicolaus Copernicus, a Polish astronomer, marked the first recorded viewing of the occultation of a star by the moon. (An occultation is the motion by one celestial body that obscures another.)

▼   **1973**   ▼

ASSOCIATIONS, SOCIETIES, UNIONS, AND GOVERNMENT DEPARTMENTS

Drug Enforcement Administration
(U.S. Department of Justice)
National Electronics Sales and Service Dealers
Association (Fort Worth, TX)
Space Education Association (Elizabethtown, PA)

MUSEUMS AND ZOOS

Arizona Historical Society Museum (Phoenix, AZ)
Children's Museum of Denver (Denver, CO)
Craft and Folk Art Museum (Los Angeles, CA)
Merritt College Anthropology Museum (Oakland, CA)
National Inventors Hall of Fame (Arlington, VA)
Reuben H. Fleet Space Theater and Science Center
(San Diego, CA)
Sea World of Florida (Orlando, FL)

IN 1973 on 1 January, all sales of DDT, a potent pesticide, were banned in the United States. Introduced commercially in 1946, DDT was enthusiastically used around the world for many years, but it was discovered to be a major destructive factor in the food chain. In 1961, Rachael Carson's book, *Silent Spring,* created the first public awareness of the negative effects of this chemical agent. At the time of its ban, about 12 million pounds of DDT were used annually in the United States.

▼ On 22 January, the Supreme Court upheld the right of women to have abortions in the case of *Roe v. Wade.* This decision restricted state regulations controlling abortions, and generally allowed abortions for the first three months of pregnancy. A related decision, also occurring on this day, eliminated restrictions on organizations that provided abortions, allowing the development of abortion clinics.

▼ On 27 January, a peace treaty was signed in Paris, ending the war in Vietnam.

▼ On 28 February, Wounded Knee, South Dakota, was the site of a takeover by the American Indian Movement (AIM), which was seeking independence and justice for Native Americans. On 8 May, 69 days later, AIM members surrendered after a siege by law enforcement personnel.

▼ On 14 May, NASA launched *Skylab,* an orbiting, manned research laboratory.

▼ On 22 September, the Dallas/Fort Worth Airport was dedicated. At the time, it was the largest airport in the world.

▼ On 6 October, Israel was attacked by Egyptian and Syrian forces during the celebration of Yom Kippur, a religious holiday. More than 20,000 lives were lost in this war—the October War—which was ended by a cease-fire on 24 October.

▼ 1973 ▼

MUSIC

Abandoned Luncheonette, by Daryl Hall and John Oates
The Adventures of Panama Red, by the New Riders of the Purple Sage
Aerosmith, by Aerosmith
Ain't No Woman, by the Four Tops
Aladdin Sane, by David Bowie
Angie, by the Rolling Stones
The Beach Boys in Concert, by the Beach Boys
Beginnings, by the Allman Brothers Band
Billion Dollar Babies, by Alice Cooper
Brothers and Sisters, by the Allman Brothers Band
The Captain and Me, by the Doobie Brothers
Chicago VI, by Chicago
Dark Side of the Moon, by Pink Floyd
Delta Dawn, by Helen Reddy
Desperado, by the Eagles
For Everyman, by Jackson Browne
Give Your Baby a Standing Ovation, by the Dells
Goodbye Yellow Brick Road, by Elton John
Half-Breed, by Cher
I Got a Name, by Jim Croce
The Joker, by the Steve Miller Band

years ago

▼ 1973 ▼

MUSIC *continued*

Killing Me Softly with His Song, by Roberta Flack
Let Me Be There, by Olivia Newton-John
Life and Times, by Jim Croce
Live and Let Die, by Paul McCartney
Living in the Material World,
    by George Harrison
Lynyrd Skynyrd, by Lynyrd Skynyrd
Made in Japan, by Deep Purple
Maria Muldaur, by Maria Muldaur
The Marshall Tucker Band,
    by the Marshall Tucker Band
Midnight Train to Georgia,
    by Gladys Knight and the Pips
The Morning After, by Maureen McGovern
Muscle of Love, by Alice Cooper
My Love, by Paul McCartney
Mystery to Me, by Fleetwood Mac
Now and Then, by the Carpenters
Overnite Sensation, by the Mothers of Invention
The Payback, by James Brown
Quadrophenia, by the Who
Sabbath Bloody Sabbath, by Black Sabbath
Tie a Yellow Ribbon,
    by Tony Orlando and Dawn

NEWSPAPERS AND MAGAZINES

Across the Board (New York, NY)
American Hunter (Herndon, VA)
Astronomy (Milwaukee, WI)
Cricket: The Magazine for Children (Peru, IL)
Entrepreneur Magazine (Los Angeles, CA)
Old House Journal (Brooklyn, NY)
Peterson's Hunting Magazine (Los Angeles, CA)
Playgirl (New York, NY)
Stone Soup (Santa Cruz, CA)

BOOKS, POETRY, AND PLAYS

The Boys on the Bus, by Timothy Crouse
Equus, by Peter Shaffer

▼   1973   ▼

MOVIES

American Graffiti (directed by George Lucas,
with Richard Dreyfuss, Ron Howard)
The Exorcist (directed by William Friedkin, with
Linda Blair, Ellen Burstyn)
The Godfather, Part II (directed by Francis Ford
Coppola, with Robert DeNiro, Al Pacino)
Last Tango in Paris (directed by Bernardo Bertolucci,
with Marlon Brando)
Paper Moon (directed by Peter Bogdanovich, with Ryan
O'Neal)
Serpico (directed by Sidney Lumet, with Al Pacino)
Sleeper (directed by Woody Allen, with Woody Allen,
Diane Keaton)
The Sting (directed by Sydney Pollack, with Paul
Newman, Robert Redford)

▼ On 10 October, Vice President Spiro Agnew resigned from office, the result of an investigation into income tax evasion. Agnew paid a $10,000 fine and received three years probation. Gerald Ford was selected to be the new vice president, and was sworn in on 6 December.

▼ On 17 October, 11 nations in the Middle East declared an embargo on oil shipments to the United States. The announcement created a rapid rise in gasoline and fuel oil prices, gasoline rationing in some areas, and the implementation of a 55 miles-per-hour speed limit on interstate highways. The embargo was lifted on 18 March 1974.

▼ Push-tabs on beverage cans arrived on the market.

▼ The NMR, or nuclear magnetic resonance scanner, was developed in Great Britain.

▼ Lynn Genesko became the first woman to receive an athletic scholarship to college. She went to the University of Miami as a swimmer.

▼ Carl Sontheimer, a retired electronics engineer, introduced the first Cuisinart food processor. Sontheimer developed this device from original designs in use in France.

▼ 1948 ▼

ASSOCIATIONS, SOCIETIES, UNIONS, AND GOVERNMENT DEPARTMENTS

American Academy of Forensic Sciences
(Colorado Springs, CO)
American Checker Federation (Baton Rouge, LA)
American Federation of Grain Millers
(Minneapolis, MN)
American Geological Institute (Alexandria, VA)
American Institute of Industrial Engineers
(Norcross, GA)
American Society of Journalists and Authors
(New York, NY)
Amusement and Music Operators Association
(Oak Brook, IL)
Blue Cross Foundation (Chicago, IL)
Central Committee for Conscientious
Objection (Philadelphia, PA)
Construction Specifications Institute
(Alexandria, VA)
Institute of Industrial Engineers (Atlanta, GA)
Plant Guard Workers of America (Roseville, MI)
Press and Radio Club (Montgomery, AL)
U.S. Information Agency (U.S. government)
Women's Professional Rodeo Association (Blanchard, OK)

IN 1948 on 28 January, the television industry awarded the first Emmys.

▼ On 30 January, Mohandas (Mahatma) Gandhi was assassinated in New Delhi, India.

▼ On 17 March, the Hell's Angels motorcycle club was formed in California.

▼ On 3 April, the Marshall Plan was signed by President Truman. Officially known as the Foreign Assistance Act of 1948, the legislation provided more than $5 billion for recovery programs in European countries.

▼ On 7 April, the World Health Organization (WHO) was founded. Originally conceived as the Health Organization of the League of Nations, dating to 1923, the WHO was established under the authority of the United Nations, with its headquarters in Geneva, Switzerland.

▼ On 30 April, the Organization of American States (OAS) was created to encourage development and cooperation among countries in the American continents. The birth of the OAS occurred in Bogota, Columbia, during an annual meeting of the Pan-American Conference.

▼ On 14 May, the independence of Israel was declared.

▼ On 25 May, a contract between General Motors and workers' unions established the first cost-of-living wage hikes.

▼ On 18 June, the American Library Association adopted the Library Bill of Rights.

▼ On 31 July, New York City opened Idlewild International Airport, then the largest such facility in the world. Idlewild was renamed John F. Kennedy (JFK) International Airport in 1963. The airfield was dedicated by President Truman; the ceremony was marked by a flyover of 900 airplanes.

▼ 1948 ▼

MUSEUMS AND ZOOS
Center of Science and Industry (Columbus, OH)
Contemporary Arts Museum (Houston, TX)
Dossin Great Lakes Museum (Detroit, MI)
Jacksonville Art Museum (Jacksonville, FL)
Mission House (Stockbridge, MA)
Orlando Science Center (Orlando, FL)
San Diego Maritime Museum (San Diego, CA)

BIRTHDAYS AND DEATH DAYS
Mahatma Gandhi died on 30 January at age 79
Orville Wright died on 30 January at age 76
Prince Charles born on 14 November

COLLEGES AND UNIVERSITIES
Brandeis University (Waltham, MA)
Gwynedd-Mercy College (Gwynedd Valley, PA)
Nicholls State University (Thibodaux, LA)
Roger Williams College (Bristol, RI)
Saint John Fisher College (Rochester, NY)
Southern College of Technology (Marietta, GA)
Stonehill College (North Easton, MA)

50 years ago

▼ 1948 ▼

MUSIC
Kiss Me Kate, by Cole Porter (first performed on 30
December in New York, NY)

NEWSPAPERS AND MAGAZINES
Archaeology (New York, NY)
Chicago Sun Times (Chicago, IL)
Fate (St. Paul, MN)
Hot Rod Magazine (Los Angeles, CA)
Skiing (New York, NY)

BOOKS, POETRY, AND PLAYS
Anne of the Thousand Days, by Maxwell Anderson
Mister Roberts, by Thomas Heggen and Joshua Logan
The Naked and the Dead, by Norman Mailer
Sexual Behavior in the Human Male, by Alfred Kinsey
Summer and Smoke, by Tennessee Williams
The Young Lions, by Irwin Shaw

MOVIES
Easter Parade (directed by Charles Walters)
Great Expectations (directed by David Lean,
   with John Mills)
The Treasure of the Sierra Madre (directed by
   John Huston, with Humphrey Bogart, Walter Huston)

▼ On 29 November, the first episode of "Kukla, Fran, and Ollie" debuted on NBC television. Kukla and Ollie, the two puppets, were the creation of Burr Tillstrom, and they first appeared in a Chicago television production known as "Kuklapolitan Players" along with Fran Allison, the human element on the show.

▼ On 10 December, the United Nations officially adopted the Universal Declaration of Human Rights. The date is recognized as Human Rights Day.

▼ The first manned dive with a bathyscaphe was completed. The bathyscaphe, invented by Auguste Piccard, a Swiss physicist, was the first undersea vehicle capable of self-controlled movement. The first manned dive reached a depth of 4,500 feet.

▼ Kurt Enoch and Victor Weybright founded New American Library, a book publishing company. New American Library—now known as NAL—was the first publisher in the United States to issue literary works in paperback.

▼ The first in-flight movies were shown to airline passengers. Pan Am introduced this concept, and the first movie shown on a flight was *Stagecoach*.

▼ The first NASCAR-sponsored race was held in Daytona Beach, Florida. NASCAR—the National Association for Stock Car Auto Racing—was established a year earlier, in 1947. The first NASCAR race was won by Red Byron driving a Ford.

▼ The origin of the universe was first linked to the theory of the "Big Bang," developed by Ralph Alpher, George Gamow, and Robert Herman.

▼ Velcro was invented by George deMestral, a Swiss engineer.

▼ The era of modern electronics began with the invention of the transistor. This electronic device was developed by American scientists Walter Amoy, John Bardeen, and William Shockley, working at Bell Laboratories. The initial announcement of the transistor's development was on 30 June; first commercial production was in 1953.

▼ The first 33 1/3 rpm long-playing record—the LP—was released. The first LPs were primarily classical music and were developed by CBS. Also, stereo sound was first reproduced on records.

▼ Little Audrey debuted as a comic book character. Little Audrey was animated in "The Lost Dream," a cartoon released in 1949. Also, Warner Brothers first introduced Wile E. Coyote and an animated *Geococcyx californianus*—a roadrunner—in "Fast and Furry-ous."

▼ Baskin-Robbins was founded from the merger of two regional ice cream store chains.

▼ Vitamin B-12 was discovered by a research team at the Merck Company.

▼ Bernard Castro introduced the Castro Convertible sofa bed.

▼ The Adidas shoe company was founded in West Germany to manufacture athletic footwear.

50 years ago

▼ The Trammel Crow Company, the largest American real estate development company, was founded in Dallas, Texas, by its namesake.

▼ Charles Lazarus opened a children's furniture store in Washington, D.C. The store was converted from a bicycle repair shop. Lazarus named his business the Baby Furniture & Toy Supermarket, and in 1957, after opening several more outlets, renamed the company Toys 'R' Us.

▼   1923   ▼

ASSOCIATIONS, SOCIETIES, UNIONS, AND GOVERNMENT DEPARTMENTS
Amateur Trapshooting Association (Vandalia, OH)
American Business Real Estate and Law Association
(Athens, GA)
American Institute of Chemists
(Bethesda, MD)
American Management Association
(New York, NY)
Association on American Indian Affairs
(New York, NY)
Marine Corps League (Arlington, VA)

MUSEUMS AND ZOOS
Carlsbad Caverns National Park (Carlsbad, NM)
Lake Superior Zoological Gardens (Duluth, MN)
Museum of the City of New York (New York, NY)
Theodore Roosevelt Birthplace National Historic Site
(New York, NY)
War Memorial Museum of Virginia (Newport News, VA)
Witte Museum (San Antonio, TX)

IN 1923 on 3 March, the first issue of *Time* magazine was published by Henry R. Luce. The first edition had 6 pages of advertisements, and was 28 pages in length. The first person illustrated on the cover was Joseph G. Cannon, a 46-year veteran of the House of Representatives as a Republican from Illinois. Contents included coverage of a bill pending in the Kansas legislature to give prison terms to anyone found with cigarettes on their person, a report on the relative military strengths of major countries, and the revelation that it cost the United States $15,450,000 to enforce the Volstead Act (prohibition) in the previous fiscal year.

▼ According to the 26 April issue of *Time* magazine, the first observed incidence of hissing by an audience in the United States occurred in that year during a New York City performance of Arnold Schoenberg's symphony, *Kammersymphonie*.

▼ On 2 August, President Warren Harding died in a hotel room in San Francisco. The president had been ill for about a week, suffering what was thought to be indigestion during a visit to Vancouver. Arriving in San Francisco, the diagnosis was changed to ptomaine poisoning and included the onset of broncho-pneumonia.

The official cause of death was cerebral apoplexy. Vice President Calvin Coolidge was sworn in as the new president on 4 August.

▼ On 25 October, a Senate subcommittee opened an investigation into the assignment of oil leases at Teapot Dome, Wyoming. This was the beginning of public disclosure of the Teapot Dome Scandal, which involved leasing oil production to private companies on land set aside for the U.S. Navy. The scandal climaxed with the indictment of Albert B. Fall, a former secretary of the interior, charged with bribery and conspiracy. Fall was eventually given a one-year prison sentence.

▼ On 6 November, a U.S. patent was issued to Jacob Schick for the first electrically powered shaver. The first electric shavers were produced by the Schick Company in Stamford, Connecticut, in 1931.

▼ 1923 ▼

BIRTHDAYS AND DEATH DAYS
Wilhelm Röntgen died on 10 February at age 78
Sarah Bernhardt died on 26 March at age 77
Gustav Eiffel died on 27 December at age 91

COLLEGES AND UNIVERSITIES
Columbia Bible College (Columbia, SC)
Lamar University (Beaumont, TX)
McMurry College (Abilene, TX)
Texas Tech University (Lubbock, TX)

MUSIC
Pictures at an Exhibition, by Modest Mussorgsky (first performed on 3 May in Paris, France)

NEWSPAPERS AND MAGAZINES
Anaheim Bulletin (Anaheim, CA)
Modern Romance (New York, NY)
National 4-H News (Washington, DC)

BOOKS, POETRY, AND PLAYS
The Ego and the Id, by Sigmund Freud
Our Betters, by W. Somerset Maugham
St. Joan, by George Bernard Shaw

75 years ago

▼ The first brain surgery using only a local anesthetic was performed by Dr. K. Winfield Ney. Operating in a New York City hospital, Ney removed a brain tumor after the patient's scalp had been treated with cocaine.

▼ Production of photoelectric cells began.

▼ A ruling from the attorney general of the United States made it legal for women to wear trousers in public.

▼ The first nonstop flight across the country was accomplished by Lts. John Macready and Oakley Kelly of the Army Air Corps. Their flight was from Roosevelt Field on Long Island to Rockwell Field, San Diego, lasting 26 hours and 50 minutes.

▼ The first dance marathons were held in the United States. These events pitted couples against each other in a battle of endurance; the winner was the pair remaining on their feet for the longest period of time. These public spectacles had their biggest run later in the decade, with such events as "The Dance Derby of the Century" in New York's Madison Square Garden, which ran for 481 hours before it was shut down by health officials. Several people died from the rigors of these marathons; the earliest fatality was in 1923. Even at the time, many social observers had little positive to say about this mania. An editorial in William Randolph Hearst's *New York American* opined at the time, "No anthropoid ape could possibly have had descendants that could display such hopeless idiocy."

▼ The Milky Way bar was created by Frank Mars. Frank's son Forrest, estranged from his father, created his own candy products, including M&Ms (in 1940). In 1964, the two companies were merged following the death of Frank Mars.

▼ The Zenith Radio Company was founded in Chicago. In 1984, the company's name was changed to Zenith Electronics.

▼ Burlington Industries was founded in Burlington, North Carolina, by J. Spencer Love. The first Burlington mill manufactured cotton products, but switched to rayon when the artificial fiber first became available. The company's success with rayon helped to finance the purchase of other mills, and it grew considerably in the process.

▼ Henry and Hillel Hassenfeld, brothers and immigrants from Poland, founded Hasbro, a company in Providence, Rhode Island, that made school supplies. The company began making toys in the 1940s, and it is now the largest toy company in the country.

75 years ago

▼ The investment banking firm Bear Stearns was founded in New York City. The company is now one of the ten largest investment bankers in the United States.

▼ John Young and Raymond Rubicam founded their advertising agency, Young & Rubicam, in Philadelphia.

▼   **1898**   ▼

ASSOCIATIONS, SOCIETIES, UNIONS, AND GOVERNMENT DEPARTMENTS

American Academy and Institute of Arts and
Letters (New York, NY)
American Optometric Association (St. Louis, MO)
American Society for Testing and Materials
(Philadelphia, PA)
Fraternal Order of Eagles (Brookfield, WI)
Medical Library Association (Chicago, IL)
National Association of Postmasters of the U.S.
(Arlington, VA)

MUSEUMS AND ZOOS

Atlanta Cyclorama (Atlanta, GA)
Erie Art Museum (Erie, PA)
Pittsburgh Zoo (Pittsburgh, PA)
State Historical Society of Missouri (Columbia, MO)

IN 1898 on 1 January, the Greater New York Charter became effective,

uniting five boroughs—the Bronx, Brooklyn, Manhattan, Queens, and Staten Island—as a single city. The preface to the charter stated: "The movement for consolidation of the cities of New York, Brooklyn and contiguous territory . . . will mark an epoch in the history of municipalities in this western continent."

▼ On 12 February, the first driver died as a result of an automobile accident. Henry Lindfield, an Englishman, was fatally injured in a single-car wreck on a road between London and Brighton. He was driving an electric car.

▼ On 15 February, the USS *Maine* blew up in the harbor at Havana, Cuba. This incident became the rallying point for American intervention to depose Spanish rule in Cuba, as it was believed at the time that Spanish sympathizers were responsible for the blast, which caused the deaths of 260 sailors. Congress voted to declare Cuba an independent country on 19 April and authorized the president to use force to support independence. For years before this, many people in the United States had opposed American intervention, believing it to be only an excuse for territorial expansion. An editorial in *Harper's Weekly* stated: " . . . at the bottom of all the pretended sympathy for Cuba lies the desire that the island shall be acquired by the United States." A state of war was initiated on 24 April with a declaration from the Spanish government, beginning the Spanish-American War. The invasion of Cuba began with the landing of Marines at Guantanamo Bay on 10 June. The war ended on 10 December with the formal signing of a peace treaty in Paris, France. President McKinley signed the treaty on 10 February 1899. Terms of the treaty included independence for Cuba; United States acquisition of Guam, the Philippines, and Puerto Rico; and the United States paying $20 million to Spain for the Philippines.

▼ On 30 April, New York passed the first law regulating advertising in the United States. The legislation was aimed at advertisements "intended to have the appearance of an advantageous offer, which is untrue or calculated to mislead."

▼ On 28 May, the U.S. Supreme Court upheld the rights of citizenship regardless of race or skin color. The case, *U.S. v. Wong Kim Ark,* established the right of citizenship for children born in this country, even if both parents were foreigners.

▼ The Los Angeles Symphony gave its first performance in Los Angeles, California. The first conductor was Harley Hamilton, and performances were held in a music hall on Spring Street.

▼   1898   ▼

BIRTHDAYS AND DEATH DAYS
C. L. Dodgson, aka Lewis Carroll, died on 14 January at
    age 65
Henry Bessemer died on 15 March at age 85
Paul Robeson born on 9 April
W. E. Gladstone died on 19 May at age 89
Otto von Bismarck died on 31 July at age 83

COLLEGES AND UNIVERSITIES
Dallas Baptist University (Dallas, TX)
DePaul University (Chicago, IL)
Friends University (Wichita, KS)
Frostburg State University (Frostburg, MD)
Husson College (Bangor, ME)
Northeastern University (Boston, MA)
Saint Norbert College (De Pere, WI)
University of Southwestern Louisiana (Lafayette, LA)

▼   **1898**   ▼

MUSIC
To Damascus, by August Strindberg

NEWSPAPERS AND MAGAZINES
American Forests (Washington, DC)
Outdoor Life (New York, NY)
Sunset (Menlo Park, CA)
Vancouver Province (Vancouver, British Columbia, Canada)

BOOKS, POETRY, AND PLAYS
Candida, by George Bernard Shaw

▼   The first virus was identified in a plant by Martinus Beijerinck. That same year, other scientists were the first to prove that foot-and-mouth disease, affecting animals, was caused by a virus.

▼   Radioactivity was discovered and named by Marie and Pierre Curie. The Curies identified polonium in July and radium in December. A Nobel Prize in physics was awarded to the Curies in 1903, along with Antoine-Henri Becquerel, who contributed to the first detection of radiation. In 1911, Marie Curie received a second Nobel Prize in chemistry.

▼   The first military submarine using modern propulsion methods was built by John Holland, an American inventor. This sub, the *Holland VI,* featured both a battery-powered electric motor for submerged running and a gasoline-powered engine for surface running. The vessel was capable of dives to 75 feet and carried a crew of seven. Years earlier, in 1881, Holland successfully tested an earlier version of his sub in New York Harbor. This underwater vessel was funded by Irish nationalists who believed it would be a useful weapon in their struggle for independence from Great Britain. However, it was not until 1895 that Holland gained interest and financial support from the U.S. military. The *Holland VI* was successfully tested by the U.S. Navy and was the first sub in the fleet. In later years, Holland's company, the Electric Boat Company, was renamed the General Dynamics Corporation. The first submarine with a modern-type ballast system was the *Narval,* a French machine built in 1899. Another important submarine development also occurred—the building of the *Argonaut I,* a vessel designed by Simon Lake and successfully sailed from Norfolk, Virginia, to New York City.

▼ The Southern Pacific Company founded *Sunset,* a magazine intended to promote travel by train in California. The title was taken from one of the company's most popular passenger trains, the Sunset Limited. The railroad sold the magazine in 1915.

▼ John Strutt (also known as Lord Ramsey), the physicist credited with the discovery of argon and helium, also isolated neon, krypton, and xenon with the assistance of Morris Travers, an English chemist. The names of these elements were derived from the Greek: neon means "new," krypton means "hidden," and xenon means "strange."

▼ Nome, Alaska, was founded in 1898.

▼ Warren Bechtel founded the Bechtel company as a contracting firm working on railroad projects in the western states. Bechtel grew into a major construction firm, building dams, pipelines, and power plants.

▼ Nabisco Brands was founded as the National Biscuit Company, a merger of 48 bakeries in Chicago. The National Biscuit Company established the first "consumer-friendly" packaging for crackers—which were previously only sold out of barrels—and invented Uneeda crackers, the first with a nationwide market.

▼ The Goodyear Tire & Rubber Company was founded in Akron, Ohio, by two brothers, Charles and Frank Seiberling. The Seiberlings chose the company name to honor the inventor of vulcanized rubber, Charles Goodyear; their first products were bicycle tires.

▼ Pepsi-Cola was invented by Caleb Bradham, a pharmacist in New Bern, North Carolina. Bradham created his carbonated beverage with kola-nut extract and other ingredients as a treatment for dyspepsia. Originally called Brad's Drink, the soda was renamed in 1903, and Pepsi-Cola became a registered trademark the same year.

▼ James Dewar, an English chemist, was the first to liquefy hydrogen. Dewar also helped in the earlier (1889) development of cordite, a smokeless explosive made from nitroglycerin.

▼ A former sheriff named Emile Ortega founded Ortega Mexican Foods.

100 years ago

▼ The International Paper Company was founded from the merger of 20 paper mills in New England.

▼ The Travelers Insurance Company issued the first car insurance policies. This insurance protected automobile drivers against lawsuits from horse owners.

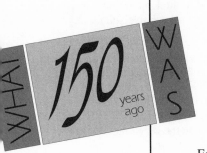

▼ **1848** ▼

**ASSOCIATIONS, SOCIETIES,
UNIONS, AND GOVERNMENT
DEPARTMENTS**
American Association for the Advancement of
Science (Washington, DC)

MUSEUMS AND ZOOS
Essex Institute (Salem, MA)

BIRTHDAYS AND DEATH DAYS
John Quincy Adams died on 23 February at age 80
François de Chateaubriand died on 4 July at age 79
Joel Chandler Harris, aka Uncle Remus, born on
8 December

IN 1848 on 24 January, gold was discovered in California near Sacra-

mento, at the confluence of the American River and the Sacramento River. The
site was owned by John Sutter, who had founded the settlement of Nueva Helvetia,
sometimes known as Sutter's Mill because of the water-powered sawmill at the
site. James Marshall, an employee of Sutter, was the first person to find the precious
metal. Despite some attempt at secrecy, the news appeared within weeks in a San
Francisco newspaper, and "gold fever" soon swept through the state. By the
following year, the news had spread to the rest of the country, and the gold rush of
1849 was on.

▼ On 2 February, at the end of the Mexican War, the Treaty of Guadalupe Hidalgo
was ratified by Mexico. The treaty granted to the United States the territory that
included Arizona, California, Colorado, New Mexico, Texas, Utah, and Wyoming.
In return, the United States paid $15 million to the government of Mexico. The
Mexican War resulted in 1,721 American combat deaths and more than 11,000
deaths from disease.

▼ On 23 February, John Quincy Adams, sixth president of the United States, died
in the Speaker's Room of the House of Representatives in Washington, D.C., after
suffering a heart attack. He was 80 years old. His last words were, "This is the last
of earth, I am content."

▼ On 29 May, Wisconsin became the thirtieth state. The state's name is a French
translation of a Native American word meaning "a gathering of waters." Western
settlement began as early as 1634, with trappers and explorers moving through the
area. In 1763, England gained control of the region from France, and in 1783, a

treaty between England and the United States ceded it to the United States as part of the Northwest Territories. The first governor of the state was Nelson Dewey, a Democrat, serving from 1848 to 1852.

▼ On 19 July, the first women's rights convention began in Seneca Falls, New York. The meeting was used to create a feminist platform modeled after the Declaration of Independence. Organized by Elizabeth Stanton, Lucretia Mott, and Sarah and Angelina Grimké, the convention attracted about 300 people. In her opening address, Lucretia Mott said, "The world has never yet seen a truly great and virtuous nation, because in the degradation of woman the very fountains of life are poisoned at their source."

▼ On 1 November, the Boston Female Medical School—the first medical school for women—opened in Boston, Massachusetts. In its first year, there were 12 women enrolled. The school became part of the Boston University School of Medicine in 1874. Its anniversary is noted as 11 March, the date in 1850 when the school was incorporated.

▼ On 7 November, the first presidential election was held under the Election Act of 1845. This act established a uniform voting day for the first time, relegating national elections to the first Tuesday in November. On this first election day, Zachary Taylor was the winner.

▼ **1848** ▼

COLLEGES AND UNIVERSITIES
Dyke College (Cleveland, OH)
Geneva College (Beaver Falls, PA)
Hahnemann University (Philadelphia, PA)
Muhlenberg College (Allentown, PA)
Rhodes College (Memphis, TN)
Rosary College (River Forest, IL)
University of Ottawa (Ontario, Canada)
University of Wisconsin–Madison (Madison, WI)

MUSIC
"Oh, Susanna!," by Stephen Foster

BOOKS, POETRY, AND PLAYS
Comedie humaine, by Honoré de Balzac
Vanity Fair, by William Makepeace Thackeray
Vision of Sir Launfal, by James Russell Lowell

▼ *The Communist Manifesto* was published by Friedrich Engels and Karl Marx. Living in Brussels, Belgium, the two were members of a group of expatriate Germans who were attempting to bring a revolution to their homeland. At the time, the 40-page pamphlet received very little attention.

▼ The world's bloodiest civil war erupted in China. Known as the Taiping Rebellion, the unrest continued for 15 years and resulted in an estimated 20 million deaths. The rebellion was led against the ruling Manchu dynasty by the leader of a religious cult who believed he was the younger brother of Jesus.

▼ The newly founded settlement of Mormons in Utah was saved from disaster when a large flock of seagulls destroyed the swarm of locusts that was eating their crops.

▼ The world's first department store was opened in New York City. This retail emporium, created by Alexander Stewart, was located on Broadway and called the Marble Dry Goods Palace.

▼ The Associated Press was conceived by a group of newspapers in New York City to help papers keep up with current events. The original organization was known as the Harbor News Association and was officially founded on 11 January 1849, after a year of informal arrangements to pool telegraphy reports. The first move by the group was to rent boats so they could quickly get to ships arriving in New York Harbor from Europe.

▼ A lieutenant in the U.S. Army discovered the Mesa Verde cliff dwellings in southwest Colorado.

▼ William Parsons (Lord Rosse), an English astronomer, discovered the Crab nebula.

▼ The American Academy of Science admitted its first woman member, Maria Mitchell. Mitchell was noted for discovering a comet a year earlier, on 1 October 1847.

▼ Scientists in Canada and the United States established the American Association for the Advancement of Science.

▼ Chewing gum first went on sale in the United States. John Curtis, of Bangor, Maine, was the first to develop a method to mass produce chewing gum; he called his product State of Maine Pure Spruce Gum.

▼ American President Companies were founded in Oakland, California. The origins of these companies began with the Pacific Mail Steamship Company, an oceangoing fleet shuttling between cities on the East Coast and San Francisco. The name was changed to American President Lines in 1938, and the company currently operates the world's largest container ships in Pacific shipping lanes.

▼ Charles Burton, an American inventor, created the first baby carriage in New York City. Burton's creation was initially the object of much public displeasure because of its tendency to bump into people on crowded sidewalks. As a result, he moved to England, where he built the first baby carriage factory. In England, the carriages were called perambulators.

▼ The first patent was issued for a hand-cranked ice cream maker. The device was invented in 1846 by Nancy Johnson, but not patented until several years later.

▼ 1798 ▼

ASSOCIATIONS, SOCIETIES, UNIONS, AND GOVERNMENT DEPARTMENTS
Public Health Service (U.S. Department of Health and Human Services)

MUSEUMS AND ZOOS
Mission San Luis Rey (San Luis Rey, CA)

BIRTHDAYS AND DEATH DAYS
Ferdinand Delacroix born on 26 April
Luigi Galvani died on 4 December at age 61

COLLEGES AND UNIVERSITIES
University of Louisville (Louisville, KY)

BOOKS, POETRY, AND PLAYS
Essay on Population, by Thomas Malthus

WHAT 200 WAS years ago

IN 1798
on 8 January, the Eleventh Amendment to the U.S. Constitution was officially ratified. This amendment limits the authority of federal courts over individual states.

▼ On 7 April, Congress established the Mississippi Territory, covering parts of what would later become the states of Mississippi and Alabama, with a territorial capital in Natchez. The territorial boundaries were expanded in 1804 and 1812.

▼ On 6 June, debtor's prisons were officially abolished by an Act of Congress. Before this time, imprisonment was a legal punishment for debt.

▼ On 11 July, an Act of Congress established the Marine Corps as part of the Department of the Navy.

▼ Thomas Malthus published a book, *Essay on Population,* describing the growth of populations by geometric progression. Malthus, an English economist, also took into account the less rapid growth of food supplies, and he concluded that exponential growth would lead to disaster and could only be balanced by natural disasters, war, disease, or famine.

▼ Lithography was invented by Aloys Senefelder, an Austrian playwright, allowing mass production of illustrations. Senefelder used special Bavarian limestone, a material still preferred by lithographers for the best quality prints. His discovery was an accident: while writing a laundry list on a piece of polished stone with a grease pencil, he got the idea of etching the stone with acid, leaving the marks of the pencil to hold ink for printing.

▼ Henry Cavendish, an English physicist, discovered a method of measuring the gravitational attraction between two objects. With this measurement, he was then able to make the first accurate calculation of the earth's mass.

WHAT WAS 250 years ago

▼ 1748 ▼

BOOKS, POETRY, AND PLAYS
Esprit des lois, by Charles Montesquieu
Semiramis, by François Voltaire

IN 1748 the industrial age was unofficially introduced with the development of the first blast furnace for iron ore. John Wilkinson built the furnace in Bilston, England.

▼ Antonio de Ulloa, a Spanish scientist, first reported the discovery of platinum, one of the rare metals. The discovery came during a trip to South America.

▼ The London-based trustees who had control over colonial Georgia passed a resolution declaring "never to permit the Introduction of Negroes into the Colony of Georgia, as the Danger which must arise from them in a Frontier Town is so evident; And as the People, Who continue to clamour for Negroes declare that the Colony can never succeed without the use of them, it is evident they don't intend by their own Industry to contribute to its Success, and must therefore rather hinder than promote it." The resolution was overturned two years later.

1998

IN 1698 the first free public library in the American colonies opened in Charleston, South Carolina.

▼ In New Jersey, the first tannery was established in the American colonies.

▼ Lutherans built the Old Swedes Church in Wilmington, Delaware, now the oldest Protestant church in continuous use in this country.

▼ The first patent was granted for a steam-powered machine. Thomas Savery, an English inventor, created the Miner's Friend, a steam-powered pump for drawing water from mines. This device was not very efficient, and predated the invention of more powerful steam-driven engines.

▼ The first voyage specifically for scientific research was undertaken by Edmund Halley, an English astronomer. Halley's exploration, lasting two years, resulted in the first world map showing magnetic declinations.

IN 1648 on 18 October, the first union in the American colonies was formalized by the Massachusetts Bay Colony, which authorized the meeting of cobblers in the city of Boston.

▼ On 24 October, Belgium and the Netherlands were granted independence from Germany when the Peace of Westphalia ended the Thirty Years War.

▼ The first person in the American colonies was executed for being a witch. Margaret Jones, in Charlestown, Massachusetts, was thought to cause illness by her touch.

▼   1598   ▼

BOOKS, POETRY, AND PLAYS
Henry IV, by William Shakespeare

IN 1598 on 15 April, Henry IV of France ended a long run of religious wars dating from 1562 with the signing of the Edict of Nantes. This document also granted political and religious rights to the Huguenots, Protestants living in France.

▼ A major settlement by Spanish colonists was begun in the Pueblo territories of northwestern New Mexico and northeastern Arizona.

IN 1548 Spanish settlers in Mexico began mining silver in Zacatecas. The Zacatecas lode was one of the richest developed during Spanish rule in the New World.

▼ During the reign of Edward VI, the English government enacted the Chantries Act. This legislation confiscated property belonging to the Church of England—only recently separated from Catholic control—and directed it to be used for education.

IN 1498 on 23 May, the Italian heretic Girolamo Savonarola was executed. Savonarola gained power within the Catholic Church and in 1494 became the political ruler of Florence. A critic of the church, he used his influential position to champion a more democratic form of government. One of his followers was ordered to be burned as an ordeal of faith, but Savonarola prevented this act, and consequently was arrested for preventing a miracle from occurring. He was tortured, tried, and hanged, and his body was then burned.

▼ On 30 May, Columbus left Spain for his third voyage to the New World, sailing in an expedition of six ships with more than 200 men. During this voyage, the explorer discovered Trinidad.

▼ The first toothbrush was invented by the Chinese, according to some sources.

▼ 1974 ▼

ASSOCIATIONS, SOCIETIES, UNIONS, AND GOVERNMENT DEPARTMENTS

Clean Energy Research Institute
(Coral Gables, FL)
Feminist Alliance Against Rape
(Washington, DC)
National Academy of Counselors and Family
Therapists (Springfield, NJ)
National Transportation Safety Board
(U.S. government)
Nuclear Regulatory Commission (U.S. government)

MUSEUMS AND ZOOS

Delaware Agricultural Museum (Dover, DE)
Lake Superior Museum of Transportation (Duluth, MN)
Metropolitan Toronto Zoo (Toronto, Ontario, Canada)
North Carolina Zoological Park (Asheboro, NC)
Presidio Army Museum (San Francisco, CA)
Riverbanks Zoological Park (Columbia, SC)
Wild Animal Habitat (Kings Island, OH)

IN 1974 on 5 February, the daughter of newspaper publisher Randolph
Hearst was kidnapped in Berkeley, California. Patty Hearst turned out to have been
captured by a terrorist group known as the Symbionese Liberation Army, which
demanded public food giveaways as part of a ransom. After eluding authorities for
more than 1 1/2 years, Hearst was found by the FBI on 18 September 1975. In the
interim, brainwashing attempts had turned Hearst into a participant in various
crimes, including bank robbery. On 20 March 1976, she was convicted of bank
robbery after a trial in San Francisco, and on 24 September was sentenced to seven
years in prison, but was released the next year under executive clemency.

▼ On 9 August, President Richard Nixon resigned the presidency, the result of an
ongoing investigation begun after a burglary of the Democratic National Headquarters at the Watergate Hotel in 1972. Gerald Ford, the vice president, was sworn in
as the new president. On 19 December, Nelson Rockefeller was sworn in as the
new vice president.

▼ On 16 September, President Ford issued a pardon that granted clemency to deserters and those who had illegally avoided the draft because of the Vietnam War.

▼ The Charles Schwab discount brokerage firm was founded in San Francisco. The founder, Charles Schwab, made his fortune with this first company to buy and sell stocks at a discounted commission. Until 1 May 1975, all stock transactions were executed at a fixed commission rate; the Securities and Exchange Commission eliminated fixed commissions after that date. As one of the first brokerage companies to take advantage of the new ruling, Charles Schwab charged less than his competition and quickly became one of the major companies in the field.

▼ 1974 ▼

MUSIC

years ago

Alice Cooper's Greatest Hits, by Alice Cooper
Annie's Song, by John Denver
Band on the Run, by Paul McCartney
Be Thankful for What You Got,
   by William DeVaughn
Before the Next Teardrop Falls, by Freddy Fender
Bennie and the Jets, by Elton John
Black Water, by the Doobie Brothers
Burn, by Deep Purple
Cat's in the Cradle, by Harry Chapin
Chicago VII, by Chicago
David Live, by David Bowie
Diamond Dogs, by David Bowie
Eldorado, by Electric Light Orchestra
Endless Summer, by the Beach Boys
Fire on the Mountain, by the Charlie Daniels Band
461 Ocean Boulevard, by Eric Clapton
Having My Baby, by Paul Anka
Heart like a Wheel, by Linda Ronstadt
I Honestly Love You, by Olivia Newton-John
I Shot the Sheriff, by Eric Clapton
If You Love Me, by Olivia Newton-John
I'm Leaving It Up to You, by Donny and Marie Osmond
Late for the Sky, by Jackson Browne
The Loco-Motion, by Grand Funk Railroad

▼ Tandem Computers was founded in Cupertino, California, by James Treybig. Tandem produced its first computer in 1976.

▼ It was discovered that the ozone layer was being destroyed by the use of chlorofluorocarbons.

▼ The first programmable pocket calculator was introduced by Hewlett Packard.

▼ The personal computer era began with the introduction of the Altair 8800. The first personal computer had 256 bytes of memory and cost $397 in kit form; by the end of 1975, Altairs generated more than $1 million in sales.

▼   1974   ▼

MUSIC *continued*
Lucy in the Sky with Diamonds, by Elton John
Photographs & Memories, by Jim Croce
So Far, by Crosby, Stills, Nash & Young
Southern Comfort, by the Crusaders
Stormbringer, by Deep Purple
Sundown, by Gordon Lightfoot
Sunshine on My Shoulders, by John Denver
Verities & Balderdash, by Harry Chapin
You Ain't Seen Nothing Yet, by Bachman-Turner Overdrive

NEWSPAPERS AND MAGAZINES
Blair & Ketchums Country Journal (Brattleboro, VT)
High Times (New York, NY)
Hustler Magazine (Los Angeles, CA)
People (New York, NY)
The Star (Tarrytown, NY)
Vegetarian Times (Oak Park, IL)

BOOKS, POETRY, AND PLAYS
All the President's Men, by Carl Bernstein and Robert
   Woodward
Jaws, by Peter Benchley

MOVIES
Chinatown (directed by Roman Polanski, with Faye
   Dunaway, Jack Nicholson)
Young Frankenstein (directed by Mel Brooks, with
   Gene Wilder)

▼   1949   ▼

ASSOCIATIONS, SOCIETIES, UNIONS, AND GOVERNMENT DEPARTMENTS

Acupuncture International Association
(St. Louis, MO)
American Business Women's Association
(Kansas City, MO)
American Ex-Prisoners of War
(Arlington, TX)
American Textile Manufacturers Institute
(Washington, DC)
Antiquarian Bookseller's Association
(New York, NY)
International Union of Electric, Electronic, Salaried,
Machine and Furniture Workers
(Washington, DC)
Italian Historical Society of America (Brooklyn, NY)
Leukemia Society of America (New York, NY)
National Assistance League (Los Angeles, CA)
National Auctioneers Association (Overland Park, KA)
National Trust for Historic Preservation (Washington, DC)
Society of Actuaries (Schaumburg, IL)
Sport Fishing Institute (Washington, DC)
United Cerebral Palsy Association (New York, NY)

IN 1949 on 20 January, Harry Truman was inaugurated for his second term as president of the United States.

▼ On 4 April, the North Atlantic Treaty Organization (NATO) was founded. The charter was signed in Washington, D.C., by Belgium, Canada, Denmark, France, Great Britain, Italy, Iceland, Luxembourg, the Netherlands, Norway, Portugal, and the United States.

▼ On 11 May, Polaroid introduced the first instant camera. The original model cost about $90 and produced a photograph in one minute.

▼ On 24 June, the first episode of "Hopalong Cassidy" appeared on television. Already a hit in "B" movies, Hopalong made the jump to the new medium along with William Boyd, who had established the role on the silver screen. Hopalong Cassidy was the first successful TV cowboy, and until the show's demise in 1953, he helped sell millions of dollars of toys, food, and licensed products.

▼ 1949 ▼

MUSEUMS AND ZOOS

American Museum of Science and Energy
 (Oak Ridge, TN)
Children's Museum (Portland, OR)
Colton Hall Museum (Monterey, CA)
Fisk University Museum of Art (Nashville, TN)
Fresno Art Museum (Fresno, CA)
Gibbs Farm Museum (St. Paul, MN)
Historic Fort Wayne (Detroit, MI)
Houston Museum (Chattanooga, TN)
John Ball Zoological Gardens (Grand Rapids, MI)
Kit Carson Foundation (Taos, NM)
Morehead Planetarium (Chapel Hill, NC)
Phoenix Art Museum (Phoenix, AZ)
University Art Museum (California State University,
 Long Beach, CA)

COLLEGES AND UNIVERSITIES

California State University (Long Beach, CA)
Grand Canyon University (Phoenix, AZ)
University of San Diego (San Diego, CA)

MUSIC

Gentlemen Prefer Blondes, music by Jule Styne
 (first performed on 8 December in New York, NY)
Rudolph the Red-Nosed Reindeer, by Gene Autry
South Pacific, by Richard Rogers and Oscar Hammerstein
 (first performed on 7 April in New York, NY)
Viola Concerto, by Béla Bartók (first performed on 2
 December in Minneapolis, MN)

NEWSPAPERS AND MAGAZINES

American Heritage (New York, NY)
Américas (Washington, DC)
Harrisburg Patriot News (Harrisburg, PA)
Historic Preservation (Washington, DC)
Magazine of Fantasy and Science Fiction (Cornwall, CT)
Modern Bride (New York, NY)
Motor Trend (Los Angeles, CA)

▼ **1949** ▼

BOOKS, POETRY, AND PLAYS

Annie Allen, by Gwendolyn Brooks
Come Back, Little Sheba, by William Inge
Death of a Salesman, by Arthur Miller
The Man with the Golden Arm, by Nelson Algren

MOVIES

Adam's Rib (directed by George Cukor, with
  Katharine Hepburn, Spencer Tracy)
All the King's Men (directed by Robert Rossen,
  with Broderick Crawford, Joanne Dru)
The Third Man (directed by Carol Reed, with
  Joseph Cotten, Orson Welles)

▼ On 1 July, Congress established the General Services Administration (GSA) to manage property and records for the government.

▼ On 23 September, the nuclear arms race began with the announcement by President Truman that the Soviet Union had developed its own atomic weapons. The Soviets exploded their first atom bomb on 22 September. The term *Cold War* was first introduced publicly on 24 October 1948, during a speech by Bernard Baruch to a U.S. Senate committee.

▼ On 24 October, the United Nations building was dedicated in New York City, where it had been built on land purchased with a monetary gift from John D. Rockefeller, Jr., in 1946.

▼ The first Sara Lee baked goods were produced in Chicago by Charles Lubin, the owner of a small chain of bake shops. Lubin's daughter was named Sara Lee, and the first Sara Lee product was Original Cream Cheese Cake.

▼ A B-50 bomber became the first plane to fly around the world nonstop. The flight took 94 hours and began and ended in Fort Worth, Texas.

▼ Gerald McBoing Boing debuted in an animated cartoon. The character was derived from a story written by Dr. Seuss. Also, Mr. Magoo first appeared in "Ragtime Bear." Quincy Magoo, with the distinctive voice of Jim Backus, later starred in *1001 Arabian Nights,* a feature-length animated film released in 1959, as well as a weekly television series.

▼ Cape Canaveral, Florida, was first opened as a testing ground for rockets by the U.S. military.

▼   1924   ▼

ASSOCIATIONS, SOCIETIES, UNIONS, AND GOVERNMENT DEPARTMENTS

American Association of Zoological Parks and
   Aquariums (Wheeling, West VA)
American Heart Association (Dallas, TX)
American Motorcyclist Association
   (Westerville, OH)
American Society of Parasitologists (Lawrence, KS)
Association of Professional Ball Players of America
   (Garden Grove, CA)
Electronic Industries Association (Washington, DC)
International Association of Torch Clubs (Chicago, IL)
International Society of Arboriculture (Urbana, IL)
National Automobile Club (San Francisco, CA)
National League of Cities (Washington, DC)
Toastmasters International (Santa Ana, CA)

MUSEUMS AND ZOOS

California Palace of the Legion of Honor
   (San Francisco, CA)
Greensboro Historical Museum (Greensboro, NC)
Hamilton Grace National Memorial (New York, NY)
Norton Simon Museum (Pasadena, CA)
Orlando Museum of Art (Orlando, FL)
Pierpont Morgan Library (New York, NY)
Shedd Aquarium (Chicago, IL)
Tucson Museum of Art (Tucson, AZ)

WHAT WAS 75 years ago

IN 1924 on 21 January, Lenin died. The head of the Soviet Union at the time of his death, Lenin was also the leader of the revolutionary movement that overthrew the previous Russian system.

▼ On 3 February, Woodrow Wilson, twenty-seventh president of the United States, died of apoplexy paralysis in Washington, D.C., at the age of 67.

▼ On 10 April, the world's first crossword puzzle book was published in New York City. The book was packaged with a pencil and was a national bestseller in its first year, inspiring the publication of several other crossword books. The cost of the first puzzle book: $1.35. Already attracting increasing attention from the public, the arrival of crossword puzzle books helped turn crossword puzzles into a national fad—puzzle designs were printed on items of clothing, competitions were created, and most daily newspapers began running crosswords as regular features. (The first daily publication of crossword puzzles was in the *New York World* in November 1924.) The company that created the first crossword book was Plaza Publishing Company, although the two partners in the company, M. Lincoln Schuster and Richard L. Simon, soon changed the name to Simon & Schuster.

▼ On 2 June, an Act of Congress granted U.S. citizenship to Native Americans. The bill stated, "All non-citizen Indians born within the territorial limits of the United States . . . are hereby declared to be, citizens of the United States."

▼ The Wrigley Building was built in Chicago, Illinois.

▼ Wheaties cereal was introduced, the first consumer product made from "bran gruel," a by-product of grain milling discovered in 1921.

▼ 1924 ▼

BIRTHDAYS AND DEATH DAYS
Vladimir Ulyanov, aka Lenin, died on 21 January
  at age 54
Woodrow Wilson died on 3 February at age 67
Joseph Conrad died on 3 August at age 67
J. A. Thibault, aka Anatole France, died on 13 October
  at age 79
Giacomo Puccini died on 29 November at age 66
C. V. Stanford died on 29 November at age 71

COLLEGES AND UNIVERSITIES
College Misericordia (Dallas, PA)

MUSIC
"Rhapsody in Blue," by George Gershwin (first
  performed on 12 February in New York, NY)

NEWSPAPERS AND MAGAZINES
Better Homes and Gardens (Des Moines, IA)
The Saturday Review (New York, NY)
True Detective (New York, NY)
True Love (New York, NY)

▼   1924   ▼

BOOKS, POETRY, AND PLAYS
Chills and Fevers, by John Crowe Ransom
Juno and the Paycock, by Sean O'Casey
So Big, by Edna Ferber
Tamar, by John Robinson Jeffers

MOVIES
Greed (directed by Erich von Stroheim, with ZaSu Pitts,
   Gibson Gowland)
The Thief of Baghdad (directed by Raoul Walsh, with
   Douglas Fairbanks)

▼ The first Popsicles were sold. These frozen fruit-flavored treats were originally called Epsicles after their inventor, Frank Epperson. The name was changed in 1929.

▼ Stanley Slotkin—upset because he could not convince a rental chair company to pay him for a pair of pants torn by one of their chairs—founded Abbey Rents in Kansas City, Missouri.

▼ The Seagram Company was founded as a liquor distillery in Montreal, Quebec, by two brothers, Allan and Samuel Bronfman. The brothers purchased another distillery in 1927, and used its name, Seagram's, to rename their enterprise.

▼ J. Fred Miles founded the Ashland Oil Company near Ashland, Kentucky.

▼ The Yellow Freight System was founded in Overland Park, Kansas. Yellow Freight is one of the five largest trucking companies in the United States.

▼ Jules Stein founded the Music Corporation of America in Chicago. Stein was an ophthalmologist with a lucrative hobby playing music in clubs and managing musicians. Now known as MCI and located in Universal City, California, his company became one of the biggest national talent agencies by the end of World War II, moving into television early in its first decade.

▼ A merger of three movie companies formed Metro-Goldwyn-Mayer (MGM). Two classic successes from the MGM studios were *The Wizard of Oz* and *Gone with the Wind.*

▼ Raymond Dart, an anthropologist, first recognized a fossilized skull that belonged to neither apes nor humans. The species was named *Australopithecus africanus,* or australopithecine.

▼ Bell Laboratories was founded.

▼ Spiral-bound notebooks first appeared for sale.

▼ The fad of flagpole sitting began when an ex-boxer named "Shipwreck" Kelly climbed a pole as a stunt for a movie being filmed in Hollywood. The feat resulted in a publicity stunt for the finished film—Kelly was paid to sit on top of a flagpole outside of the theater where the film was showing. Asked to perch for 10 hours, he chose to stay for 13 hours, 13 minutes, and attracted enough of a crowd to turn the stunt into a career. Kelly's feats soon became a national story, and other flagpole sitters, including many amateurs, took to the heights in various cities.

▼ The Kimberly Clark company began marketing disposable tissues made from cellulose. The tissues, originally labeled Celluwipes, were later renamed Kleenex.

WHAT 100 years ago WAS

▼ **1899** ▼

ASSOCIATIONS, SOCIETIES,
UNIONS, AND GOVERNMENT
DEPARTMENTS
American Astronomical Society (Washington, DC)
American Ceramic Society (Westerville, OH)
American Hospital Association (Chicago, IL)
American Rose Society (Shreveport, LA)
American Society for Microbiology (Washington, DC)
American Society of Landscape Architects (Washington, DC)
Colonial Dames of America (New York, NY)
International Gideons (Nashville, TN)
National Institute of Social Sciences (New York, NY)
Tea Association of the U.S.A. (New York, NY)
Veterans of Foreign Wars of the U.S. (Kansas City, MO)

IN 1899 on 11 February, the first person died in a motorcycle accident. Holding this distinction is George Morgan, the driver of a motorized tricycle who was killed while driving in Exeter, England.

▼ On 20 May, the first speeding ticket was issued to an automobile driver in the United States. This event took place in New York City; the recipient was a cab driver who was caught by a policeman on a bicycle while driving at 12 miles per hour.

▼ On 13 September, Henry Bliss, age 68, had the dubious distinction of becoming the first pedestrian to be killed by an automobile in the United States. The car, driven by Arthur Smith, hit Mr. Bliss as he was getting off a streetcar at the corner of 74th Street and Central Park West in New York City. (The world's first automotive death occurred on 17 August 1896 in England.)

▼ On 11 October, hostilities between British and Dutch settlers in South Africa turned into a war with a declaration issued by the Dutch states of Transvaal and the Orange Free State. The South African War, also known as the Boer War, introduced the concepts of guerrilla fighting and concentration camps. The war was ended on 31 May 1902 with the Treaty of Vereeniging, which formally ceded the Dutch territories to British rule.

▼ The first juvenile court in the United States was established in Chicago. The principal motivators for this institution were Jane Addams and Julia Lathrop. Addams had earlier created Hull House in Chicago, a community center that developed programs to help the urban poor.

▼ 1899 ▼

MUSEUMS AND ZOOS
Brooklyn Children's Museum (Brooklyn, NY)
Camden County Historical Society (Camden, NJ)
New York Zoological Park (Bronx, NY)
Oklahoma Museum of Natural History (Norman, OK)
Stearns Collection of Musical Instruments (University
    of Michigan, Ann Arbor, MI)
Toledo Zoological Gardens (Toledo, OH)

BIRTHDAYS AND DEATH DAYS
Johann Strauss died on 3 June at age 74
Charles Laughton born on 1 July
Noel Coward born on 16 December

COLLEGES AND UNIVERSITIES
Appalachian State University (Boone, NC)
Azusa Pacific University (Azusa, CA)
College of Saint Elizabeth (Convent Station, NJ)
Elizabethtown College (Elizabethtown, PA)
Northern Arizona University (Flagstaff, AZ)
Northern Michigan University (Marquette, MI)
San Francisco State University (San Francisco, CA)
Simmons College (Boston, MA)
Southern Nazarene University (Bethany, OK)
Southwest Texas State University (San Marcos, TX)
Tarleton State University (Stephenville, TX)
Western Illinois University (Macomb, IL)

▼ 1899 ▼

MUSIC

Finlandia, by Jean Sibelius (first performed on 4 November in Helsingfors, Finland)
"The Maple Leaf Rag," by Scott Joplin
"On the Banks of the Wabash," by Paul Dresser
Shéhérazade, by Maurice Ravel
Symphony No. 1 in E Minor, by Jean Sibelius (first performed on 26 April in Helsingfors, Finland)

NEWSPAPERS AND MAGAZINES

Audubon (New York, NY)
Technology Review (Cambridge, MA)

BOOKS, POETRY, AND PLAYS

The Interpretation of Dreams, by Sigmund Freud
McTeague, by Benjamin Franklin Norris
Uncle Vanya, by Anton Chekhov

▼ United Telecom was founded in Westwood, Kansas, as a company that wired homes and municipalities for telephone service. In the 1980s, United Telecom began expanding into long-distance services, telecommunications equipment, and telephone directory publishing.

▼ American Telephone and Telegraph (AT&T) was founded after a reorganization of the Bell Telephone Company. Originally located in Boston and begun by Alexander Graham Bell, the Bell Telephone Company moved to New York City in 1899 and changed its name. In its earliest days, AT&T was controlled by J. P. Morgan, the most powerful banker in the United States, who succeeded in the phone business by buying up competitors or killing them off with business tactics. In 1913, the U.S. government allowed the company to gain an effective monopoly over all telephone service in the country as a compromise to avoid being prosecuted for attempting to run a monopoly. It was one of the best deals ever struck in American business history.

▼ The Tandy Corporation was founded in Fort Worth, Texas, as a leather store. Charles Tandy, the son of the store's founder, turned the concept into a national chain by the 1950s. In 1963, Tandy purchased Radio Shack, a chain of nine electronics stores, and pursued the same plan, making the chain a national landmark by the 1960s.

▼ The Fiat company was founded in Turin, Italy, by Giovanni Agnelli, a former cavalry officer in the Italian army. The company's official name was Fabbrica Italiana di Automobili Torino.

▼ The Renault Company was founded in Paris by the three Renault brothers: Fernand, Louis, and Marcel. The Renault—the world's first sedan model automobile—was produced during the same year.

▼ A U.S. patent was issued for the first rubber shoe heels. Humphrey O'Sullivan invented this product in Lowell, Massachusetts, as a safety improvement.

▼ The Gideons were founded by a group of traveling salesmen. It was not for another nine years, in 1908, that the first Gideon Bible was donated for placement in a hotel room.

▼ The United Fruit Company was founded by Captain Lorenzo Baker. United Fruit's principal business when it was created was to import bananas into the United States.

▼ Ragtime music became popular with the publication of "The Maple Leaf Rag," by Scott Joplin.

▼ The Pittsburgh Symphony was established in Pittsburgh, Pennsylvania.

▼ A patent was issued for the first motorized vacuum cleaner. The patent described this device as a "pneumatic carpet renovator."

▼ 1849 ▼

ASSOCIATIONS, SOCIETIES, UNIONS, AND
GOVERNMENT DEPARTMENTS
Department of the Interior (U.S. government)

MUSEUMS AND ZOOS
Minnesota Historical Society (St. Paul, MN)
Tennessee Historical Society Museum
(Nashville, TN)

BIRTHDAYS AND DEATH DAYS
August Strindberg born on 22 January
Edgar Allan Poe died on 7 October at age 40
Frédéric Chopin died on 17 October at age 39

▼ 1849 ▼

COLLEGES AND UNIVERSITIES

Austin College (Sherman, TX)
Central Connecticut State University (New Britain, CT)
Eastern Michigan University (Ypsilanti, MI)
Linfield College (McMinnville, OR)
Pacific University (Forest Grove, OR)
Waynesburg College (Waynesburg, PA)
William Jewell College (Liberty, MO)

MUSIC

Concerto No. 1 in A Major, by Franz Liszt
Le Prophete, by Giacomo Meyerbeer

NEWSPAPERS AND MAGAZINES

New Mexican (Santa Fe, NM)
St. Paul Pioneer Press (St. Paul, MN)

BOOKS, POETRY, AND PLAYS

The California and Oregon Trail, by Francis Parkman
Poems, by John Greenleaf Whittier
The Prophet, by Giacomo Meyerbeer
Who's Who (St. Martin's Press)

IN 1849 on 3 March, Congress established the Home Department, later known as the Department of the Interior.

▼ On 5 March, Zachary Taylor was inaugurated as the twelfth president of the United States. Born on 24 November 1784, Taylor served in various military campaigns, including the Black Hawk War in 1832 and the Battle of Lake Okeechobee in 1837. His greatest success was as the American military leader during the Mexican War. This made him a national hero and a candidate for the presidency as a member of the Whig party, although he had never before participated in politics or even voted in a national election. During his only term in office, he accomplished little because of growing threats of Southern secession. After little more than a year in office, he died suddenly from illness on 9 July 1850.

▼ On 7 March, Luther Burbank was born in Lancaster, Massachusetts. Burbank, a biologist who specialized in breeding plants, is noted for developing more than

600 varieties of fruits, vegetables, and flowers. Among his successes were the Burbank potato, developed during his early research near Lunenburg, Massachusetts, before he moved to Santa Rosa, California, in 1875. Burbank is quoted as saying, "I shall be contented if, because of me, there shall be better fruits and fairer flowers." He died on 11 April 1926 in Santa Rosa. In some areas 7 March is recognized as Burbank Day.

▼ On 10 April, the first patent was issued for the safety pin. This ubiquitous device was designed by Walter Hunt, an American inventor. Hunt was driven to create the safety pin to pay off a debt of $15 he owed a draftsman. In three hours, he developed several variations of a self-clasping pin; all rights to his invention were sold to the draftsman for $400. In the patent, the invention is described as a dress-pin, and the applicant states: "Another great advantages [*sic*] unknown in other plans is found in the perfect convenience of inserting these into the dress, without danger of bending the pin, or wounding the fingers, which renders them equally adapted to either ornamental, common dress, or nursery uses."

▼ On 15 June, James Knox Polk, eleventh president of the United States, died in Nashville, Tennessee, at the age of 53.

▼ On 7 October, Edgar Allan Poe died. His death was most likely caused by a brain tumor or a diabetic coma, although it was popularly attributed to alcoholism.

▼ On 7 October, James Whitcomb Riley was born in Greenfield, Indiana. Riley was a widely published poet, writing in the local Hoosier dialect. Known as the Hoosier poet, his works include "When the Frost Is on the Punkin," "The Raggedy Man," and "Little Orphan Annie." He died on 22 July 1916. His birthday is recognized as Riley Day in Indiana.

▼ Harriet Tubman began her career by escaping from slavery in Maryland. On at least 20 trips back to slave states, Tubman led more than 300 blacks to freedom in the North. Her home in Auburn, New York, was another of her projects, a refuge for the old and indigent.

▼ Price Waterhouse, an accounting firm, was founded in London; it later moved to the United States.

▼ Pfizer, Inc. was founded in Brooklyn, New York. Now a major pharmaceutical company, the firm was established by cousins Charles Pfizer and Charles Erhart, both immigrants from Germany. The pair's first product was a candy-coated dewormer.

▼ The Burlington Northern Company was founded as a regional railroad by James J. Hill, a legendary character often described as a robber baron by his contemporaries. Hill's original railroad line was the Great Northern, a route that included the northern Midwest and states in the Northwest. In the early 1900s, Great Northern (now the Burlington Northern) attempted to merge with other railroads, but this was prevented until 1970, when a Supreme Court decision ruled in the company's favor.

▼ A medical degree was awarded to a woman for the first time in the United States. Elizabeth Blackwell, the degree recipient, later founded a hospital for women and children in New York City.

▼ The Waltham Watch Company was founded in Roxbury, Massachusetts. The company's original name was the American Horologe Company.

▼ Joseph Monier, a French inventor, created a new method of adding strength to concrete by forming internal skeletons of iron bars, now referred to as reinforced concrete.

▼ **1799** ▼

MUSEUMS AND ZOOS
Peabody Museum of Salem (Salem, MA)

BIRTHDAYS AND DEATH DAYS
Honoré de Balzac born on 20 May
Alexander Pushkin born on 7 June
George Washington died on 14 December at age 67

NEWSPAPERS AND MAGAZINES
Keene Sentinel (Keene, NH)

IN 1799 on 7 February, a taxpayer's rebellion ended with the arrest of its leader, John Fries. Fries had organized a few hundred men in several counties of eastern Pennsylvania, hoping to forcibly stop the U.S. government from collecting taxes that were intended to support a war with France. Fries was convicted of treason and sentenced to death, but he received a pardon from President Adams.

▼ On 14 December, George Washington, first president of the United States, died after being bled by physicians who were trying to cure his cold. He was 67 years old. As he lay dying, he told his physician, "Doctor, I die hard, but I am not afraid to go." His last words were, "It is well."

▼ Alessandro Volta first produced an electrical current from a chemical cell, a container with zinc and copper plates. In 1746, earlier experiments by van Musschenbroek and von Kleist had succeeded in storing static electricity, but Volta's breakthrough was the first device capable of producing electricity on its own. Volta, a physicist from Italy, was made a count by Napoleon in 1801 following a demonstration of his invention.

▼ The Rosetta Stone was discovered near the Nile River in Egypt by soldiers of Napoleon's army. This inscribed slab, containing text in hieroglyphics, was originally created during the reign of Ptolemy V.

▼ The initial companies that were eventually to form Chase Manhattan Bank were founded in New York City. One of them was the Manhattan Company, a business supplying water to the city. Created by Aaron Burr and Alexander Hamilton, it was authorized by the city and state to provide a safe water supply as a result of a local outbreak of yellow fever. The law authorizing the creation of the Manhattan Company included a clause, written secretly by Burr, that allowed for expansion of the business into areas other than water supply. Six months after the Manhattan Company began operating, the Bank of Manhattan was opened, a factor that reportedly helped turn a disagreement between the two partners into an eventual duel: in 1804, Hamilton was killed by Burr. In 1955, the Bank of Manhattan merged with the Chase National Bank, itself founded in 1877.

▼   1749   ▼

COLLEGES AND UNIVERSITIES
Washington and Lee University (Lexington, VA)

BOOKS, POETRY, AND PLAYS
Tom Jones, by Henry Fielding

IN 1749 Halifax, Nova Scotia, was founded.

▼ The English-speaking world was introduced to the term *psychology* with the publication, in England, of *Observations on Man,* by David Hartley.

▼ The first patent was issued for ball bearings, originally created for the axles on horse-drawn carriages.

▼ Benjamin Franklin invented the lightning rod. The first one was installed on top of his house in Philadelphia. Fascinated with the concept of electricity, Franklin also experimented with electrical storage devices and was one of the first to discover—accidentally—the power of this energy source. During a demonstration at his home during the Christmas holidays in 1750, he received a severe shock. According to his account, "The Company present Say that the flash was very great and the crack as loud as a pistol, yet my Senses being instantly gone, I neither Saw the one nor heard the other; nor did I feel the Stroke on my hand, though I afterwards found it raised a round swelling where the fire enter'd."

IN 1699 the French explorer Pierre Le Moyne created a settlement at Biloxi Bay (near the present town of Ocean Springs) in what is now the state of Mississippi. Fort Maurepas, built at that location, established the southern limits of the Louisiana Territory—also known as New France—which extended to the Gulf of St. Lawrence. Fort Maurepas served as the capital of the Louisiana Territory until 1702.

▼ Changes to the voting laws in the colony of Virginia excluded voting rights for anyone who did not own land.

IN 1649 Charles I, King of England, was executed and the ruling power for the country was passed to a commonwealth, with Oliver Cromwell as the leader.

▼ **1599** ▼

BOOKS, POETRY, AND PLAYS
Henry V, by William Shakespeare
Much Ado about Nothing,
   by William Shakespeare

IN 1599
the science of zoology was established with the publication of *Natural History,* a work by the Italian scientist Ulisse Aldrovandi, who also studied the properties of drugs and wrote one of the first pharmaceutical guides in 1574.

▼ The first known book auction was held in the Netherlands.

IN 1549
on 15 August, six years after the first Europeans arrived in Japan, St. Francis Xavier, a Jesuit missionary from Spain, landed on the island of Kyūshū. Although he was already an established missionary, having previously converted pagans in India and the Malay Islands, he wrote that the Japanese were "the best people yet discovered." Shortly after his arrival, however, the local warlord forbade conversion to Christianity, the punishment being death. Xavier soon developed the notion that the best way to reach these non-Christians was through China, which at the time was considered the center of knowledge by the Japanese. While attempting to enter China, the  priest died of an unknown illness on 3 December 1552. Francis Xavier was canonized as a saint in 1622; the day of his death was established as his feast day.

▼ *The Book of Common Prayer,* by the archbishop of Canterbury, was published. Commissioned by the English Parliament, it was the first simplified guide to church service in England, and it became even more influential when Parliament banned all other prayer books.

IN 1499
on 22 September, the Peace of Basel was signed by the Swiss and King Maximilian I of Germany, ending the Swabian War, a conflict that resulted from increasing control and taxation placed on the Swiss subjects by the German king. The treaty, for all practical purposes, made Switzerland independent, although it was not formerly considered a separate state until 1648.

▼ The Portuguese explorer Vasco da Gama returned home after a voyage to Africa. Among the cargo brought back from this exploration were cloves, nutmeg, and pepper—spices that became important in the establishment of world trade routes.

2000

▼   1975   ▼

ASSOCIATIONS, SOCIETIES, UNIONS, AND GOVERNMENT DEPARTMENTS
American Narcolepsy Association (San Carlos, CA)
American Society of Interior Designers
(New York, NY)

MUSEUMS AND ZOOS
Flandrau Planetarium (Tucson, AZ)
The Mexican Museum (San Francisco, CA)
Northwest Trek Wildlife Park (Eatonville, WA)
Parque Zoológico Nacional (Santo Domingo,
Dominican Republic)

MUSIC
All the Love in the World, by Mac Davis
Another Somebody Done Somebody Wrong Song,
by B.J. Thomas
Between the Lines, by Janis Ian
Blood on the Tracks, by Bob Dylan
Blow by Blow, by Jeff Beck

IN 1975 on 30 April, the final evacuation of U.S. personnel from the U.S. embassy in Vietnam was completed. On that date, communist troops from North Vietnam occupied the city, ending the war. Final death toll: more than 1 million.

▼ On 12 May, the *Mayaguez,* a merchant ship owned by an American company, was captured by Cambodian forces who charged that the crew had been spying and the ship illegally sailing within the 12-mile coastal zone belonging to Cambodia. U.S. Navy and Marine forces staged a rescue operation on 14 May. The 39 crew members were freed at a loss of 16 American lives.

▼ On 26 June, a Supreme Court decision ended the practice of locking up mental patients who were not a danger to society.

▼ On 17 July, American astronauts and Soviet cosmonauts linked their spacecraft in a joint maneuver in space. The *Apollo* and *Soyuz* vehicles were connected for two days while the crews cooperated in research projects.

▼ On 1 August, the Superdome was dedicated in New Orleans.

▼ On 29 November, legislation was signed by President Ford to provide equal educational opportunities for children with disabilities.

▼ The first "lite" beer was introduced to the public.

▼ The American public was temporarily struck dumb with the concept of "mood rings." These rings contained temperature-sensitive crystals that changed color as the wearer's body temperature changed, a signal of mood, according to popular belief. Mood rings were a major consumer fad in 1975, with an estimated 20 million sold. Another consumer fad in that year was Pet Rocks, the creation of Gary Dahl, a unemployed Californian. The Pet Rock was a perfect example of a product fad, with a rapid, enthusiastic acceptance by consumers followed by a drop in interest that was just as quick.

▼ Microsoft was founded by William Gates, along with Paul Allen. In its first year, this computer software company developed the BASIC language, the most widely used programming language in the first generation of personal computers. Later Microsoft accomplishments included the MS-DOS operating system and the Windows program.

years ago

▼ **1975** ▼

MUSIC *continued*
Chicago VIII, by Chicago
Chicago IX, by Chicago
Convoy, by C. W. McCall
Diamonds and Rust, by Joan Baez
Face the Music, by Electric Light Orchestra
Fame, by David Bowie
Fifty Ways To Leave Your Lover, by Paul Simon
Gratitude, by Earth, Wind and Fire
Have You Never Been Mellow, by Olivia Newton-John
He Don't Love You, by Tony Orlando and Dawn
The Heat Is On, by the Isley Brothers
Horizon, by the Carpenters
I Write the Songs, by Barry Manilow
Jive Talkin', by the Bee Gees
Judith, by Judy Collins
Love Will Keep Us Together, by Captain & Tennille
Main Course, by the Bee Gees

2000

▼ 1975 ▼

MUSIC *continued*
Oh What a Night, by the Four Seasons
One of These Nights, by the Eagles
Pieces of the Sky, by Emmylou Harris
Red Headed Stranger, by Willie Nelson
Rhinestone Cowboy, by Glen Campbell
Shining Star, by Earth, Wind and Fire
Spirit of America, by the Beach Boys
Thank God I'm a Country Boy, by John Denver
That's the Way of the World, by Earth, Wind and Fire
Wasted Days and Wasted Nights, by Freddy Fender
The Way I Want To Touch You, by Captain & Tennille
Welcome to My Nightmare, by Alice Cooper
Wildfire, by Michael Murphey
Win, Lose or Draw, by the Allman Brothers Band
Wind on the Water, by Graham Nash and David Crosby
Young Americans, by David Bowie

NEWSPAPERS AND MAGAZINES
American Film (New York, NY)
Bon Appétit (Los Angeles, CA)
Soldier of Fortune (Boulder, CO)

BOOKS, POETRY, AND PLAYS
Looking for Mr. Goodbar, by Judith Rossner
Ragtime, by E. L. Doctorow

MOVIES
Jaws (directed by Steven Spielberg, with Richard
    Dreyfuss, Roy Scheider)
The Man Who Would Be King (directed by John Huston,
    with Michael Caine, Sean Connery)
Nashville (directed by Robert Altman, with Karen
    Black, Henry Gibson)
One Flew over the Cuckoo's Nest (directed by Milos
    Forman, with Jack Nicholson)
The Sunshine Boys (directed by Herbert Ross, with
    George Burns, Walter Matthau)

▼　**1950**　▼

ASSOCIATIONS, SOCIETIES, UNIONS, AND GOVERNMENT DEPARTMENTS

Alpha Beta Alpha (Denton, TX)
Army Association of the United States (Arlington, VA)
Association for Retarded Citizens of the U.S. (Arlington, TX)
Muscular Dystrophy Association (New York, NY)
National Association of Legal Secretaries (Tulsa, OK)
National Science Foundation (U.S. government)
Society of Women Engineers (New York, NY)

MUSEUMS AND ZOOS

Akron Zoological Park (Akron, OH)
Carillon Historical Park (Dayton, OH)
Castle Clinton National Monument (New York, NY)
Columbia Museum of Art and Gibbes Planetarium (Columbia, SC)
Dearborn Historical Museum (Dearborn, MI)

IN 1950 on 11 May, President Truman dedicated the Grand Coulee Dam on the Columbia River in Washington.

▼ On 25 June, North Korean military forces crossed the 38th parallel, attacking South Korea. On 27 June, the United Nations Security Council voted to accept a resolution calling for armed reaction. On 30 June, the use of U.S. forces was authorized by President Truman; the first American troops landed in Korea on 1 July.

▼ On 29 November, the National Council of the Churches of Christ in the U.S.A. was founded.

▼ The Triple Crown trophy was established in horse racing to signify the winners—past and future—of the three Triple Crown series races: the Kentucky Derby, the Belmont Stakes, and the Preakness.

▼ The first National Basketball Association championship series was held. The winning team was the Minneapolis Lakers, beating the Syracuse Nationals four games to two.

▼ 1950 ▼

MUSEUMS AND ZOOS *continued*
Fort Kearney Museum (Kearney, NE)
Jefferson Barracks Historic Park (St. Louis, MO)
Las Vegas Art Museum (Las Vegas, NV)
MIT-List Visual Arts Center (Cambridge, MA)
National Museum of Racing (Saratoga Springs, NY)
Old Salem (Winston-Salem, NC)
Palomar Observatory (Pasadena, CA)
Pony Express Museum (St. Joseph, MO)
Riverside Zoo (Scottsbluff, NE)
San Jose Historical Museum (San Jose, CA)
Siskin Museum of Religious and Ceremonial Art
    (Chattanooga, TN)
Temple Museum of Jewish Religious Art (Cleveland, OH)

BIRTHDAYS AND DEATH DAYS
George Bernard Shaw died on 2 November at age 94

▼ The first automated pin-setting machines were installed in bowling alleys in the United States. Another milestone in bowling was a change in rules by the American Bowling Congress, allowing nonwhite males to participate in professional competition for the first time.

▼ The word game Scrabble was first offered for sale. The game was invented in 1933 by Alfred Butts, who was unsuccessful in finding a company to market his creation for many years.

▼ The first computerized weather forecasts were made.

▼ The era of plastic money began with the introduction of charge cards. Diners Club was the first company to offer this concept of payment, the idea of Francis McNamara, a New York businessman. Some retail stores, however, had previously issued charge cards for use only in their stores.

▼ Racquetball was invented by Joe Sobek in Greenwich, Connecticut. Sobek, a former professional tennis player, created this game—originally called paddle rackets—by combining elements of squash and handball.

▼ William Rosenberg opened the first Dunkin' Donuts in Quincy, Massachusetts.

▼ Cyclamate, the first artificial sweetener, was offered to consumers.

▼ The first commercial instant coffee was distributed by Maxwell House.

▼ The first Timex watches were sold in the United States. This inexpensive timepiece was designed by Joakim Lehmkuhl, a Norwegian immigrant living in Middlebury, Connecticut. Lehmkuhl's business, the Waterbury Clock Company, had developed mass production techniques to make accurate timing devices for bombs. After the war, the factory was redesigned to produce accurate, low-cost watches.

▼ **1950** ▼

COLLEGES AND UNIVERSITIES
Baptist Bible College (Springfield, MO)
Brescia College (Owensboro, KY)
Marymount University (Arlington, VA)
Notre Dame College (Manchester, NH)
Oklahoma Christian University of Science and Arts
  (Oklahoma City, OK)
Rutgers, State University of New Jersey, University
  College Camden (Camden, NJ)
State University of New York Health Science Center at
  Syracuse (Syracuse, NY)
University of Alabama in Huntsville (Huntsville, AL)

NEWSPAPERS AND MAGAZINES
Atlanta Journal Constitution (Atlanta, GA)
Children's Digest (Indianapolis, IN)
Golf Digest (Trumbull, CT)
Prevention (Emmaus, PA)

BOOKS, POETRY, AND PLAYS
Betty Crocker's Picture Cook Book,
  by Betty Crocker [pseud.]
The Cardinal, by Henry Robinson

MOVIES
All about Eve (directed by Joseph Mankiewicz,
  with Anne Baxter, Bette Davis)
Cyrano de Bergerac (directed by Michael Gordon,
  with José Ferrer)
Sunset Boulevard (directed by Billy Wilder,
  with William Holden, Gloria Swanson)

50 years ago

2000

▼ **1925** ▼

ASSOCIATIONS, SOCIETIES, UNIONS, AND GOVERNMENT DEPARTMENTS
American Speech-Language-Hearing Association (Rockville, MD)
Appalachian Trail Conference (Harpers Ferry, WV)
Atheist Association (San Diego, CA)
Grand United Order of Antelopes (East Orange, NJ)
International Amateur Radio Union (Newington, CT)
National Rehabilitation Association (Alexandria, VA)
Portuguese Continental Union of the U.S.A. (Boston, MA)
Society of Woman Geographers (Washington, DC)

MUSEUMS AND ZOOS
Children's Museum (Indianapolis, IN)
Cigna Museum (Philadelphia, PA)
J. B. Speed Art Museum (Louisville, KY)
Jacksonville Zoological Gardens (Jacksonville, FL)

BIRTHDAYS AND DEATH DAYS
Sun Yat-sen died on 12 March at age 58
H. Rider Haggard died on 14 May at age 69
Peter Sellers born on 18 September

IN 1925 on 5 January, Nellie Tayloe Ross was inaugurated as governor of Wyoming, the first woman to be elected to this post in the United States. Twenty days later, Miriam "Ma" Ferguson was inaugurated as governor of Texas. Both women were elected on the same date in 1924, but Ross was inaugurated first, giving her the historical honor. Ross's husband, William B. Ross, was the previous governor of Wyoming; he had died in office three months earlier.

▼ On 4 March, Calvin Coolidge was inaugurated for his second term as president of the United States.

▼ On 10 July, the Scopes trial began in Dayton, Tennessee. Defended by Clarence Darrow and prosecuted by William Jennings Bryan, this trial was a showcase for a major argument between science and a fundamentalist interpretation of the Bible, with John T. Scopes, a public schoolteacher, the defendant. Several years earlier, the term *fundamentalist* was first coined to describe the Bryan-led argument against the science of evolution. The trial ended with John Scopes being convicted, although the ruling was later overturned by the Supreme Court of Tennessee.

▼ On 12 December, the first motel was opened. Located in Monterey, California, this motor inn was called the Milestone Motel.

▼ According to some sources, 1925 marked the introduction of the Charleston, a dance often associated with the Roaring Twenties.

▼ American physicist Robert Millikan first reported the existence of cosmic rays, which he named.

▼ The New York Giants professional football team was founded in New York City.

▼ The *Louisville Courier Journal* initiated the first National Spelling Bee. Scripps-Howard, a newspaper chain, has sponsored this competition since 1939.

▼ The Grand Old Opry was first broadcast as a radio program, featuring country music from Nashville, Tennessee.

---

years ago

▼ 1925 ▼

COLLEGES AND UNIVERSITIES
Augusta College (Augusta, GA)
Mesa State College (Grand Junction, CO)
Mount Saint Mary College (Los Angeles, CA)
Southeastern Louisiana University (Hammond, LA)
University of Baltimore (Baltimore, MD)
University of Miami (Coral Gables, FL)
Xavier University of Louisiana (New Orleans, LA)

MUSIC
Concerto in F Major, by George Gershwin (first
    performed on 3 December in New York, NY)
No, No, Nanette, by Vincent Youmans, Otto Harback,
    Frank Mandel, and Irving Caesar (first performed on
    16 September in New York, NY)

NEWSPAPERS AND MAGAZINES
Arizona Highways (Phoenix, AZ)
Automotive News (Detroit, MI)
Baton Rouge Advocate (Baton Rouge, LA)
Fur-Fish-Game (Columbus, OH)
Philadelphia Daily News (Philadelphia, PA)

▼ Edwin Armstrong, an American electronics engineer, invented frequency modulation—usually referred to as FM—as a method of transmitting radio waves.

▼ Bennett Cerf founded Random House in New York City. The company's first and only line of books was the Modern Library, already an established money-maker. In 1927, original titles were first published, and Cerf and his partner, Donald Klopfer, changed the name of the business from Modern Library to Random House, as they chose some of their first authors randomly.

▼ Winn-Dixie Stores were founded in Lemon City, Florida, by W. M. Davis. The Winn-Dixie name was adopted in 1955; previously, the company was known as Table Supply.

▼ Dry ice was first made commercially available.

▼ United Technologies was formed as an airline manufacturing consortium that was then known as United Aircraft and Transportation Corporation. United Airlines separated from the company in 1934 following a congressional ruling on airline monopolies, leaving such manufacturing companies as Pratt & Whitney, Boeing, and Sikorsky.

▼ Walter Chrysler put his name on the Maxwell Motor Company, the beginning of the Chrysler Corporation. In 1928, Chrysler bought up Dodge and became one of the three largest automobile companies in the United States, along with Ford and GM.

▼   1925   ▼

BOOKS, POETRY, AND PLAYS
An American Tragedy, by Theodore Dreiser
Arrowsmith, by Sinclair Lewis
Cantos, by Ezra Pound
Gentlemen Prefer Blondes, by Anita Loos
The Great Gatsby, by F. Scott Fitzgerald
Manhattan Transfer, by John Dos Passos

MOVIES
The Battleship Potemkin (directed by Sergi Eisenstein)
The Big Parade (directed by King Vidor, with John Gilbert)
The Gold Rush (directed by Charlie Chaplin, with Charlie Chaplin)
The Phantom of the Opera (directed by Rupert Julian, with Lon Chaney)

▼ **1900** ▼

ASSOCIATIONS, SOCIETIES, UNIONS, AND GOVERNMENT DEPARTMENTS

American Booksellers Association (New York, NY)
American Philosophical Association (Newark, DE)
Association of American Universities
  (Washington, DC)
The College Board (New York, NY)
International Ladies Garment Workers Union
  (New York, NY)
Motor Vehicle Manufacturers Association (Detroit, MI)
Rabbinical Assembly (New York, NY)
Society of American Foresters (Bethesda, MD)
Workmen's Circle (New York, NY)

IN 1900 in January, Frank Nelson Doubleday and Walter Hines Page founded Doubleday, Page & Company in New York City. The name of this book publishing business was changed to Doubleday, Doran & Company in 1928, and then to Doubleday & Company in 1946.

▼ On 14 March, Congress passed the Gold Standard Act, establishing a gold reserve.

▼ On 30 April, "Casey" Jones died in the wreck of the Cannonball. Jones, whose real name was John Luther, was the engineer of Locomotive Number 382 on the Illinois Central Railroad. When it collided with another train, Jones was immortalized in a ballad published in 1909.

▼ On 29 May, the Otis Elevator Company registered a trademark for their new invention, the escalator. The first escalator made by Otis was displayed at the Paris Exposition in 1900 and installed in 1901 in a building in Philadelphia.

▼ On 2 July, the first rigid airship was flown by Count Ferdinand von Zeppelin. Zeppelin's dirigible was made possible by the development of low-cost supplies of aluminum, with which he built a frame that was streamlined to minimize wind resistance. The dirigible was the first aircraft that could be steered in any direction.

▼ On 27 August, a hurricane hit Galveston, Texas. Between 6,000 and 7,000 people lost their lives during this blow.

2000

▼ On 17 November, the College Entrance Examination Board was established in New York City. In 1901, the first college entrance exams were held, with 973 students participating at 67 testing stations throughout the country. The original tests included questions in English, language (Latin, Greek, German, or French), mathematics, history, chemistry, and physics.

▼ On 14 December, Max Planck, a German physics professor, first announced his discovery of the quantum theory. This concept theorized that energy is released in specified amounts, or quantums, rather than continuously. Planck's theory earned him the Nobel Prize in 1918.

▼ The first camera to use film in rolls was introduced to the public. The Kodak Brownie cost $1, and film cost 15 cents a roll. The Brownie was an instant hit, opening the era of snapshots and amateur photography.

▼ The Eatery in New Haven, Connecticut, is credited with making the first hamburger.

▼ The first Daisy air rifles hit the market. The gun was the creation of Clarence Hamilton, who was the first to make an air rifle out of metal. The company manufacturing the rifles was originally called the Plymouth Iron Windmill Company; the name was later changed as these BB guns proved a popular item.

▼   1900   ▼

MUSEUMS AND ZOOS
Alaska State Museum (Juneau, AK)
Denver Museum of Natural History (Denver, CO)
Isabella Stewart Gardner Museum (Boston, MA)
Mineral Museum (Butte, MT)
Museum of Fine Arts (Houston, TX)

BIRTHDAYS AND DEATH DAYS
John Ruskin died on 20 January at age 81
Stephen Crane died on 5 June at age 28
Lord Louis Mountbatten born on 25 June
Friedrich Nietzsche died on 25 August at age 56
Aaron Copland born on 14 November
Oscar Wilde died on 30 November at age 44

COLLEGES AND UNIVERSITIES
Carnegie Mellon University (Pittsburgh, PA)
Coppin State College (Baltimore, MD)
Lees-McRae College (Banner Elk, NC)

▼ 1900 ▼

MUSIC
Nocturnes I and II, by Claude Debussy (first performed on 9 December in Paris, France)
Tosca, by Giacomo Puccini (first performed on 14 January in Rome, Italy)

NEWSPAPERS AND MAGAZINES
Natural History (New York, NY)

BOOKS, POETRY, AND PLAYS
Lord Jim, by Joseph Conrad
Sister Carrie, by Theodore Dreiser
Three Plays for Puritans, by George Bernard Shaw
To Have and To Hold, by Mary Johnston
Up from Slavery, by Booker T. Washington

▼ The archaeological excavation of the Palace of Knossos on the island of Crete was begun, a project that lasted more than 25 years. Financed by Arthur Evans, an Englishman, the excavation uncovered unique frescoes of ancient Greek myths, ceremonial rooms, and important evidence of the use of the Greek language hundreds of years earlier than previously thought.

▼ The first oil wells were drilled in an offshore location, near Santa Barbara, California.

▼ Blood types were discovered by Karl Landsteiner, a doctor in Austria. Landsteiner's work classified blood into four types and identified which types could be combined without clotting. This discovery allowed for the use of blood transfusions, which had previously been avoided by doctors because of the occasional deadly results. Landsteiner was awarded the Nobel Prize in 1930. Later, during further research in the United States, he also contributed to the discovery of Rh factors in blood.

▼ Paul Ulrich, a French scientist, discovered gamma rays.

▼ Frederick Hopkins, an English biologist, discovered tryptophan, the first essential amino acid to be isolated.

▼ Harry Stevens, the catering director at the Polo Grounds in New York City, invented the hot dog. They were originally called "red hots," and the first recorded use of the term *hot dog* was by T. A. Dorgan in a cartoon in a Hearst newspaper in 1901.

2000

▼ The Hershey Foods Company was founded by Milton Hershey to manufacture candy. Hershey began his operation with an imported chocolate molding machine that he saw demonstrated at the Chicago Exposition of 1893. The first Hershey factory was built in Derry Church, Pennsylvania, a town that renamed itself after its major employer in 1906.

▼ Firestone Tire & Rubber (now Bridgestone-Firestone, Inc.) was founded in Akron, Ohio, by Harvey Firestone. Firestone began selling horse-drawn buggies in 1892 and early on believed that rubber tires were an important improvement for vehicles. His first business venture was a tire supply company in Chicago, which provided the capital with which he started Firestone Tire & Rubber. The first original Firestone tires were manufactured in 1903, and the company succeeded by developing new and efficient methods for attaching tires to rims.

▼ Booker T. Washington's autobiography, *Up from Slavery,* was published. Already a prominent leader and founder of the Tuskegee Institute, Washington's life story was credited with focusing new attention on American racial attitudes. The following year, President Theodore Roosevelt invited the author to dinner at the White House, an event that upset many white Southerners.

▼ The first Davis Cup tennis tournament was held.

▼ The Philadelphia Orchestra was founded in Philadelphia, Pennsylvania. Since its inception, the orchestra has presented its programs in the Academy of Music building, constructed in 1857.

▼   **1850**   ▼

BIRTHDAYS AND DEATH DAYS
Samuel Gompers born on 27 January
William Wordsworth died on 23 April at age 80
Henry Cabot Lodge born on 12 May
Zachary Taylor died on 9 July at age 65
Guy de Maupassant born on 5 August
Honoré de Balzac died on 17 August at age 51
Robert Louis Stevenson born on 13 November

COLLEGES AND UNIVERSITIES
Defiance College (Defiance, OH)
Heidelberg College (Triffin, OH)
Hiram College (Hiram, OH)
Illinois Wesleyan University (Bloomington, IL)
University of Dayton (Dayton, OH)

▼   1850   ▼

COLLEGES AND UNIVERSITIES
continued
University of Rochester (Rochester, NY)
University of Utah (Salt Lake City, UT)
Urbana University (Urbana, OH)

MUSIC
Lohengrin, by Richard Wagner (first performed on 28 August in Weimar, Germany)

NEWSPAPERS AND MAGAZINES
Portland Oregonian (Portland, OR)
Richmond Times Dispatch (Richmond, VA)
Savannah News (Savannah, GA)

BOOKS, POETRY, AND PLAYS
David Copperfield, by Charles Dickens
Representative Men, by Ralph Waldo Emerson
The Scarlet Letter, by Nathaniel Hawthorne
Sonnets from the Portuguese, by Elizabeth Barrett Browning
The Wide, Wide World, by Susan Bogert Warner

IN 1850 in June, *Harper's Magazine* began publication in New York City. The original name was *Harper's New Monthly Magazine,* a periodical intended to promote the books of its publisher, the House of Harper. The title was changed to *Harper's Monthly Magazine* in 1900 and changed again, to its present title, in 1925.

▼ On 9 July, Zachary Taylor, twelfth president of the United States, died in office at the age of 65. His death was caused by "bilious fever," typhoid fever, and cholera. His last words were, "I regret nothing, but am sorry that I am about to leave my friends." He was succeeded in office by Millard Fillmore, the vice president, on July 10.

▼ On 28 August, Richard Wagner's opera, *Lohengrin,* was performed for the first time. The first performance was produced by Franz Liszt and played in Weimar, Germany. At the time, Wagner was hiding in Zurich, Switzerland, avoiding a warrant that had been issued for his arrest in Dresden. The warrant was the result of his participation in the Dresden uprising in 1849, a disturbance organized by German revolutionaries.

▼ On 9 September, California was admitted to the Union as the thirty-first state. The state was named after an imaginary island written about by a Spanish author, Garcia Ordonez de Montalvo, in 1500. The first western exploration was by the Spanish in 1542, and missionary outposts were quickly established throughout the region. American settlers first moved into the state in large numbers during the early 1800s, eventually creating a movement to make the territory part of the United States. At the conclusion of the Mexican War in 1848, Mexico ceded the land to the United States. The first governor was Peter H. Burnett, a Democrat, who served from 1849 to 1851.

▼ On 28 September, the U.S. Congress prohibited flogging on U.S. Navy vessels and American merchant ships.

▼ The Aetna Life Insurance Company offered its first life insurance policies for clients.

▼ The Stroh Brewery Company was founded in Detroit by Bernhard Stroh, a German immigrant who came to this country with a family history of beer making.

▼ Three competing delivery companies in Buffalo, New York, merged to form American Express. One of the earliest successes for the new company was the founding of Wells, Fargo & Company; two of the original American Express founders were Henry Wells and William Fargo. Wells, Fargo prospered and became an independent company, and the American Express founders stayed home to lead their business through a prosperous period of growth. American Express created the first money orders in 1882 and introduced traveler's checks in 1891.

▼ Levi Strauss & Company was founded in San Francisco by Levi Strauss, a 20-year-old German immigrant. Strauss had intended to sell tents to miners, but a lack of demand forced him to turn his supply of canvas into work pants. According to company lore, it was the customers who began referring to the pants as Levis. The addition of rivets to the pants came from a suggestion from a tailor in Nevada, who had been paid to repair torn pockets on the jeans. In a letter to Levi Strauss, he wrote, "The secratt of them Pents is the Rivits that I put in those Pockets."

▼ Emanuel Leutze completed the painting *Washington Crossing the Delaware.* Leutze, a German immigrant, also painted the mural in the U.S. House of Representatives wing of the Capitol building, a work titled *Westward the Course of Empire Takes Its Way*—also known as *Westward Ho.*

▼ The teletype was invented by Francis Galton.

▼ Sixteen English sparrows were deliberately imported into Brooklyn, New York, from England. The sparrows were intended to be a natural control over insect pests, but their population increased so rapidly that the sparrows themselves became pests in only a few decades. In 1890, an attempt to control the sparrows was made with the importation of starlings, but now starlings are also a major pest in most cities.

▼ 1800 ▼

MUSEUMS AND ZOOS
Library of Congress (Washington, DC)

BIRTHDAYS AND DEATH DAYS
Millard Fillmore born on 7 January
John Brown born on 9 May
Thomas Macaulay born on 25 October

MUSIC
Piano Concerto No. 1, by Ludwig van Beethoven
   (first performed on 2 April in Vienna, Austria)
Symphony No. 1 in C Major, by Ludwig van Beethoven
   (first performed on 2 April in Vienna, Austria)

IN 1800 on 7 January, Millard Fillmore was born in Locke, New York. An attorney, Fillmore was a state assemblyman for several terms and was elected to the U.S. House of Representatives in 1833, serving until 1843. Affiliated with several parties, he became a Whig in 1834 and was elected as vice president under Zachary Taylor in 1848. Fillmore became the thirteenth president of the United States on 9 July 1850, following the death of President Taylor in office. Beaten in the presidential election of 1852, he ran for president again in 1856 as a member of the Know-Nothing party, but was unsuccessful in this bid as well. Retiring from politics, he helped found the University of Buffalo (New York). He died in Buffalo on 8 March 1874 at the age of 74.

▼ On 4 April, the U.S. Congress established the Library of Congress. Among the first books for the library were more than 7,000 titles in a collection owned by Thomas Jefferson. The first librarian of Congress was James Beckley, appointed in 1802 by President Jefferson.

2000

▼ On 17 November, the first session of a U.S. Congress was held in Washington, D.C. Congress met in the north wing of the Capitol building, the only finished part of the structure at that date. Until the completion of government buildings in Washington, the federal government did most of its business in Philadelphia. Also, the White House was first occupied—by John and Abigail Adams—although it was still unfinished.

▼ Water was first separated into oxygen and hydrogen using the process of electrolysis.

▼ Water purification using chlorine was carried out for the first time.

▼ The first coffee percolator was created by Jean Baptiste de Belloy, the archbishop of Paris.

▼ Marie Francois Xavier Bichat, a French doctor, published *The Treatise on Membranes,* the first medical book describing types of living tissue. The science of histology developed from this beginning.

▼ The first report was published describing the existence of infrared radiation, a discovery made by William Herschel, a German astronomer. Herschel is also credited with the discovery of Uranus in 1781, several satellites of Saturn, the satellites of Uranus, and hundreds of deep-sky objects. William's sister, Caroline Lucretia Herschel, also was an important astronomer, discovering eight comets and other stellar objects; William's son, Sir John Frederick William Herschel, published one of the first reference guides to deep-sky objects and made important developments in photography.

▼ **1750** ▼

BOOKS, POETRY, AND PLAYS
Discours sur les arts et les sciences, by
Henri Rousseau

IN 1750 the first Conestoga wagons were built to transport residents of Pennsylvania to the western territories.

▼ Dr. Thomas Walker, an American explorer, discovered the Cumberland Gap in the Appalachian Mountains (near the present-day town of Middlesboro, Kentucky). The natural passage, named after the Duke of Cumberland, proved to be an important gateway for the development of the West.

▼ The Redwood Library in Newport, Rhode Island, was constructed, the oldest library building in continuous use in this country.

▼ The modern science of anatomy was introduced with the publication of an essay describing the dissection of the body of a murderer who was executed in New York City.

IN 1700 William Kidd, better known as Captain Kidd, turned himself in to the colonial governor of New York after being accused of piracy and murder.

Kidd had been commissioned by royal order in 1695 to attack pirates preying on English ships. According to some accounts of his exploits, he himself turned to piracy after unsuccessfully pursuing his mission. Despite his attempts to prove the charges false, he was found guilty in London in 1701 and hanged.

IN 1650 the first tea was brought to England; in 1651, the first tea was sold to the public in that country. The cultivation of tea for beverages in China dates

to about A.D. 350. It was first described to the western world in 1560 in the published journals of Portuguese explorer Jesuit Gaspar da Cruz, and it was first brought to Europe in 1610.

▼ The first coffee house in England was opened in Oxford.

▼   **1600**   ▼

BOOKS, POETRY, AND PLAYS
As You Like It, by William Shakespeare
Julius Caesar, by William Shakespeare

IN 1600 on 31 December, the British East India Company was incorporated under a royal charter. Established to compete with the successful spice trading monopolies developed by Spain and Portugal, the original name of this organization was the Governor and Company of Merchants of London Trading with the East Indies. The company went out of business in 1873 after 273 years of operation.

▼ William Gilbert, an English doctor and physicist, published the first book outlining the properties of magnetism and the behavior of compasses. Gilbert's book, *De magnete, magneticisque corporibus, et de magno magnete tellure* (Concerning magnetism, magnetic bodies, and the great magnet earth), was the first to list the terms *electrical force* and *magnetic pole*. During his life, Gilbert was the court physician to Queen Elizabeth I and later to King James I.

IN 1550 on 12 June, the city of Helsinki—originally called Helsingfors—was founded in Finland by King Gustav Vasa of Sweden. The settlement was created as a trading center when Finland was part of the Swedish empire. The Finnish capital was moved from Turku to this location in 1812 when the country was under Russian rule.

IN 1500 the first recorded successful cesarean section on a living woman was performed in Switzerland. The deed was performed by Jacob Nufer, a pig farmer, and the patient was his wife.

▼ The territory of Brazil in South America was officially declared part of the Portuguese empire by Pedro Álvares Cabral. Cabral "discovered" Brazil after being blown off course while searching for a new sea route to India. The explorer was doubly lucky on this trip, establishing Portuguese rule despite the fact that the territory had earlier been discovered by the Spanish (the Portuguese had some help from an earlier treaty signed by both countries) and eventually succeeding in making a round-trip to and from his original destination, India.

▼ Drawings by Leonardo da Vinci introduced the concept of the helicopter, a machine that would not become reality until more than 400 years later. Other da Vinci drawings made in 1500 depicted one of the first-known versions of a hand-held firearm, the musket.

2001

▼ 1976 ▼

MUSEUMS AND ZOOS
Knoxville Zoological Gardens (Knoxville, TN)
Omnisphere and Science Center (Wichita, KA)
Shoreline Historical Museum (Seattle, WA)
The Texas Zoo (Victoria, TX)

MUSIC
Alice Cooper Goes to Hell, by Alice Cooper
Boston, by Boston
Changesonebowie, by David Bowie
Chicago X, by Chicago
Children of the World, by the Bee Gees
Disco Duck, by Rick Dees and His Cast of Idiots
Dreamboat Annies, by Heart
Fly Like an Eagle, by the Steve Miller Band
Fooled Around and Fell in Love, by Elvin Bishop
Greatest Stories—Live, by Harry Chapin
Hotel California, by the Eagles
A Kind of Hush, by the Carpenters
Lonely Night, by Captain & Tennille
Love So Right, by the Bee Gees
Love To Love You Baby, by Donna Summer
Natalie, by Natalie Cole

WHAT **25** years ago WAS

IN 1976 on 22 April, Barbara Walters, with ABC, became the first woman to anchor a network news program.

▼ On 24 May, supersonic passenger service between Europe and the United States began with two flights of *Concorde* SSTs to Washington, D.C., one coming from London and one from Paris.

▼ On 5 June, 14 people died after the Teton River Dam in Idaho collapsed.

▼ On 19 June, *Viking I* became the first man-made object to land in a controlled manner on the surface of another planet. On the surface of Mars, *Viking I* transmitted photographs and data about the planet back to earth.

▼ On 31 July, a flash flood in Big Thompson Canyon in Colorado killed 139 people.

▼ On 15 October, the first debate was held between candidates for the vice presidency. Participants were Democrat Walter Mondale and Republican Robert Dole.

▼ Liz Claiborne founded her fashion company in New York City.

▼ The country's largest chain of retail computer stores was founded as Computer Shacks; later the name was changed to Computerland.

▼ Steven Jobs and Stephen Wozniak founded Apple Computer, Inc. in California.

▼ Genentech was founded in San Francisco by Herbert Boyer and Robert Swanson. Genentech developed and manufactured the first genetically engineered drug with FDA approval, a form of insulin.

▼ The U.S. military academies began admitting female students for the first time.

▼ The "MacNeil-Lehrer Report" debuted on the Public Broadcasting Service (PBS).

▼ The ink-jet printer was introduced by IBM.

25 years ago

▼ 1976 ▼

MUSIC *continued*
New Kid in Town, by the Eagles
The Pretender, by Jackson Browne
Run with the Pack, by Bad Company
Saddle Tramp, by the Charlie Daniels Band
Song of Joy, by Captain & Tennille
The Sound in Your Mind, by Willie Nelson
Station to Station, by David Bowie
Takin' It to the Streets, by the Doobie Brothers
Torn between Two Lovers, by Mary MacGregor
We Sold Our Soul for Rock 'n' Roll, by Black Sabbath
Wired, by Jeff Beck
You Should Be Dancing, by the Bee Gees

NEWSPAPERS AND MAGAZINES
Arts and Leisure Magazine (Custer, SD)
Mother Jones (San Francisco, CA)
New West Magazine (Los Angeles, CA)
Outside Business Magazine (Chicago, IL)
Teen Beat (New York, NY)
Wilson Quarterly (Washington, DC)
Working Woman (New York, NY)

▼ 1976 ▼

BOOKS, POETRY, AND PLAYS
The Deep, by Peter Benchley
Roots, by Alex Haley

MOVIES
All the President's Men (directed by Alan Pakula, with
   Dustin Hoffman, Robert Redford)
Network (directed by Sidney Lumet, with Faye
   Dunaway, Peter Finch)
Rocky (directed by John Avildsen, with Sylvester
   Stallone)
Taxi Driver (directed by Martin Scorsese, with Robert
   DeNiro, Jody Foster)

▼ College football's first Independence Bowl was held in Shreveport, Louisiana. In that first game, McNeese State beat Tulsa, 20-16.

▼ 1951 ▼

ASSOCIATIONS, SOCIETIES, UNIONS, AND GOVERNMENT DEPARTMENTS
Air Line Employees Association (Chicago, IL)
National Hearing Aid Society (Livonia, MI)
Nature Conservancy (Arlington, VA)
Society of Fire Protection Engineers (Boston, MA)

IN 1951 on 26 February, the Twenty-Second Amendment to the U.S. Constitution was enacted, limiting presidential terms to two.

▼ On 25 June, CBS made the first commercial broadcast of a television program in color. The broadcast was a one-hour show featuring Arthur Godfrey, Ed Sullivan, and other celebrities.

▼ On 4 September, the first simultaneous transmission of a television program throughout the country occurred. The program covered President Truman's remarks at a conference in San Francisco for the signing of a Japanese peace treaty with 48 nations. The broadcast was carried on 94 local television stations.

▼ On 20 December, at Arco, Idaho, the first electricity was generated with nuclear fission at an experimental atomic power plant.

▼ Wang Laboratories was founded by An Wang, an immigrant from China. Wang received his doctorate in physics from Harvard before starting his company with $600. A patent sale for his first invention earned the company enough money to begin manufacturing electronics, and Wang eventually introduced a successful word-processing computer in 1976.

▼ Abstract expressionism first attracted public attention in the United States, beginning a new era for the art industry. The turning point was a major exhibition at the Museum of Modern Art in New York City.

50 years ago

▼ 1951 ▼

MUSEUMS AND ZOOS
Birmingham Museum of Art (Birmingham, AL)
Corning Museum of Glass (Corning, NY)
Denver Botanic Gardens (Denver, CO)
National Maritime Museum (San Francisco, CA)
Roanoke Museum of Fine Arts (Roanoke, VA)
Sacramento Science Center (Sacramento, CA)
Southern Baptist Historical Library and Archives
    (Nashville, TN)
Utah Museum of Fine Arts (University of Utah, Salt
    Lake City, UT)

BIRTHDAYS AND DEATH DAYS
Arnold Schönberg died on 13 July at age 76

COLLEGES AND UNIVERSITIES
Belmont College (Nashville, TN)
Calumet College of Saint Joseph (Whiting, IN)
Mercy College (Dobbs Ferry, NY)
Mount Olive College (Mount Olive, NC)
Purdue University Calumet (Hammond, IN)
University of Connecticut at Stamford (Stamford, CT)

▼ 1951 ▼

MUSIC
Amahl and the Night Visitors, by Gian Carlo Menotti
Billy Budd, by Benjamin Britten
Imaginary Landscapes No. 4, by John Cage
The King and I, by Richard Rogers and Oscar Hammerstein
    (first performed on 29 March in New York, NY)
Paint Your Wagon, by Alan Lerner and Frederick Loewe

NEWSPAPERS AND MAGAZINES
Jet (Chicago, IL)
Navy Times (Washington, DC)
Read (Middletown, CT)
Skin Diver (Los Angeles, CA)

BOOKS, POETRY, AND PLAYS
Barbary Shore, by Norman Mailer
The Caine Mutiny, by Herman Wouk
The Catcher in the Rye, by J. D. Salinger
Collected Poems, by Marianne Moore
From Here to Eternity, by James Jones
The Rose Tattoo, by Tennessee Williams
The Sea around Us, by Rachel Carson

MOVIES
The African Queen (directed by John Huston, with
    Humphrey Bogart, Katharine Hepburn)
An American in Paris (directed by Vincente Minnelli,
    with Leslie Caron, Gene Kelly)
The Death of a Salesman (directed by Laslo Benedek,
    with Fredric March)
Oliver Twist (directed by David Lean, with Alec Guinness)
A Place in the Sun (directed by George Stevens, with
    Montgomery Clift, Elizabeth Taylor)
Quo Vadis (directed by Mervyn LeRoy, with Deborah
    Kerr, Robert Taylor)
Rashomon (directed by Akira Kurosawa, with Toshiro
    Mifune)
A Streetcar Named Desire (directed by Elia Kazan, with
    Marlon Brando, Vivian Leigh)
The Thing (directed by Christian Nyby, with Kenneth Tobey)

▼ The Circle K Corporation was founded in El Paso, Texas. The company founder was Fred Hervey, an ex-mayor of the city, and the convenience store chain was created with the purchase of three existing stores, operating as Kay's Food Stores. The Circle K name was adopted in 1957.

▼ Alcoholics were first treated with antabuse, a compound that, when ingested by a patient, elicits a painful reaction if any alcohol is consumed.

▼ The heart-lung machine was invented by John Gibbon, an American doctor.

▼ The first computers were made commercially available. The first model was a UNIVAC I, produced by Remington Rand. UNIVAC, or Universal Automatic Computer, was designed by Eckert and Mauchly, who also designed the ENIAC in 1946. UNIVAC was the first computer to use magnetic tape.

▼ The first Pan-American Games were held in Buenos Aires, Argentina. Winners in these games, held from 27 February–9 March, included the Cuban baseball team, the U.S. basketball team, the Argentinian boxing team, and the Argentinian soccer team.

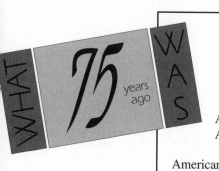

WHAT

75 years ago

WAS

▼ 1926 ▼

ASSOCIATIONS, SOCIETIES, UNIONS, AND GOVERNMENT DEPARTMENTS

American Arbitration Association (New York, NY)
American Association of Teachers of German (Cherry Hill, NJ)
American Shore and Beach Preservation Association (Walnut Creek, CA)
International Brotherhood of Magicians (Lynn, MI)
International Chiropractors Association (Washington, DC)
International Electrical Manufacturers Association (Washington, DC)
Medieval Academy of America (Cambridge, MA)
National Association for the Education of Young Children (Washington, DC)

IN 1926 on 7 March, the first wireless voice transmission across the Atlantic was broadcast between New York and London.

▼ On 16 March, Robert Goddard, an American scientist, launched the world's first liquid-fueled rocket. The vehicle flew to a height of 184 feet. This anniversary is traditionally known as Goddard Day.

2001

▼   1926   ▼

MUSEUMS AND ZOOS
American Swedish Historical Foundation
    Museum (Philadelphia, PA)
Dittrick Museum of Medical History
    (Cleveland, OH)
Grand Army of the Republic Memorial Museum
    (Philadelphia, PA)
James R. Slater Museum of Natural History (Tacoma, WA)
Liberty Memorial Museum (Kansas City, MO)
Little Rock Zoological Gardens (Little Rock, AR)
Longyear Historical Museum (Brookline, MA)
Museum of Science and Industry (Chicago, IL)
Rodin Museum (Philadelphia, PA)
Santa Barbara Botanic Garden (Santa Barbara, CA)
Siouxland Heritage Museum (Sioux Falls, SD)

BIRTHDAYS AND DEATH DAYS
Queen Elizabeth II born on 21 April
Claude Monet died on 5 December at age 66
Rainer Maria Rilke died on 29 December at age 51

▼ On 17 April, the first regular airline service began with a flight from Los Angeles to Salt Lake City. The first flight was operated by Western Airlines, the oldest airline company in the United States. The flight delivered only mail, but Western added passenger service in May by putting folding chairs next to the sacks of mail. In 1987, Western Airlines was merged into Delta Airlines.

▼ On 9 May, Lieutenant Commander Richard E. Byrd made the first flight over the North Pole. The flight originated from Kings Bay, Spitzbergen (an island in the Barents Sea), and the round-trip took 15 hours and 51 minutes. Flying a tri-motor Fokker airplane, he made the flight despite a serious oil leak in one of the engines. At the time, Byrd was a commissioned officer in the U.S. Navy, and he flew with Floyd Bennett, an experienced Arctic pilot.

▼ On 2 July, the Army Air Corps was established by Congress.

▼ On 6 August, Gertrude Ederle became the first woman to swim the English Channel. Ederle, from New York, not only became the first woman to accomplish this feat, but in doing so she set a new record, beating the best time set by a man by more than two hours.

▼ On 31 October, Harry Houdini died. An internationally known magician, he was famous for performing spectacular escapes from precarious positions. Born Ehrich Weiss in Budapest, Hungary, in 1874, Houdini emigrated to the United States with his family just after he was born. He chose his name in commemoration of a famous French magician, Robert-Houdin. His death was caused by peritonitis, which developed after he received a blow to the stomach. According to a prior arrangement with his wife, he planned to send her a message telepathically "from the grave" if there were life after death. His wife died in 1943, after spending years waiting in vain for communication from her dead spouse. The anniversary of Houdini's death is celebrated as National Magic Day.

▼ The first hybrid corn seed was marketed to farmers. The corn hybrid was first developed in 1921 at the Connecticut Agricultural Experiment Station. The first agricultural experiment station was founded in 1875 and located at Wesleyan University in Middletown, Connecticut; Congress began federal support of these research outposts in 1887.

▼ Volvo began producing its first automobiles in Gothenburg, Sweden. The Volvo Corporation was founded in 1915 as a subsidiary of a ball bearing company. The first Volvo cars used engines and components manufactured by other companies, with the first all-Volvo designs produced in 1935.

▼   1926   ▼

COLLEGES AND UNIVERSITIES
Center for Creative Studies (Detroit, MI)
Long Island University (Brooklyn, NY)
Sarah Lawrence College (Bronxville, NY)

NEWSPAPERS AND MAGAZINES
Parents' Magazine (New York, NY)
Science News (Washington, DC)

BOOKS, POETRY, AND PLAYS
Abraham Lincoln: The Prairie Years, by Carl Sandburg
Desire under the Elms, by Eugene O'Neill
The Plough and the Stars, by Sean O'Casey
The Sun Also Rises, by Ernest Hemingway

MOVIES
Metropolis (directed by Fritz Lang)

2001

▼ The Toyota Motor Corporation was founded in Japan by Ki-ichiro Toyoda.

▼ Safeway was established as a grocery store chain in the western states, starting with a single store in American Falls, Idaho. The original stores were called United Stores and were renamed Safeway when United Stores merged with another chain in 1926.

▼ Q-tips were developed.

75 years ago

▼ The National Broadcasting Company (NBC) was founded as a radio network by David Sarnoff, the head of RCA. In its original form, NBC aired two broadcasts, the Blue Network and the Red Network. The Blue Network eventually became the American Broadcasting Company (ABC).

▼ Columbia Broadcasting System (CBS) was founded. Two years later, there were 22 stations in the network, and William Paley became the new company head. Paley introduced the concept of affiliates, with centralized broadcasting made available free to member stations. This ploy, which brought in more stations and more listeners, was the beginning of a national radio audience that was sold to advertisers.

▼ Delta Airlines was founded by Collett Everman Woolman. Woolman started and operated a crop dusting company in Louisiana, moving to passenger service in 1926. The first Delta flights connected cities in Texas, Louisiana, and Mississippi.

▼ Northwest Airlines was founded in Minneapolis. Originally known as Northwest Airways, the company established the first regular airline connections between Chicago and Minneapolis, with the first passenger flights in 1927.

▼ United Airlines was begun with the founding of Varney Air Lines. Varney and other airline companies—including Pacific Air Transport, National Air Transport, Stout Air Services, the Pratt & Whitney Company, and Boeing—ended up merged into United Airlines in 1931, with headquarters in New York City. United was the first airline to train stewardesses, offer coast-to-coast service, and fly to all 50 states (not until 1985). In 1934, a congressional ruling to control monopolization required airline companies to be separate from companies that manufactured airplanes, forcing United to end its ownership of Pratt & Whitney and Boeing.

▼ General Telephone (GTE) was founded by Sigurd Odegard as a small, independent telephone company in southern California. Originally called Associated Telephone Utilities, the company was renamed General Telephone in a bankruptcy reorganization during the depression years. In 1959, with the acquisition of Sylvania, the company's name was changed to General Telephone and Electronics; the name General Telephone was adopted in 1971.

▼ Book clubs were introduced in the United States, with the formation of the Book-of-the-Month Club and the Literary Guild. The Book-of-the-Month Club gained 40,000 subscribers in its first year.

▼ Herman Muller, an American biologist, discovered that X rays produce genetic mutations.

▼ Pop-up toasters were first marketed.

▼ William Randolph Hearst founded the *National Enquirer* in New York City as a weekly, Sunday afternoon tabloid. The paper was purchased in 1952 by Generoso Pope, Jr., and moved to Florida in 1971.

▼ 1901 ▼

ASSOCIATIONS, SOCIETIES, UNIONS, AND GOVERNMENT DEPARTMENTS

4-H Clubs (Washington, DC)
National Bureau of Standards (U.S. Department of Commerce)
National Society for the Study of Education (Chicago, IL)
Society of Illustrators (New York, NY)
United Textile Workers of America (Vorhees, NJ)

MUSEUMS AND ZOOS

Brookline Historical Society (Brookline, MA)
Busch-Reisinger Museum (Cambridge, MA)
Grand Army of the Republic Memorial Hall Museum (Madison, WI)
Lowie Museum of Anthropology (University of California, Berkeley, CA)
Madison Art Center (Madison, WI)
Modern Art Museum of Fort Worth (Fort Worth, TX)

IN 1901 on 10 January, the first oil strike in Texas was made on the Spindletop claim outside of Beaumont.

▼ On 28 January, professional baseball organizations formed the American League. The original teams in this league were located in Baltimore, Boston, Chicago, Cleveland, Detroit, Milwaukee, Philadelphia, and Washington, D.C.

▼ On 4 March, William McKinley was inaugurated for his second term as president of the United States.

▼ On 13 March, Benjamin Harrison, twenty-third president of the United states, died of pneumonia in Indianapolis, Indiana, at the age of 67. His last words were, "Are the doctors here?"

▼ On 23 March, Emilio Aguinaldo, the leader of a rebellion in the Philippines against U.S. forces, was captured in Luzon. Aguinaldo had been fighting against Spanish forces before the outcome of the Spanish-American War transferred official control of the islands to the United States. With the surrender of Spanish forces in Manila on 13 August 1898, guerrilla fighting kept U.S. soldiers busy for several years. One of the commanders in the field, Colonel Frederick Funston, was quoted at the time by *Harper's Weekly Magazine*: "After the war, I want the job of Professor of American History in Luzon University, when they build it, and I'll warrant that the new generation of natives will know better than to get in the way of the bandwagon of Anglo-Saxon progress and decency."

▼   1901   ▼

MUSEUMS AND ZOOS *continued*
Museum of American Illustration (New York, NY)
Robinson State Museum (Pierre, SD)
Toledo Museum of Art (Toledo, OH)

BIRTHDAYS AND DEATH DAYS
Giuseppe Verdi died on 27 January at age 88
Benjamin Harrison died on 13 March at age 68
William McKinley died on 14 September at age 58
Walt Disney born on 5 December
Margaret Mead born on 16 December

COLLEGES AND UNIVERSITIES
California Polytechnic State University (San Luis
    Obispo, CA)
Golden Gate University (San Francisco, CA)
Grambling State University (Grambling, LA)
Idaho State University (Pocatello, ID)
Millikin University (Decatur, IL)
Texas Woman's University (Denton, TX)
Trevecca Nazarene College (Nashville, TN)
University of Portland (Portland, OR)

years ago

▼ 1901 ▼

MUSIC
Concerto No. 2 in C Minor, by Sergei
Rachmaninoff (first performed on 14 October
in Moscow, Russia)
Dance of Death, by August Strindberg
Nocturne III, by Claude Debussy (first performed
on 27 October in Paris, France)

NEWSPAPERS AND MAGAZINES
Delaware State News (Dover, DE)
Editor and Publisher (New York, NY)
House and Garden (New York, NY)
Houston Chronicle (Houston, TX)
Kansas City Times (Kansas City, MO)
Travel/Holiday (New York, NY)

BOOKS, POETRY, AND PLAYS
Buddenbrooks, by Thomas Mann
Kim, by Rudyard Kipling
Life of the Bee, by Maurice Maeterlinck
Mrs. Wiggs of Cabbage Patch, by Alice Caldwell
Hegan Rice
Poems of the Past and Present, by Thomas Hardy
The Psychopathology of Everyday Life, by Sigmund Freud

▼ On 14 September, William McKinley, twenty-fourth president of the United States, died eight days after being shot by an assassin in Buffalo, New York, where he was attending the Pan-American Exposition. He was 58 years old at the time of his death. His last words were, "It is God's way. His will be done, not ours. . . . We are all going, we are all going, we are all going. Oh, dear." Vice President Theodore Roosevelt succeeded McKinley as president.

▼ On 18 November, the United States and Great Britain signed the Hay Paunce-forte Treaty, allowing the United States to build the Panama Canal connecting the Atlantic Ocean and Pacific Ocean in Central America.

▼ On 5 December, Walt Disney was born in Chicago, Illinois. Disney became involved in animated films in the early 1920s in Kansas City, Missouri, and began developing a unique production team in Los Angeles in 1923. In 1928, Disney created his first and most memorable animated character, Mickey Mouse, who debuted in a cartoon that year. Disney died on 15 December 1966 at the age of 65.

▼ On 10 December, Nobel Prizes were first awarded. Funds for the prizes were provided by the will of Alfred Nobel, who died on 10 December 1896. The annual Nobel Prize awards are made annually on this date.

▼ On 12 December, the date often cited as the birth of the radio era, the first long-distance broadcast of a radio signal was made by Marchese Guglielmo Marconi, an Italian electrical engineer. Earlier, in 1894, he had built the first radio transmitter, which could only transmit to a distance of about 30 feet. By the following year, however, Marconi was successfully broadcasting over a distance of several miles. He made the famous 1901 broadcast from the south-eastern coast of England with a balloon pulling an antenna high into  the air. The signals—comprised of a three dot pattern making the letter "S"—were received in Newfoundland, about 2,000 miles distant. (In its early years, radio was called wireless telegraphy and could only be used to send and receive nonverbal messages, consisting of standard telegraphic code.) This achievement was generally ignored at the time or believed to have little significance. In 1924, the *New York Times* printed an article about this event, remarking, "The apathy or downright indifference of the public following the announcement of the first transatlantic wireless message seems almost incredible."

▼ U.S. Gypsum (USG) was founded in Chicago with the merger of 35 companies involved in the production of gypsum products.

▼ The Walgreen Company was founded as a single drugstore in Chicago. It was started by Charles Walgreen, who opened a second store in 1909. Ice cream and soda concessions were made part of the stores, the first soda fountains in the country.

▼ Bergdorf Goodman opened a store in New York City to sell furs and tailoring services to women.

▼ John W. Nordstrom opened a shoe store in Seattle. An immigrant from Sweden, Nordstrom had three sons who stayed in their father's business, expanding the store into the country's largest chain of shoe outlets. In 1963, the Nordstrom company branched out into department store retailing with a single store in Seattle; by the 1980s, Nordstrom's was one of the country's largest department store chains.

▼ The Gerber Products Company was founded in Fremont, Michigan. Originally a commercial cannery, the company began making the country's first pre-made baby food in 1928 at the suggestion of the founder's wife. The first Gerber products were carrots, peas, prunes, spinach, and vegetable soup. Price: 15 cents a can.

▼ The Henbe Manufacturing Company in Springfield, Massachusetts, began producing the first motorcycle made in the United States—the Indian. In 1953, the company moved its operations to England.

▼ The Cleveland Cap Screw Company was founded in Cleveland, Ohio. After several name changes—including the Electric Welding Company, Steel Products Company, Thompson Products, and Ramo-Wooldridge—it became Thompson Ramo Wooldridge in 1958, now called TRW. Originally a manufacturer of steel products, the company began developing other technologies after World War II. TRW was the first company in the United States to construct a spacecraft, *Pioneer I.*

▼ The Edison General Electric Company in Harrison, New Jersey, marketed the first electric lights for Christmas trees.

▼ Quaker Oats was founded as a manufacturer of rolled oats cereal.

▼ Monsanto was founded by John Queeny. The company's name was inspired by his wife's maiden name. The original products Monsanto manufactured included caffeine, vanillin, and saccharin.

▼ J. P. Morgan, one of the nation's wealthiest bankers, bought out the controlling interest in the Carnegie Steel Company from its founder, Andrew Carnegie. The deal, for $480 million, was the largest financial transaction to date in U.S. business. The new head of the company changed the name to U.S. Steel, which eventually became the USX Corporation, headquartered in Pittsburgh, Pennsylvania.

▼ A Russian scientist named Ilya Ivanov opened the first artificial insemination laboratory.

▼ The Heublein Company, in Hartford, Connecticut, began making A-1 Sauce.

▼ Sigmund Freud published *The Psychopathology of Everyday Life,* containing his explanation of what are now known as Freudian slips.

▼ The Pan-American Exposition opened in Buffalo, New York. More than 9 million visitors came to see this fair, a multicultural extravaganza lit up by "new-fangled" electric lights. The fair was also referred to as the Rainbow City of Lights; it featured exhibits from many different countries and cultures, as well as some of the first disaster shows—staged events reproducing catastrophes such as the Chicago Fire and the Johnstown Flood.

▼ The first electric typewriter appeared.

▼ The Gillette Safety Razor Company was founded by King Camp Gillette, the inventor of the disposable razor blade. Gillette dated his initial brainstorm to 1895, when he conceived the idea of a disposable razor and blade, but it took six years of development to turn the idea into a product. Several more years elapsed before the product caught on.

▼ Lionel trains were first manufactured by Joshua Lionel in New York City. Lionel's original concept was to build scale models of Brooklyn trolleys for use in window displays. These trains proved so successful at attracting attention the first year that Lionel quickly shifted marketing plans and began selling them to the public. In the company's catalog for 1902, he wrote: "We received so many inquiries from the students and their friends for duplicate outfits that we decided to manufacture them in larger quantities, thereby reducing their cost and enabling us to offer them at a popular price." The original toy trolleys weighed 12 pounds, were 16 1/2 inches long, and ran on 2 7/8-inch track. They sold for $6, including several cars and track. For customers who did not yet have electrical power to their buildings, the catalog also offered a battery setup with glass jars filled with acid. In 1918, the company was incorporated.

▼ A U.S. medical commission officially concluded that yellow fever was transmitted by mosquitoes. Walter Reed, an American doctor working as an Army surgeon, first discovered this connection in 1900 after several years of work in Cuba. Earlier work by Ronald Ross had established that malaria was transmitted in a similar fashion.

▼   1851   ▼

ASSOCIATIONS, SOCIETIES, UNIONS, AND GOVERNMENT DEPARTMENTS
American Geographical Society (New York, NY)
International Association of Rebekah Assemblies (Winston-Salem, NC)

BIRTHDAYS AND DEATH DAYS
James Fenimore Cooper died on 14 September at age 61

IN 1851 on 5 June, the first installment of *Uncle Tom's Cabin,* or *Life among the Lowly,* by Harriet Beecher Stowe, was printed in the *National Era,* a weekly antislavery newspaper published in Washington, D.C. The author said at the time, "I feel that the time is come when even a woman or a child who can speak a word for freedom and humanity is bound to speak." The story, which ran in 40 installments and was later issued as a book in 1852, was considered to be a major factor in focusing public attention in the Northern states for abolition of slavery.

▼ 1851 ▼

COLLEGES AND UNIVERSITIES
Carson-Newman College (Jefferson City, TN)
Catawba College (Salisbury, NC)
Coe College (Cedar Rapids, IA)
College of Notre Dame (Belmont, CA)
Marian College (Indianapolis, IN)
Northwestern University (Evanston, IL)
Ripon College (Ripon, WI)
Saint Joseph's University (Philadelphia, PA)
Santa Clara University (Santa Clara, CA)
Spring Garden College (Philadelphia, PA)
University of Minnesota, Twin Cities Campus
   (Minneapolis, MN)
University of the Pacific (Stockton, CA)

▼ On 12 August, Isaac Singer received a patent for his sewing machine. Earlier, in 1846, Elias Howe was awarded the first patent for a sewing machine, and Howe ended up suing Singer for copying part of his design. Singer lost this case—and $15,000—but was the ultimate winner, as his manufacturing company produced machines that were enthusiastically accepted by the public.

▼ On 22 August, the first America's Cup race was held in the waters off the Isle of Wight. The trophy became known as the America's Cup because the first winner was the yacht *America,* which beat the favored British boats. The America's Cup is considered to be the oldest continuously held sporting event in the world.

▼ On 18 September, the first issue of the *New York Times* was published in New York City. The original name was the *New York Daily Times;* the word *Daily* was dropped in 1857. The opening statement by the paper's founder, Henry Raymond, said, "We do not mean to write as if we were in a passion, unless that shall really be the case, and we shall make it a point to get in a passion as rarely as possible." In its first year, the paper was sold for a penny a copy. The *New York Times* was purchased in 1896 by Adolph Ochs; Ochs introduced a new slogan for the paper on 25 October 1896: "All the news that's fit to print."

▼ The U.S. government signed the Treaty of Fort Laramie with Plains Indian tribes. The tribes ended hostilities against white settlers in exchange for the guarantee of exclusive use of a specified region of land. The land was later divided into the states of Colorado, Kansas, Montana, Nebraska, North Dakota, South Dakota, and Wyoming.

▼   1851   ▼

MUSIC

Rigoletto, Giuseppe Verdi (first performed on 11 March in Venice, Italy)
"Swanee River" (also known as "Old Folks at Home"), by Stephen Foster

NEWSPAPERS AND MAGAZINES

San Jose Mercury (San Jose, CA)

BOOKS, POETRY, AND PLAYS

Moby Dick, by Herman Melville
The House of the Seven Gables, by Nathaniel Hawthorne

150 years ago

▼ The Illinois Central Railroad was chartered in Chicago, the first in the country organized as a land-grant railroad.

▼ The city of Chicago hired its first detective, Allan Pinkerton. Pinkerton later established the first national private detective agency, The Pinkerton Agency, with this motto: The Eye That Never Sleeps. One of the company's first major jobs was providing security for President Abraham Lincoln, whom Pinkerton met while Lincoln was working as a lawyer for a railroad company. Pinkerton agents also worked as spies for the North in the Civil War, and specialized in strike-breaking and industrial security.

▼ The Blatz Brewing Company opened in Milwaukee, Wisconsin.

▼ The concept of absolute zero was proposed by William Thomson (Lord Kelvin).

▼ Jean Bernard Leon Foucault first demonstrated his pendulum, an oscillating weight that indicated the rotation of the earth. The next year, Foucault invented the gyroscope.

▼ Herman Melville's *Moby Dick* and Nathaniel Hawthorne's *The House of the Seven Gables* were published. *Moby Dick* was poorly received by the reading public, selling few copies in its first few years, but Hawthorne, already an established author, had an immediate hit. At the time, the two authors were neighbors in Lenox, Massachusetts.

▼ The first world's fair, the Great International Exhibition, opened in London. Features of this exposition included many technological inventions, industrial advances, and the construction of the Crystal Palace, a unique glass building.

▼ The first U.S. chapter of the Young Men's Christian Association (YMCA) was opened in Boston. The YMCA was founded in England in 1844.

▼ Gail Borden created evaporated milk in Brooklyn, New York. Borden's invention led to the establishment of the Borden Milk Company in the 1860s. Before his foray into dairy products, Borden had been a successful surveyor, creating the first topographic map of the Texas territory. He was also involved in the war for Texas independence, founding and publishing a pro-independence newspaper. After the war, working as an agent for the city of Galveston, he conceived the idea of developing food products that could be carried by settlers and immigrants. The invention of evaporated milk was inspired by his witnessing the use of a vacuum-pan method of producing maple syrup in a Shaker settlement in New Lebanon, New York. His invention was patented in 1856. Borden left his company in 1861, and moved to a town named after him in Texas.

▼ The first electrically powered railroad system in the United States began operating, with trains running from Washington, D.C., to Bladensburg, Maryland.

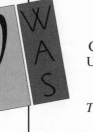

▼ 1801 ▼

COLLEGES AND UNIVERSITIES
University of South Carolina (Columbia, SC)

MUSIC
The Seasons, by Franz Joseph Haydn (first
    performed on 24 April in Vienna, Austria)
Sonata in C Sharp Minor (*Moonlight* Sonata),
    by Ludwig van Beethoven

NEWSPAPERS AND MAGAZINES
New York Post (New York, NY)

BOOKS, POETRY, AND PLAYS
The Maid of Orleans, by Friedrich von Schiller

IN 1801 on 1 January, the first asteroid was discovered by Giuseppe Piazzi, an Italian astronomer. Piazzi named the asteroid Ceres.

▼ On 4 March, Thomas Jefferson was inaugurated as the third president of the United States. Jefferson was elected after 36 ballots in the House of Representatives on 17 February, and he became the first president to be inaugurated in Washington, D.C.,

where government buildings had only recently been completed. During his first term, the Barbary Wars were fought with Tripoli and other states in the Mediterranean region. Jefferson was elected to a second term in 1804, and he retired to his estate in Monticello, Virginia, in 1809. On 4 July 1826, he died at the age of 83.

▼ On 14 May, Tripoli declared war on the United States. The war, marked by the first assignment for the U.S. Marine Corps, lasted until 1805.

▼ On 16 November, the *New York Evening Post* was founded by Alexander Hamilton. The *Post* survived many changes of ownership and editorial control; it was purchased in 1977 by Rupert Murdoch.

▼ On 24 December, the first steam-powered vehicle was demonstrated by Richard Trevithick, an English engineer. Trevithick had built the first engine to run on high-pressure steam the previous year; earlier steam-powered engines used low-pressure steam and were relatively inefficient.

▼ Pierre du Pont and his son founded the E.I. du Pont de Nemours and Company in Wilmington, Delaware. The Du Pont Company started with the manufacture of gunpowder and expanded into other explosive products later in the century. After World War I, Du Pont began making artificial fabrics, developing cellophane, rayon, and nylon, among others. Teflon was discovered at a Du Pont laboratory in 1938, and later discoveries included Orlon, Dacron, Mylar, and Freon. Explosives continued to be a part of the company's tradition; Du Pont constructed and ran the first plant to produce plutonium, which was used in one of the atomic bombs dropped on Japan.

▼ Josiah Bent opened a bakery in Milton, Massachusetts. Biscuits produced at this bakery were so crisp that they inspired the name "crackers" for the sound made when they were chewed.

▼ Joseph-Marie Jacquard, a French inventor, developed the first weaving loom capable of producing patterns. This device, soon referred to as the Jacquard loom, relied on interchangeable cards to guide machine movement.

▼ Robert Fulton, an American inventor, constructed the first submarine capable of diving, resurfacing, and running while submerged.

▼ Ultraviolet radiation was discovered by Johann Ritter, a German physicist.

▼ The first suspension bridge in the United States was constructed by James Finney. The bridge spanned Mahantango Creek in Uniontown, Pennsylvania.

▼ Jean-Baptiste de Lamarck, a French naturalist, developed the first system to identify and organize animals without backbones. Lamarck is known for creating the terms *vertebrate* and *invertebrate,* and he is the founder of the science of invertebrate zoology.

▼ 1751 ▼

BIRTHDAYS AND DEATH DAYS
James Madison born on 16 March

BOOKS, POETRY, AND PLAYS
Elegy Written in a Country Churchyard, by Thomas Gray

IN 1751 on 16 March, James Madison was born in Port Conway, Virginia. A graduate of the College of New Jersey (later renamed Princeton University), Madison was elected to the Constitutional Convention as a representative from Virginia in 1776; in 1780, following the founding of the republic, he was elected to the first U.S. Congress. Madison was a significant contributor to the U.S. Constitution—he is often referred to as the "father of the Constitution"—and, with Alexander Hamilton and John Jay, he wrote the *Federalist* papers. President Jefferson selected Madison as his secretary of state in 1800, and, after a successful campaign, he became the fourth president of the country in 1808. Madison's two terms in office were dominated by the War of 1812. At the close of his second term in 1817, he moved to Montpelier, Virginia, and he died on 28 June 1836.

▼ Axel Fredrick Cronstedt, a Swedish scientist, first discovered nickel. The metal was found in an ore that miners had named "kupfernickel" (Old Nick's copper) because no useful metal could be extracted from it.

▼ The world's first insane asylum was opened in London.

▼ Plantation owners in Louisiana first planted sugarcane.

▼ Denis Diderot, a French writer, published the first volume of *L'Encyclopedie,* the first encyclopedia. The work was completed in 1772.

▼ 1701 ▼

COLLEGES AND UNIVERSITIES
Yale University (New Haven, CT)

IN 1701 on 24 July, Antoine de la Mothe Cadillac created the settlement of Fort Pontchartrain, later named Detroit, in the territory of Michigan.

▼ On 16 October, Yale College was founded in Killingworth, Connecticut, as the Collegiate School. The college was moved in 1745 to New Haven, Connecticut, where it was given its current name.

▼ The first inoculations against smallpox were administered to children in Constantinople by Giacomo Pylarini.

IN 1651 Thomas Hobbes, the English phi-
losopher, published his most important work, *Leviathan*. In this book, Hobbes argued that people are incapable of thriving without the authoritarian control of a government.

▼ Giambattista Riccioli, an Italian astronomer, published the first atlas of the surface of the moon. Riccioli's book, *Almagestum Novum,* was the first to label lunar features, including the craters Copernicus, Kepler, Ptolemaeus, and Tycho, named after famous astronomers and scientists.

IN 1601 the English Parliament estab-
lished the first official public welfare legislation. The "Act for the relief of the poor" included provisions for creating jobs and apprenticeships and for aiding those unable to work.

IN 1551 Erasmus Reinhold published the
first book of astronomical tables that confirmed that the earth and the other planets revolved around the sun, as proposed by Copernicus in 1543.

▼ The theodolite was invented by Leonard Digges. This device was created to improve the science of surveying.

IN 1501 in Santo Domingo, the first black slaves were introduced by Spanish colonists. This was the first arrival of blacks in the New World.

▼ In Italy, Michelangelo completed the *Pietà*, a marble statue of the Virgin Mary and the dead body of Christ that was commissioned by the abbot of St. Denis. The Italian artist also began work on his statue of David during this year.

▼ Movable type was first used for printing music, although it had already been established as a new technology for printing (around 1450). This *noteworthy* innovation was created by Ottaviano dei Petrucci, a Venetian printer.

BIBLIOGRAPHY

ABC Sports. *The Complete Book of Sportsfacts*. Reading, MA: Addison-Wesley Publishing Company, 1981.

Adams, James Truslow. *Album of American History*. New York: Charles Scribner's Sons, 1945.

Asimov, Isaac. *Asimov's Chronology of Science and Discovery*. New York: Harper & Row, 1989.

Basalla, George. *The Evolution of Technology*. New York: Cambridge University Press, 1988.

Bernardo, Stephanie. *The Ethnic Almanac*. New York: Doubleday & Company/Dolphin Books, 1981.

Britannica Book of the Year. Chicago, IL: Encyclopaedia Britannica, annual.

Brooks, Tim, and Marsh, Earle. *The Complete Directory to Prime Time Network TV Shows*. Rev. ed. New York: Ballantine Books, 1981.

Bunch, Bryan, and Alexander Hellemans. *The Timetables of Science: A Chronology of the Most Important People and Events in the History of Science*. New York: Simon & Schuster/Touchstone, 1988.

Carruth, Gorton, and Associates, eds. *The Encyclopedia of American Facts and Dates*. New York: Thomas Y. Crowell Company, 1978.

Carruth, Gorton, and Eugene Ehrlich. *Facts and Dates of American Sports*. New York: Harper & Row/Perennial Library, 1988.

Carter, E. F., ed. *Dictionary of Inventions and Discoveries*. New York: Frederick Muller, 1974.

Chinquilla. *The Old Indian's Almanac*. Jamaica, NY: Indian Craft Museum, 1938.

Cohen, Hennig, and Tristam Potter Coffin, eds. *The Folklore of American Holidays*. Detroit, MI: Gale Research Company, 1987.

Collins, Dan, and Gale Collins. *The Millennium Book*. New York: Doubleday & Company/Dolphin Books, 1991.

Congressional Quarterly's Guide to U.S. Elections. Washington, DC: Congressional Quarterly, 1975.

BIBLIOGRAPHY

Dearling, Robert, and Celia Dearling. *The Guinness Book of Music Facts and Feats.* Enfield, England: Guinness Superlatives, 1976.

Dennis, Henry C. *The American Indian 1492–1970: A Chronology and Fact Book.* Dobbs Ferry, NY: Oceana Publications, 1971.

Dickson, Paul. *Timelines.* Reading, NY: Addison-Wesley Publishing Company, 1990.

Douglas, George William. *The American Book of Days.* Bronx, NY: H. W. Wilson Company, 1948.

Du Vall, Nell. *Domestic Technology: A Chronology of Developments.* Boston, MA: G. K. Hall & Company, 1988.

Eggenberger, David. *A Dictionary of Battles.* New York: Thomas Y. Crowell Company, 1967.

Ewen, David. *Popular American Composers: From Revolutionary Times to the Present.* Bronx, NY: H. W. Wilson Company, 1962.

Foner, Eric, and John A. Garraty, eds. *The Reader's Companion to American History.* Boston, MA: Houghton Mifflin Company, 1991.

Furer, Howard B., ed. *Chicago: A Chronological and Documentary History.* Dobbs Ferry, NY: Oceana Publications, 1974.

———. *New York: A Chronological and Documentary History.* Dobbs Ferry, NY: Oceana Publications, 1974.

Gebhart, John Robert. *Your State Flag.* Philadelphia, PA: Franklin Publishing Company, 1971.

Gregory, Ruth W. *Anniversaries and Holidays.* Chicago, IL: American Library Association, 1975.

Gusikoff, Lynne. *Guide to Musical America.* New York: Facts on File Publications, 1984.

Hadden, Briton, and Henry R. Luce. *Time Capsule/1923: A History of the Year Condensed from the Pages of Time.* New York: Time Life Books, 1967.

Hoffman, Mark S., ed. *The World Almanac and Book of Facts.* New York: Pharos Books, annual.

Hoover, Gary, Alta Campbell, and Patrick J. Spain, eds. *Hoover's Handbook: Profiles of Over 500 Major Corporations.* Austin, TX: The Reference Press, 1990.

Horn, Maurice, ed. *The World Encyclopedia of Cartoons.* New York: Chelsea House Publishers, 1980.

Hornsby, Alton, Jr. *Chronology of African-American History: Significant Events and People from 1619 to the Present.* Detroit, MI: Gale Research Company, 1991.

Hudson, Robert V. *Mass Media: A Chronological Encyclopedia of Television, Radio, Motion Pictures, Magazines, Newspapers, and Books in the United States.* New York: Garland Publishing, 1987.

Jackson, Michael. *The World Guide to Beer.* Philadelphia, PA: Running Press, 1977.

Johnson, David E. *From Day to Day: A Calendar of Notable Birthdays and Events.* Metuchen, NJ: Scarecrow Press, 1990.

Johnson, Richard A. *American Fads: From Silly Putty and Swallowing Goldfish to Hot Pants and Hula Hoops, 40 Crazes that Swept the Nation.* New York: William Morrow and Company/Beech Tree Books, 1985.

Kane, Joseph Nathan. *Famous First Facts: A Record of First Happenings, Discoveries and Inventions in the United States.* Bronx, NY: H. W. Wilson Company, 1964.

Kelly, R. Gordon. *Children's Periodicals of the United States.* Westport, CT: Greenwood Press, 1984.

Kouwenhoven, John A. *Adventures of America: A Pictorial Record from Harper's Weekly.* New York: Harper & Brothers Publishers, 1938.

Krug, Edward A. *Salient Dates in American Education.* New York: Harper & Row, 1966.

Linton, Calvin. *The American Almanac.* Nashville, TN: Thomas Nelson, 1977. (Previously published as *The Bicentennial Almanac,* 1975).

Long, Kim, and Terry Reim. *Kicking the Bucket.* New York: William Morrow and Company/Quill, 1985.

McGrath, Molly Wade. *Top Sellers, USA: Success Stories behind America's Best-Selling Products, from Alka-Seltzer to Zippo.* New York: William Morrow and Company, 1983.

Maleska, Eugene T. *Down and Across: The Crossword Puzzle World.* New York: Simon & Schuster/Fireside. 1984.

Moore, Elizabeth. *An Almanac for Music Lovers.* New York: Henry Holt & Company, 1940.

Moskowitz, Milton, Robert Levering, and Michael Katz. *Everybody's Business: A Field Guide to the 400 Leading Companies in America.* New York: Doubleday & Company/Currency, 1990.

The New Encyclopaedia Britannica. 15th ed. Chicago, IL: Encyclopaedia Britannica, 1977.

Panati, Charles. *Panati's Parade of Fads, Follies, and Manias: The Origins of Our Most Cherished Obsessions.* New York: HarperCollins, 1991.

Perry, J. Tavenor. *The Chronology of Mediaeval and Renaissance Architecture: A Date Book of Architectural Art, from the Building of the Ancient Basilica of S. Peter's, Rome, to the Consecration of the Present Church.* London, England: John Murray, 1893.

Robinson, Richard. *United States Business History, 1602–1988: A Chronology.* Westport, CT: Greenwood Press, 1990.

Schlesinger, Arthur M., Jr., ed. *The Almanac of American History.* New York: G. P. Putnam's Sons, 1983.

Schwartz, Hillel. *Century's End: A Cultural History of the Fin de Siécle, from the 990s through the 1990s.* New York: Doubleday & Company, 1990.

Shapiro, Larry. *A Book of Days in American History.* New York: Charles Scribner's Sons, 1987.

Smith, Josephine Metcalfe. *A Chronology of Librarianship.* Metuchen, NJ: Scarecrow Press, 1968.

Steinberg, S. H. *Historical Tables: 58 BC–AD 1985.* Updated by John Paxton. New York: Garland Publishing, 1986.

The United States Government Manual. Washington, DC: U.S. Government Printing Office/National Archives and Records Administration, annual.

Urdang, Laurence, ed. *The World Almanac Dictionary of Dates.* New York: World Almanac Publications, 1982.

Van Doren, Charles, ed. *Webster's American Biographies.* Springfield, MA: G. & C. Merriam Company, 1974.

Wallace, Amy, David Wallechinsky, and Irving Wallace. *The Book of Lists #3.* New York: William Morrow and Company, 1983.

Wallace, Irving, and David Wallechinsky. *The People's Almanac.* New York: Doubleday & Company, 1975.

————. *The People's Almanac #2.* New York: Bantam Books, 1978.

————. *The People's Almanac #3.* New York: Bantam Books, 1981.

Wallace, Irving, David Wallechinsky, Amy Wallace, and Sylvia Wallace. *The Book of Lists #2.* New York: William Morrow and Company, 1980.

Wallechinsky, David, Irving Wallace, and Amy Wallace. *The Book of Lists.* New York: William Morrow and Company, 1977.

Wetterau, Bruce. *The New York Public Library Book of Chronologies.* New York: Prentice Hall Press/Stonesong Press, 1990.

White, Adam. *The Billboard Book of Gold & Platinum Records.* New York: Watson-Guptill Publications/Billboard Books, 1990.

Williams, Neville. *Chronology of the Modern World: 1763 to the Present Time.* New York: David McKay Company, 1966.

Wilson, Mitchell. *American Science and Invention.* New York: Simon & Schuster, 1954.

Zoological Parks and Aquariums in the Americas. Wheeling, WV: American Association of Zoological Parks and Aquariums, annual.

INDEX

217

INDEX

INDEX

INDEX

INDEX

INDEX

INDEX

INDEX

INDEX

INDEX

INDEX

INDEX

INDEX

INDEX

INDEX

INDEX